Screening Queer Memory

Library of Gender and Popular Culture

From *Mad Men* to gaming culture, performance art to steampunk fashion, the presentation and representation of gender continues to saturate popular media. This series seeks to explore the intersection of gender and popular culture, engaging with a variety of texts - drawn primarily from Art, Fashion, TV, Cinema, Cultural Studies and Media Studies – as a way of considering various models for understanding the complementary relationship between 'gender identities' and 'popular culture'. By considering race, ethnicity, class, and sexual identities across a range of cultural forms, each book in the series adopts a critical stance towards issues surrounding the development of gender identities and popular and mass cultural 'products'.

For further information or enquiries, please contact the library series editors:

Claire Nally: claire.nally@northumbria.ac.uk
Angela Smith: angela.smith@sunderland.ac.uk

Advisory Board:
Dr Kate Ames, Central Queensland University, Australia
Prof Leslie Heywood, Binghamton University, USA
Dr Michael Higgins, Strathclyde University, UK
Prof Asa Kroon, Orebro University, Sweden
Dr Niall Richardson, Sussex University, UK
Dr Jacki Willson, Central St Martins, University of Arts London, UK

**Library of Gender
& Popular Culture**

Published and forthcoming titles:

The Aesthetics of Camp: Post-Queer Gender and Popular Culture
By Anna Malinowska

Ageing Femininity on Screen: The Older Woman in Contemporary Cinema
By Niall Richardson

All-American TV Crime Drama: Feminism and Identity Politics in Law and Order: Special Victims Unit
By Sujata Moorti and Lisa Cuklanz

Bad Girls, Dirty Bodies: Sex, Performance and Safe Femininity
By Gemma Commane

Beyond: Celebrity Feminism in the Age of Social Media
By Kirsty Fairclough-Isaacs

Conflicting Masculinities: Men in Television Period Drama
By Katherine Byrne, Julie Anne Taddeo and James Leggott (Eds)

Fat on Film: Gender, Race and Body Size in Contemporary Hollywood Cinema
By Barbara Plotz

Fathers on Film: Paternity and Masculinity in 1990s Hollywood
By Katie Barnett

Film Bodies: Queer Feminist Encounters with Gender and Sexuality in Cinema
By Katharina Lindner

Gay Pornography: Representations of Sexuality and Masculinity
By John Mercer

Gender and Austerity in Popular Culture: Femininity, Masculinity and Recession in Film and Television
By Helen Davies and Claire O'Callaghan (Eds)

The Gendered Motorcycle: Representations in Society, Media and Popular Culture
By Esperanza Miyake

Gendering History on Screen: Women Filmmakers and Historical Films
By Julia Erhart

Girls Like This, Boys Like That: The Reproduction of Gender in Contemporary Youth Cultures
By Victoria Cann

The Gypsy Woman: Representations in Literature and Visual Culture
By Jodie Matthews

Love Wars: Television Romantic Comedy
By Mary Irwin

Masculinity in Contemporary Science Fiction Cinema: Cyborgs, Troopers and Other Men of the Future
By Marianne Kac-Vergne

Moving to the Mainstream: Women On and Off Screen in Television and Film
By Marianne Kac-Vergne and Julie Assouly (Eds)

Paradoxical Pleasures: Female Submission in Popular and Erotic Fiction
By Anna Watz

Positive Images: Gay Men and HIV/AIDS in the Culture of 'Post-Crisis'
By Dion Kagan

Queer Horror Film and Television: Sexuality and Masculinity at the Margins
By Darren Elliott-Smith

Queer Sexualities in Early Film: Cinema and Male-Male Intimacy
By Shane Brown

Steampunk: Gender and the Neo-Victorian
By Claire Nally

Television Comedy and Feminity: Queering Gender
By Rosie White

Gender and Early Television: Mapping Women's Role in Emerging US and British Media, 1850–1950
By Sarah Arnold

Tweenhood: Femininity and Celebrity in Tween Popular Culture
By Melanie Kennedy

Women Who Kill: Gender and Sexuality in Film and Series of the Post-Feminist Era
By David Roche and Cristdle Maury (Eds)

Wander Woman: Feminism, Culture and the Body
By Joan Ormrod

Young Women, Girls and Postfeminism in Contemporary British Film
By Sarah Hill

Bad Girls, Dirty Bodies: Sex, Performance and Safe Femininity
By Gemma Commane

Are You Not Entertained? Mapping the Gladiator across Visual Media
By Lindsay Steenberg

Screening Queer Memory

LGBTQ Pasts in Contemporary Film and Television

Anamarija Horvat

BLOOMSBURY ACADEMIC
LONDON • NEW YORK • OXFORD • NEW DELHI • SYDNEY

BLOOMSBURY ACADEMIC
Bloomsbury Publishing Plc
50 Bedford Square, London, WC1B 3DP, UK
1385 Broadway, New York, NY 10018, USA
29 Earlsfort Terrace, Dublin 2, Ireland

BLOOMSBURY, BLOOMSBURY ACADEMIC and the Diana logo are trademarks of
Bloomsbury Publishing Plc

First published in Great Britain 2021
Paperback edition published in 2023

Copyright © Anamarija Horvat, 2021

Anamarija Horvat has asserted her right under the Copyright, Designs and
Patents Act, 1988, to be identified as Author of this work.

For legal purposes the Acknowledgements on pp. x–xi constitute an
extension of this copyright page.

Cover design by Charlotte Daniels
Cover image: *Pride* (2014) (© Photofest NYC)

All rights reserved. No part of this publication may be reproduced or
transmitted in any form or by any means, electronic or mechanical, including
photocopying, recording, or any information storage or retrieval system,
without prior permission in writing from the publishers.

Bloomsbury Publishing Plc does not have any control over, or responsibility for,
any third-party websites referred to or in this book. All internet addresses given
in this book were correct at the time of going to press. The author and publisher
regret any inconvenience caused if addresses have changed or sites have
ceased to exist, but can accept no responsibility for any such changes.

A catalogue record for this book is available from the British Library.

A catalog record for this book is available from the Library of Congress.

ISBN:		
	HB:	978-1-3501-8765-8
	PB:	978-1-3501-8840-2
	ePDF:	978-1-3501-8766-5
	eBook:	978-1-3501-8767-2

Series: Library of Gender and Popular Culture

Typeset by Integra Software Services Pvt. Ltd.

To find out more about our authors and books visit www.bloomsbury.com
and sign up for our newsletters

Contents

List of figures	viii
Series editor's foreword	ix
Acknowledgements	x
Introduction: Locating queer memory	1
Part One Queer memories of the screen	**17**
1 The picture of Arthur Stuart: Todd Haynes's *Velvet Goldmine* and queer fan memory	25
2 Going on Faith: Cheryl Dunye's *The Watermelon Woman* and the invention of Black lesbian memory	41
Part Two Queer memory, intergenerationality and television	**61**
3 Haunting and queer histories: Representing postmemory in Joey Soloway's *Transparent*	67
4 New spies, old tricks: Intergenerational narratives and memories of the AIDS crisis in *London Spy*	82
Part Three Remembering queer activism	**103**
5 Reimagining LGSM: Gendered activism and neoliberalism in Matthew Warchus's *Pride*	109
Conclusion: The borders of memory: Transnational trends in LGBTQ representation	136
Notes	140
Bibliography	163
Film and television references	180
Index	183

List of figures

1	Arthur looks furtively at the television	26
2	The fan imagines coming out	26
3	Fan fantasies – Arthur's drawing of Brian	31
4	Curt as a Ken doll	33
5	Cheryl mimics Fae's mammy next to a recording of *Plantation Memories*	47
6	Diana and Cheryl framed by cinema, in the video store	50
7	Cheryl and Diana watch a film of Fae's before they first have sex	50
8	Cheryl and Diana positioned directly in front of a poster of Isaac Julien's *The Attendant*	53
9	The season two opening credits and lesbian counter-memory	74
10	National memory – a female couple looks at the Statue of Liberty	75
11	Ali and the young grandma Rose hold hands	79
12	The terrified Gittel looks back through time at her family	79
13	The salacious media treatment of Alex's death and his relationship with Danny	85
14	Danny at the warehouse	88
15	Danny during his encounter with the police	89
16	The 'Blue' room and Scottie's partner on the bed	95
17	Scottie recounts his partner's illness	99
18	Danny swims in blue	100
19	Stella squeezes between 'Martha' Scargill and Joe to tell a displeased Steph about LAPC	116
20	*Pride*'s closing frame – a banner pointing towards the significance of solidarity for the world	127

Series editor's foreword

As with many books in the Bloomsbury Library of Gender in Popular Culture, Anamarija Horvat's *Screening Queer Memory: LGBTQ Pasts in Contemporary Film and Television* shows how marginalized or occluded narratives can enter the realm of popular culture. In this book, she offers a robust and theoretically astute examination of queer cinema, television and LGBTQ history. Horvat's research navigates the critical terrain of queer theory and specifically the idea of LGBTQ memory. In examining material like Amazon's *Transparent* (2014–19) and *Pride* (2014) and the identification of queer histories, Horvat uncovers the complexities of intergenerational memory (and its absence) as well as the tensions involved in such representations. This material is exceptionally timely and shows a studied attention to developments in critical thinking such as affect and intersectionality, as well as contextual issues such as the debates surrounding trans access to women-only spaces. Horvat also draws extensively on archival material, which in many instances uncovers a new history of queer identities and debates within the community.

Such an engagement with queer visibility and narrative also situates this volume alongside several others in the Library of Gender and Popular Culture, including Darren Elliott-Smith's *Queer Horror Film and Television: Sexuality and Masculinity at the Margins* (2016), Katherine Lindner's *Film Bodies: Queer Feminist Encounters with Gender and Sexuality in Cinema* (2017) and Shane Brown's *Queer Sexualities in Early Film: Cinema and Male-Male Intimacy* (2016). Horvat's attention to the AIDS crisis in the 1980s, and its subsequent representation on screen, draws many comparisons with Dion Kagan's book *Positive Images: Gay Men and HIV/AIDS in the Culture of 'Post Crisis'* (2018). Ultimately, this book testifies to the urgency and sensitivity of these intellectual debates within and outside of LGBTQ cultures.

Acknowledgements

I am very lucky to have had the support of wonderful people while writing this book. I am immensely thankful to Rosie White and Victoria Bazin, whose indefatigable support, unmatched generosity as researchers and insightful comments have made it possible for this work to exist. My heartfelt thanks also go out to Claire Nally, whose insights and encouragement first as my doctoral examiner and later as my editor have been invaluable. I am also deeply grateful to Angela Smith and Camilla Erskine for their interest in this book, as well as their editorial support. I would also greatly like to thank Rachel Carroll for her constant academic generosity, support and insight, as well as Julie Scanlon, whose support for this project's 'baby steps' was truly indispensable.

My profound gratitude goes out to Inmaculada Sánchez-García, who has inspired me as a person and as a researcher in ways that are impossible to properly convey. Our conversations, her own wonderful writing, and warmth as a person and a reader have affected me in ways beyond the capacity of words, and I feel deeply lucky to have her in my life.

This project would not have been possible without Northumbria University, whose generous funding of my doctoral research made this book a reality. I am also immensely thankful to the Institute for Advanced Studies in the Humanities at the University of Edinburgh, where my postdoctoral fellowship granted me the opportunity to turn my doctorate into this book.

I would also like to thank the People's History Museum in Manchester – access to their archive has been invaluable to me. My thanks also go out to the journal *Feminist Media Studies* for allowing the reproduction of my work on 'Haunting and queer histories: Representing memory in Joel Soloway's *Transparent*' in this book.

I have had the support of wonderful colleagues and friends during the writing of this book. My special thanks go out to Bianca, Eleni, Pankaj, Ilke, Thiago and Martina, whose warmth and encouragement have made the Toon something it never could have been without them.

A heartfelt thank you goes out to my parents, Davorka and Zdenko, who have supported and encouraged me to pursue the work that I care about, for which I am tremendously thankful. I am grateful to them both for never implying the pursuit of the humanities was a 'fool's errand' and for steering me towards doing work that I love and not just what was practical. My thanks also go out to my wonderful grandfather Željko, as well as those who could not be here to witness this, my grandmothers Ksenija and Marija, and grandpa Zdravko. I want here to recognize your warmth and kindness, which is unforgettable.

Introduction: Locating queer memory

This book begins with a boycott. In 2015, the trailer for the film *Stonewall* was released, tracking the journey of Danny (Jeremy Irvine) to New York, where he eventually ends up acting as one of the leading figures in the eponymous Stonewall Riots. While the film dramatizes real events, Danny is an entirely fictional protagonist – white, blond and cisgendered. Rather than focusing on BAME (Black, Asian and Minority Ethnic) trans icons such as Marsha P. Johnson and Sylvia Rivera, or Stormé DeLarverie, the butch lesbian to whom the spark of the riot is often credited, the film gives Danny a central role in the rebellion, even seeing him throwing the fabled 'first brick' of the riots while Latinx and African American queers yell in admiration. Upon seeing the trailer, the reaction of numerous queer viewers was swift; a petition to boycott the film was started, soon amassing more than 20,000 signatures. 'Do not support a film that erases our history,' the petition urged: 'Do not watch *Stonewall*.'[1] News of the boycott were soon picked up by the media with articles appearing in *The Guardian* and on the *BBC News* website, and parodies of the film being shared on Twitter under the hashtag *#notmystonewall*, with memes inserting the fictional Danny into other historical events ranging from Civil Rights marches, the Black Panther Party meetings and iconic images of Second Wave Feminism.[2] When told of the boycott, director Roland Emmerich responded that 'you have to understand one thing: I didn't make this movie only for gay people, I made it also for straight people. I kind of found out, in the testing process, that actually, for straight people, [Danny] is a very easy in. Danny's very straight-acting. He gets mistreated because of that. [Straight audiences] can feel for him.'[3]

In the end, this focus on a white 'straight-acting' protagonist did not end up endearing *Stonewall* to audiences, with the film earning less than $200,000 at the box office, and being met with near-unanimous critical disapproval, with a Rotten Tomatoes score of only 9 per cent.[4] It is also worth noting here that many reviewers criticized precisely the film's historical inaccuracy, thus raising the question of whether such criticism would have been readily apparent to the average reviewer had the boycott not happened.[5] Taken together, both the critical and audience rejection of the film testifies to the awareness of activists of the potential influence of cinema on audience perceptions of LGBTQ (Lesbian, Gay, Bisexual, Transgender and Queer) history.[6] In this sense, the boycott that marked *Stonewall*'s release serves as an especially apt introduction to this book, illuminating precisely the issues which lie at its core. How, in other words, is the queer past represented? Which narratives of LGBTQ history are being commemorated and reified, and which obscured? Whose stories are being told, and whose conveniently forgotten? How do cinema and television comment on and influence the formation of queer memory?

In this book, I examine how queer memory is represented on and created by contemporary US and UK film and television. Following Iwona Irwin-Zarecka, who argues that we should look for collective memory 'not in the minds of individuals, but in the resources they share', I look at cinema and television as technologies through which LGBTQ community memory is both reflected and formed.[7] While interest in queer temporalities and the historical permutations of sexuality has blossomed in academia over the past decades, there has been notably less analysis of the role of cinema and television in shaping our view of the past and the ways in which on-screen works act as makers of queer memory.[8] At the same time, while scholars in the field of memory studies have long accepted the crucial role of cinema and television in the formation of societal memory, a sustained study of its role in the creation of LGBTQ memory specifically has yet to be undertaken.[9] This lack of interest is especially paradoxical when taking into account events like the boycott against *Stonewall*, which clearly demonstrates the importance that many queer viewers themselves attach to such films. In writing this book, I have thus aimed to fill this gap and to provide the first sustained academic interrogation of queer memory in cinema and television.

In focusing on this issue, I draw on the work of memory scholars who have transformed our perception of the concept of memory from a solitary, individual issue – how I, as an individual, remember my own life – to include how social groups and nations narrativize their own past and which stories they tell about their own histories. As Maurice Halbwachs notes, the memories of a society should not be thought of simply as a reconstruction of the past by numerous people. Rather, memory depends on our present outlook and is (re)created by each group according to its present needs. Halbwachs writes that a society creates its collective memories by reconstructing 'an image of the past which is in accord, in each epoch, with the predominant thoughts of the society'.¹⁰ Consequently, how the past is mobilized by a certain group can be said to reveal more about its contemporary ambitions and tendencies, rather than simply illuminating the details of its history. In this sense, how a society approaches the histories and memories of minorities is particularly relevant, as it also testifies towards their position in the present.

This book focuses specifically on queer on-screen memory for a number of reasons. On the one hand, the question of LGBTQ histories is a complex one, as queer people were often forced to stay hidden and to deliberately destroy the evidence of their existence in order to survive.¹¹ On the other, the specific history of discrimination and persecution that marks both the LGBTQ past and present has often meant that queer histories have been deliberately erased and removed from official narratives. In the UK, Scotland is the only member state which, by virtue of regulations passed in 2018, mandates the teaching of LGBTQ history as part of its national curriculum.¹² In the United States, four countries mandate such an inclusion, with only California, Colorado, New Jersey and Illinois emphasizing the relevance of LGBTQ history in the state curriculum.¹³ At the same time, even when LGBTQ histories are included into national commemorative projects, such inclusion has often been met with virulent opposition, as is for example evident from the Berlin Memorial to Homosexuals Persecuted under Nazism being repeatedly vandalized, most recently in 2019, and the same happening to the LGBT Holocaust Memorial in Tel Aviv in 2018.¹⁴ The vandalization of these monuments serves as not only an attack on the LGBTQ community, but also as an attack on queer memory itself and on the notion that queer people *have* a history.

In spite of such obstacles, representations of queer histories have for long been found on cinema and television screens, with a particular proliferation of such works happening in recent years. Whether it be the film *Pride* (2014), which depicts the queer activism that marked the British Miners' Strike in 1984–5; the television series *Transparent* (2014–19), which looks back at the development of sexology in Magnus Hirschfeld's Institute in 1930s Germany; the film *Carol* (2015), which depicts a romance between two women in 1950s America; or the TV series *Pose* (2018–), which reimagines the AIDS crisis through the eyes of BAME ballroom communities during the 1980s, the preoccupation of both queer film and television with the past is easy to notice. While these works are part of a longer tradition in queer on-screen representation of looking back (a tradition which encompasses works as different as the deliberate historical anachronism of Derek Jarman's oeuvre on the one hand and *heritage* television like *Brideshead Revisited* (1981) on the other), the sheer number of queer memory works produced in recent years points towards the cinematic and televisual popularity of reimagining the queer past and of creating non-heteronormative visions of history.[15]

In turn, such works are particularly important considering the fact that LGBTQ communities do not have the same ways of passing on memory as other minority communities do. In queer communities, contact between people of different generations is limited, prompting researchers like Glenda M. Russell and Janis S. Bohan to go as far as to argue that this lack of intergenerational contact is precisely what differentiates LGBTQ communities from other minority communities, be they racial, ethnic or religious.[16] They note that 'in these communities/families, contacts between youths and elders are not an intrinsic element of social systems [as these] tend to be age-segregated (youths cannot go to bars; adults cannot participate in youth coming-out groups)'.[17] Similarly, researchers like Rachel Gelfand have also pointed towards the lack of queer memory transfer within the family, with the family itself often being the primary source of trauma encountered by the LGBTQ person, in turn leading to queer histories being hidden from view.[18] As Sarah Schulman has argued:

> Most social movements have been constructed by people who were related: civil rights and labor movements involve multi-generations of rebellion by the same families. Even feminism has tried to be a movement of mothers and daughters. But the gay and lesbian movement, like the disability movement, is made up of people who stand apart from the fate of their family members, and whose most intense oppression experiences may be at the hand of those same relatives.[19]

As Schulman describes, both the queer community and queer activism can often be defined as *in opposition to* or simply as 'outside' the family – a development which has profound consequences on the formation of community memory. The concept of queer memory is therefore a complex one, as it is impossible to speak of LGBTQ people as a minority community constructed in the same manner as either ethnic or religious minority groups, though the queer community will of course find itself formed across the intersections of many such groups. In other words, while the passage of memory in other minority communities frequently occurs along familial intergenerational lines, LGBTQ memory is more often omitted from how families choose to narrate their own past.

The lack of queer memory formed along familial lines raises the question of whether and how LGBTQ communities pass on what Marianne Hirsch terms 'postmemory'. Originally postulated within the context of Holocaust studies, Hirsch uses the concept of postmemory 'to describe the relationship of children of survivors of cultural or collective trauma to the experience of their parents, experiences that they "remember" only as stories and images with which they grew up, but that are so powerful, so monumental, as to constitute memories in their own right'.[20] Her work thus emphasizes the ways in which the memory of individual trauma can travel from the person who originally experienced it to others who have heard and been emotionally affected by their remembrance. Such a transfer of memory can often have powerful effects not only on the individual for whose identity postmemory becomes an important part, but also for the formation of minority communities along the lines of shared memories.

For queer people, what Hirsch terms 'familial postmemory' has rarely been possible. However, this does not mean that queer postmemory is not passed on – instead, this book argues that media such as film and television play a crucial role in creating such postmemory. My work on queer on-screen memory thus builds on scholars like Rachel Gelfand, who stresses that 'thinking queerly about [the transfer of memory from one generation to another means] detaching inheritance from biology' and instead looking at other ways in which ideas about LGBTQ pasts have been passed on.[21] In this sense, one of the main arguments of my work on queer memory is precisely the fact that it is shaped in greater measure by on-screen representation than other types of minority community memories, which do not have to deal with the same obstacles to familial memory transfer.

In turn, queer commemorative cinema and television can serve complex functions, not only through combating a lack of queer familial postmemory, but also through countering the effects of the lack of intergenerational contact brought about by the AIDS crisis, which has had a tremendous impact on the generational make-up of the LGBTQ community. A good example of this comes from a recent interview with activist Cleve Jones, whose own work on the NAMES Project AIDS Memorial Quilt exemplifies the vast activist labour which has gone into preserving queer seropositive legacies. In the interview, Jones commented on the influence of trauma on the fading of Harvey Milk's legacy, as well as the effects of Gus Van Sant's Oscar-winning film about Milk being released. Jones commented that:

> [The film] was a very important symbol that went out there. One of many terrible things about AIDS was that it disrupted the transmission of information from one generation to the next, because half of my generation got out and those who survived, many of us don't want to talk about any of it because it's so painful still. So, his memory was beginning to recede ... I would go and speak at universities with tons of LGBT people in the audience and I'd say 'How many of you know

who Harvey Milk was?' and maybe one or two hands would go up. But Gus changed that with *Milk*.[22]

I mention Jones's quote here because it illustrates how cinema can serve as a substitute for the types of in-person contact which might have existed had the AIDS crisis not happened or had activists like Harvey Milk been embraced earlier by the US government as a beloved part of officially sanctioned national narratives of memory. The effects of the film's popularity are perhaps most evident in the establishment of Harvey Milk Day in California, where its Republican Party governor Arnold Schwarzenegger had vetoed the measure in 2008 prior to the film's release but signed it into law the following year.[23] In explaining this change of heart, the governor's spokesperson cited Milk's Presidential Medal of Freedom and the film's influence in making him 'much more of a symbol of the gay community' and, by implication, barring Schwarzenegger from once again arguing that he should be honoured on a local level instead of a state one.[24] Apart from making Milk a symbol for the LGBTQ movement in the United States, the film also made him a transnational symbol, with tributes to his life ranging from the Stratford LGBT student society's tribute to Milk in England, to the Guarani LGBTQ organization Somosgay in Paraguay creating a mural of Milk as part of their 'Graffities for Equality' artistic action.[25]

All of this emphasizes the importance of contemporary queer cinema and television in countering the generational segregation that otherwise pervades LGBTQ communities, as well as in creating queer memory. This does not mean that cinema and television are the sole channels through which queer memory is passed on, with LGBTQ groups working diligently to preserve and excavate their histories and creating numerous community archives. Nonetheless, such archives are in many cases only beginning to be digitised and are as such far less accessible to the average LGBTQ person than a film like *Milk* would be, as it is screened transnationally and is available for streaming. Similarly, a plethora of books have been published on LGBTQ history, but they require a person to actively seek them out, while cinema and television function as technologies of memory a person can even stumble upon accidentally. For example, 2017 saw a wave of queer commemorative programming in the UK, as the fiftieth anniversary of the partial decriminalization of male homosexuality in England and Wales was celebrated in the BBC's *Gay Britannia* season, as well as on Channel 4's unfortunately titled *50 Shades of Gay* line-up. In documentaries such as *Prejudice and Pride: The People's History of LGBTQ Britain* (BBC) and *Convicted for Love* (Channel 4), as well as in historical drama such as *Queers* (BBC) and *The Man in the Orange Shirt* (BBC), the question of gay rights was directly linked with national memory, bringing the matter of queer memory onto the television screens of even accidental viewers.

In contemplating the commemorative function of film and television in this way, it is of course necessary to acknowledge that access to these mediums is a privilege countless millions of people do not possess. Equally importantly, the fact of one's access to these mediums does not automatically preclude that they are liberated from censorship, as can for example be seen in the recent censoring of gay sex scenes in the British film *God's Own Country* (2017) on Amazon Prime in the US or the removal of similar scenes in the Elton John biopic *Rocketman* (2019) in Russia.[26] Nonetheless, the prevalence of such media among people who *do* have access to them makes them an especially significant memory resource for LGBTQ people, allowing it to counter the lack of intergenerational contact mentioned above. At the same time, looking at how queer memory is being constructed by and represented in the media also means taking into account the broader positionality of LGBTQ memory within wider society. As Ann Cvetkovich comments, 'that gay and lesbian history even exists has been a contested fact', and it is with this in mind that this book questions whether LGBTQ people and communities are being allowed what Anna Reading terms the 'right to memory'.[27] For Reading, this concept refers to international legislature and the possibility of enshrining a 'right to memory' as a legally protected category (most pertinently with regard to crimes against humanity and human rights violations). Within the context of this work, however, I borrow Reading's concept in relation to queer people as a minority who are often denied this right through their deliberate erasure and exclusion from state-sanctioned commemorative projects. While this is changing in both the UK and US contexts on which this book focuses, the very fact that it is possible to count on the one hand the number of US states which mandate the teaching of LGBTQ history points towards how far it is from becoming the norm. In the UK, both the inclusion of queer history into Scottish educational guidelines and the silence which still surrounds the issue in other parts of the UK highlight the crucial role played by national memory regimes in the (lack of) preservation and transmission of LGBTQ memory.

Drawing from this, it becomes clear that cinematic and televisual works of queer memory also exist as rhetorical interventions into heteronormative narratives of collective memory. Through provoking affective engagement, on-screen works create new memories in the viewer and raise complex questions about the experiences they commemorate. Such cinematic and televisual acts of memory can either uphold or subvert the political contexts within which they are entrenched and can serve as fertile ground for further memory work and activism in the future. At the same time, like national archives and state-sanctioned events of commemoration, the media also often commemorate the experiences of those powerful enough to control discursive spaces.[28] Michel Foucault thus warns against the danger of cinema, which he locates in the possibility that it will convince the viewer that political resistance was not part of their past and is therefore impossible in their future.[29] He contends that 'if one controls people's memory, one controls their dynamism. And one controls their experience, their knowledge of previous struggles.' In Foucault's view, the appearance of cheap books and, more relevantly, cinema has led to a '*reprogramming*' of popular memory. He comments that, in cinema, 'people are shown not what they were, but what they must remember having been', pointing thus towards the ways in which even the memories of a personal experience can be reshaped by the media.[30] Media retellings of events can be so powerful as to shape the memories even of those who participated in the events being depicted, as is for example evidenced by Marita Sturken's work on Vietnam War veterans who report having their own memories of the war irrevocably transformed by cinematic representations of it.[31] The importance of the media as a maker of memory in contemporary society therefore cannot be overstated, as it not only creates new memories, but also influences the possibility of political action.

However, while Foucault focuses on the negative potential of cinema as a creator of remembrance, this book also emphasizes the positive potential of media memories. I draw here on the work of Alison Landsberg and her concept of prosthetic memory to emphasize the potential of cinema and television to transcend national and group boundaries, and to inspire an affective reaction in the viewer. Landsberg describes the potential of 'mass culture [to make] particular memories more widely available, so that people who have no "natural" claim to them might nevertheless incorporate them into their own archive of experience'.[32] Created by technologies such as cinema, these 'prosthetic memories' can be 'acquired by anyone, regardless of skin color, ethnic background, or biology'.[33] Landsberg notes the 'transportable' nature of such memories, which 'therefore challenge more traditional forms of memory that are premised on claims of authenticity, "heritage," and ownership'.[34] She elaborates that

> [t]he idea of prosthetic memory, then, rejects the notion that all memories – and, by extension, the identities that those memories sustain – are necessarily and substantively shaped by lived social context. Prosthetic memories are not 'socially constructed' in that they do not emerge as the result of living and being raised in particular social frameworks. At the same time, prosthetic memories are transportable and hence not susceptible to biological or ethnic claims of

ownership. These memories are thus neither essentialist nor socially constructed in any straightforward way: they derive from a person's mass-mediated experience of a traumatic event of the past.[35]

I draw here on Landsberg's insights when approaching queer cinematic and televisual works and their potential to at once create politically potent prosthetic memories in the viewer, as well as to potentially obscure the historical realities which they represent. 'Calling them "prosthetic"', Landsberg points out, 'signals their interchangeability and exchangeability and underscores their commodified form.' For Landsberg, 'these memories, like an artificial limb, are actually worn on the body; these are sensuous memories produced by an *experience* of mass-mediated representations'.[36] In this sense, the potency of on-screen representations of the queer past lies precisely in the potential of sensuous and sympathetic immersion while, at the same time, remaining a commodity whose reach is primarily limited to viewers who are able to afford it and wish to access it.

In spite of this affective and, by extension, political potential, memory remains a severely underutilized concept in queer studies, with writers prioritizing concepts such as nostalgia, history, temporality and the archive.[37] This is especially paradoxical considering the so-called turn to temporality within the last two decades of predominantly American queer theory, during which a number of authors have also pointed towards the porous borders between the present and past, and have noted the affective dimensions of such ghostly presences. Carolyn Dinshaw, for example, notes 'a queer desire for history' – the need for 'a different kind of past, for a history that is not Straight'.[38] She sees 'queer histories [as] made of affective relations' and argues for a formation of queer 'communities across time'.[39] In a similar move, Elizabeth Freeman's concepts of 'temporal drag' and 'erotohistoriography' echo Dinshaw's work by highlighting how the past can still be felt in the present.[40] In this sense, the present *drags* with it parts of the past, and so Freeman's work focuses on artistic representations of the past which depict the present as itself a hybrid between past and present temporalities. Louise Fradenburg and Carla Freccero also write that 'the past may not be the present, but it is sometimes in the present, haunting, even if only through our uncertain knowledges of it'.[41] For Freccero, Derrida's concepts of 'spectrality' and 'hauntology' are particularly useful, as they acknowledge the ways in which the social is haunted by the past.[42] While there are many differences between these authors, what unites them is the approach to the past and the present as categories that are far from either separate or stable. In spite of this, the concept of memory remains largely unused in works dealing with queer temporalities and media studies, with work focusing on this intersection mostly limited to single case studies or book chapters.[43]

In recent years, Gilar Padva and a number of authors have utilized the concept of nostalgia to analyse on-screen representations of the queer past in Anglophone film, and while this is a constructive approach, it is necessary here to outline the differences between it and a focus on memory.[44] For Padva, nostalgia represents a yearning for an idealized past and as such offers a respite from both history and reality, giving us a window into a utopian world. He argues that nostalgia can be both better and more real than what has actually happened, and writes that 'sometimes our memory is just a scaffolding to construct something much realer: nostalgia is the place where life's really happening, where pain becomes bearable'.[45] While not as ready to highlight the utopian potential of nostalgia as Padva is, the editors of the 2017 special issue of the journal *Queer Studies in Media and Popular Culture* have also wondered 'why popular media [is] so eager to turn to the past to tell stories about queer people and for whom these stories were being told'.[46] They also mobilize the concept of nostalgia as what they consider the most productive lens through which to survey these developments.

This theoretical position raises a number of issues. As Padva argues, 'the nostalgic recollection is a major part of any collective memory,' and while this is correct, it is precisely the reason I privilege the concept of memory over nostalgia, as the former contains the latter.[47] Differently put, while both memory and nostalgia are marked by an affective and sometimes idealized engagement with the past, memory encompasses within itself a wide range of affect, sometimes startlingly negative, sometimes painful, and sometimes marked with utopian potential. In privileging the concept of memory over that of nostalgia, I thus focus in more detail on how on-screen works have commented on the passage (or lack thereof) of painful memories from one generation of queers to another, and how they have portrayed the affective costs of such hidden histories, which are examined in Chapters 3 and 4. Similarly, on-screen works have commented on the very process of how the media remembers LGBTQ people and how they themselves remember the media, which is dealt with in Chapters 1 and 2 of this work. Finally, while Padva is correct that nostalgia carries utopian potential, even (and perhaps especially) if idealized, utopian representations of the past also need to be regarded with respect to what they leave out and misremember, and what the political consequences of such misremembering are, as is the case in Chapter 5 and the analysis of activist representation therein.

In taking such an approach to queer media works, I am interested in the interrelationship between queer media memory and community, and how one is constituted through the other. Through travelling across national boundaries and being viewed by different audiences, such media memories have the potential of forming new collectivities and of shaping the outlook of existing ones.[48] From this, it is possible to survey mass media in general and on-screen media in particular as creators of memory and to pay particular attention to the narratives it selects as worthy of representation. In this book, I focus specifically on how American and British cinema and television create queer memories. Such a focus was influenced by the global reach of media works from these regions, which contributes to their potential in creating prosthetic memories beyond national boundaries. Sometimes, this transnational exchange is referenced explicitly by queer media works, as can be seen in Maryam Keshavarz's *Circumstance* (شرایط, 2011), which focuses on the experiences of young lesbians in Iran and shows its central protagonists dubbing Gus Van Sant's *Milk* (2008) into Persian. Similarly, another example can be found in Srđan Dragojević's *The Parade* (*Parada*, 2011), which utilizes William Wyler's *Ben-Hur* (1959) in its exploration of homophobia and xenophobia in Serbia and displays clips from the film in pivotal moments of the developing relationship between its gay and straight central protagonists. In both films, these references raise the question of a common cinematic queer heritage, which Keshavarz and Dragojević deploy in the service of analysing their own national contexts. The reach of British and, in particular, American film and television thus clearly transcends their own national frameworks, which in turn carries the potential of influencing the memory of innumerable queer communities around the world.

The concept of global memory, advanced most prominently by Daniel Levy and Natan Sznaider, is here immensely useful.[49] While drawing on Roland Robertson's notion of 'glocalization' in their description of how transnational communication transforms our perception of the local and increases our awareness of its position within the global, Levy and Sznaider argue that memory itself has become glocalized. While their arguments focus on the Holocaust, I draw here on their notion of global memory in my approach to the transnational reach of British and especially American queer cinema and television works. The notion of globalized memory is of course not unproblematic. Ross Poole has rightfully argued against its Western bias and has also pointed towards the lack of an affective connection which transnational subjects might feel towards events which, no matter how terrible, are not part of their personal or national consciousness.[50] While I agree with these arguments, it is not my intention here to suggest that any event might reasonably be considered a universalizing memory. On the contrary, I wish to emphasize precisely the cultural colonialism inherent in the over-representation of media stemming from the United States and Britain, with the dangers of homonationalism being especially prominent.[51] In fact, it is precisely *because* of the inherent disparity of power which the over-representation of British and especially American media creates in local media contexts that this book focuses on them in such detail, as it is relevant to understand precisely what type of narratives is being promoted. Consequently, this book stresses the potential of prosthetic memories to create affect that transcends national boundaries and, in turn, influences community and activist formations. Transnational communication between activists has already exerted a profound influence on how LGBTQ politics is shaped on a glocal level. This extends to the popularity of Pride marches as a method of political action, activist actions promoting same-sex marriage, as well as the transnational popularization of the history of the Stonewall Riots. When taking into account the global reach and availability of particularly American and British queer cinema and television, the ability of media from these areas to shape transnational narratives of queer history becomes clear.

In all of this, the question of how cinematic and televisual constructions of queer memory shape not only our perception of the past, but our hopes for the future is paramount. This book thus builds on the arguments of scholars like Yifat Gutman, Adam D. Brown and Amy Sodaro, who emphasize both the negative and positive political potential of the mobilization of memory for future goals.[52] By arguing for what they term a 'Janus-faced view of memory', looking simultaneously backwards and forwards, they highlight the ways in which memory itself functions as a temporally unstable category.[53] In this way, their work echoes that of Jose Esteban Muñoz, who also argues that 'the present must be known in relation to the alternative temporal and spatial maps provided by a perception of past and future affective worlds' and emphasizes the constructed and political nature of memory.[54] Crucially, such a backward glance is neither for Muñoz nor for this book a simple turning away from the present or from the future. Rather, as Muñoz argues, 'our remembrances and their ritualized tellings – through film, video, performance, writing, and visual culture [carry within themselves] world-making potentialities', and it is precisely this potential for world-making that this book focuses on.[55]

To give an example of this, one needs to look no further than the considerable public visibility granted by the film *Pride* to the activist group Lesbians and Gays Support the Miners, whose legacy had fallen into near-total obscurity prior to the film's release, but who have since inspired the young activist group Lesbians and Gays Support the Migrants.[56] In drawing a link between cinematic representations of groups like LGSM and LGSMigrants, I do not intend to claim that one would not have existed without the other. However, the popularization of the former's legacy makes it easier for the latter to be aware of the precedent for their own activism and to claim, as LGSMigrants do, that their work builds 'on a proud history of queer solidarity'.[57] In this sense, filmic and televisual constructions of queer memory can function as an affective and critical resource for political action and the building of future worlds. To talk of queer memory therefore signifies not only reflecting on the recollections of LGBTQ individuals and how they are represented, but rather a queer imaginative engagement with the past. On-screen depictions of queer histories have the power to influence the viewer's perception of community history and by extension their political consciousness, and so it is for this reason that this book focuses on them in such detail.

Drawing from this, this book interrogates what sort of visions of the queer past are being promoted through cinematic and televisual representation, as well as how on-screen representation influences queer processes of memory more broadly. In Part One, I look at the relevance of queer media representation to the construction and self-narrativization of the queer subject. I focus on the relationship between LGBTQ people and film – on how queers remember the screen and how it, in turn, remembers them. Due to the particular history of censorship and misrepresentation which marks queer on-screen representation, LGBTQ people have a different relationship to the screen than their heterosexual counterparts. Stretching from the Hays Code, which banned representations of queerness in US cinema from the 1930s to 1968, to televisual representations which depicted LGBTQ people as villainous and deranged, the development of cinema and television has been littered with homophobia, biphobia and transphobia.[58] Similarly, while recent years have seen a notable rise in the number of LGBTQ people represented in film and television, queers are still summarily excluded from certain movie genres and role types. Drawing on this, I focus here on the specificity of the queer relationship to the screen, as well as how this has influenced LGBTQ memory. This entails looking at filmic representations of memories *of* the media and of the ways in which queerness is often deliberately forgotten. How, in other words, do queers tell stories of their past in relation to on-screen representation? How do they remember overtly queer media works and celebrities, as well as heterocentrist representation? And finally, how are these queer media memories represented on-screen?

Chapter 1 focuses on the memories of queer fans and looks at one of the classic texts of New Queer Cinema, Todd Haynes's *Velvet Goldmine* (1998). Through examining the film, I analyse the formative role which out queer celebrities can play in the self-narrativization of LGBTQ fans – in how they remember not only the screen, but themselves. While the film focuses specifically on memories of glam rock and its own fictionalized version of David Bowie, I read its depiction of queer fandom as surpassing this specific context and as a commentary on the broader utopian possibilities of drawing on the memories of queer fans. After this, Chapter 2 continues its focus on queer fan memory, this time looking at another crucial New Queer Cinema text, Cheryl Dunye's *The Watermelon Woman* (1996). In approaching the question of Black lesbian memory in cinema, *The Watermelon Woman* uses its subject to provide a broader critique of how both Black LGBTQ artists and interracial queer relationships have been screened away from memory projects. Through looking at Dunye's mockumentary, I thus analyse how it comments on the racist misremembering of Black lesbians, as well as how echoes of discriminatory representation find their way into queer interracial relationships.

After this, the second section moves on to representations which thematize the issue of queer postmemory and how it is passed on among LGBTQ people of different generations. It focuses on recent developments in both American and British television, which are set apart from their predecessors through their focus on older queer protagonists, intergenerational contact and the effects of memories left unsaid and unshared. It looks at the passage of queer memory within the family, friends and different subgroups within the LGBTQ spectrum, as well as paying particular attention to transgender memory and to the AIDS crisis. In Chapter 3, I focus on Joey Soloway's *Transparent* (Amazon Prime, 2014–19), a crucial text for contemporary transgender representation, approaching the series to see how it presents the passage of transgender memory within the family, and among transgender and cisgender queer women. In particular, I look at how pain and privilege affect how we remember the past, as well as the potential of imagination in establishing a renewed connection with the Other. Considering the current prominence of transphobic narratives even among certain feminist circles, the question of connection among opposed individuals is all the more relevant, with the series presenting a vital commentary on the passage of memory across different generations and among LGBTQ subgroups.

Chapter 4 continues its analysis of queer postmemory by looking at Tom Rob Smith's miniseries *London Spy* (BBC, 2015) and its depiction of an intergenerational friendship between gay men. Released in 2015, *London Spy* focuses on the presence of discrimination in contemporary Britain, questioning how memories of homophobia travel between one generation to the other, as well as how seropositive legacies are passed on. The series invokes a decidedly queer cinematic heritage in its approach to gay postmemory with an especially prominent homage to Derek Jarman's *Blue* commenting on the ways in which queer cinema acts as affective memory resources. In doing so, the series comments on the role of cinema and television in the construction of queer memory more broadly and the ways in which these technologies can serve to combat institutional homophobia and the erasure of LGBTQ histories.

The third part of the book looks at how LGBTQ activism is commemorated and recreated in contemporary film and television. Within the field of memory studies, the focus on war, trauma and genocide has often meant that memories of non-violent activism remain less examined, while the impact of memories on social movements has also not been much analysed.[59] At the same time, the question of how the past of queer activism is narrativized is of particular relevance at the present moment, seeing as a number of contemporary Anglo-American LGBTQ activist organizations face criticism for embracing neoliberal politics, homonormativity, as well as homonationalism.[60] One of the central issues in how the LGBTQ movement is commemorated on-screen thus becomes whether the movement itself is depicted as neoliberal and whether the legacy of queer activism which fought against economic inequality risks being forgotten. This part of the monograph thus presents a comparative analysis of the cinematic and televisual trends which can be observed in American and British representations of LGBTQ activism, particularly with respect to depictions of collective action and the activism of lesbian, bisexual, transgender and ethnic minority queers.

Chapter 5 focuses in detail on Matthew Warchus's film *Pride*, which I have already noted in this Introduction as popularizing the unprecedented collaboration between openly queer activists and mining communities which took place during the 1984–5 Miners' Strike in Britain. In my analysis of the film, I focus on two aspects of *Pride*'s presentation of LGSM: firstly, I am interested in how the film (mis)remembers the activism of queer women, and secondly, how it locates LGSM's activism with respect to broader issues of neoliberal reform. In analysing *Pride*, I draw on the archival research I have undertaken at the People's History Museum in Manchester, which hosts an extensive collection of materials relating to LGSM and thus presents an invaluable resource for looking at which aspects of the group's story Warchus's film chooses to commemorate and which to forget. I draw on this archive not due to the belief that historical film must adhere absolutely to historical fact – rather, I do so in order to gauge what version of the queer activist memory is being promoted by the film and how this comments on both the present and past of the LGBTQ rights movement.

Taken together, these three sections focus on three key aspects of queer memory – the media, intergenerationality and activism. The conclusion returns again to the broader terrain of queer on-screen memory, commenting briefly on transnational cinematic trends in depicting LGBTQ pasts. By looking at these cinematic and televisual tendencies, it emphasizes the ways in which queer on-screen works intervene in national heterocentrist memory discourses, as well as the ways in which they not only comment on, but also create queer memory. The issue of who commemorates queer history, profits from it and influences community memory is thus of the utmost importance, as are questions of what sort of vision of the past is being promoted by these works. As I have noted earlier, how we imagine the past has the potential not only to influence our present, but our future, and it is precisely such a belief in the political, world-making potentialities of memory that guides this project.

Part One

Queer memories of the screen

An older man, demonstrably serious, walks into a cinema. He is a writer by profession and has just purchased tickets for an E. M. Forster adaptation, but as he sits in the darkness, he begins to doubt if he is in the right place. On screen, a group of young voyeurs gather in front of the dorm room window, watching unabashedly as two women undress. Behind them, a short-haired woman, overweight and lesbian-coded, catches sight of this and rushes to attack them. 'This isn't E.M. Forster!', exclaims the writer. The scene's humour stems from its incongruity; the movie is crude, its characters are crass, and the older man most definitely should not be there. And yet, just as he gets up to leave the cinema, Jason Priestley appears on screen. Struck by the young man's beauty, the writer stays and returns the next day to see the film again. Soon enough, he has seen all of Priestley's films, each of which is a similar example of B movie trash cinema, and is collecting newspaper clippings about him. Shortly after, he leaves London and attempts to track Priestley down in the United States. This is the plot of Richard Kwietniowski's film *Love and Death on Long Island* (1996), which stars John Hurt as the aforementioned writer and revolves around his obsession with the up-and-coming actor. While not a film directly concerned with the matter of queer memory, it nonetheless deals with the specificity of queer spectatorship and fandom. Through depicting Hurt's fascination with Priestley, it also depicts his entrance into a type of cinema he would not otherwise have considered or taken seriously. All of the films he watches are relentlessly heteronormative and yet, for him, they reflect his own queerness.

Like Hurt's character, LGBTQ people have a long history of repurposing heterosexist media.[1] In his book *Gay Men at the Movies: Cinema, Memory and the History of a Gay Male Community* (2016), Scott McKinnon recounts his own similar experience of engaging with heteronormative film in a queer way.² 'I remember', he writes, 'with perhaps only slight exaggeration, that I almost wore out the tape on the video of the film *Lethal Weapon* (1987), having frequently rewound and replayed a scene in which Mel Gibson climbed out of bed and walked across a room naked.'³ For McKinnon, then a young boy whose awareness of his own sexuality was just beginning to evolve, 'this memory gives a sense of sexuality developing through movies'; of 'moments in which [he] could secretly explore, via the movies, possibilities that [he] felt [he] must keep hidden from the world'.⁴ Such an experience is far from foreign to LGBTQ people – rather, it forms an intrinsic part of queer spectatorship.

In part, this specificity can be attributed to the history of censorship and discrimination which marks the development of LGBTQ film and television representation. Be it during the Hays Code era, which prohibited depictions of queerness in American cinema from the 1930s to 1968, or during more recent cinematic and televisual history, which often portrayed LGBTQ people as murderous and duplicitous, the evolution of both mediums has been littered with transphobia, biophobia and homophobia.⁵ Similarly, the scarcity of queer characters in both film and television has also had a notable effect on queer viewing practices. As filmmaker Jan Oxenberg comments in Rob Epstein and Jeffrey Friedman's documentary *The Celluloid Closet* (1995), queer people have been 'pathetically starved for images of ourselves', and this has shaped the ways in which they approach media works. In this sense, it is impossible to think of queer viewing practices without also considering the 'symbolic annihilation' to which LGBTQ individuals have often been subject.⁶

Since the 1990s and Oxenberg's interview, there has been an unprecedented increase in LGBTQ on-screen visibility and diversity on screen. In 2020, GLAAD's *Where We Are on TV* report (which measures LGBTQ on-screen representation in US television) found an unparalleled 10.2 per cent of regular series characters on US screens to be LGBTQ.⁷ This increase in number is particularly notable with regard to LGBTQ protagonists of colour, who for the first time outnumber white queer characters, as well as the slightly higher number of queer women represented as opposed to the number of represented LGBTQ men. In terms of the film industry, the results of GLAAD's *Studio Responsibility Index* are less impressive – while LGBTQ characters appeared in 18.2 per cent of the major studio releases analysed in the report, more than half of the LGBTQ characters therein had only three minutes of screen time, while 35 per cent had less than a minute.⁸ Taken together, GLAAD's surveys point towards the somewhat paradoxical position inhabited by the queer spectator with regard to contemporary US film and television; on the one hand, this viewer will find themselves faced with more representation than they might have previously thought possible. On the other, they can still count on being summarily excluded and erased from certain film and television genres, as well as portrayed only as fleeting, cursory figures. Finally, while it is now easier for LGBTQ people to find themselves reflected on screen than it once was, numerous generations of queer individuals have grown up in circumstances where this was not the case and have vivid memories of such media silence and discrimination. In all of these cases, the LGBTQ viewer can still often find themselves defined in opposition to mainstream on-screen representation, and not mirrored within it.

Moreover, the proposed dichotomy between visibility and invisibility is in fact anything but simple and clear cut.[9] As Melanie Kohnen argues, the screen is 'both projection surface and filtering device' and can itself act as a closet. 'Whenever a particular form of queer visibility is projected on film and TV screens', Kohnen writes, 'other possibilities are filtered or screened out', often leading to the normalization of queerness as white male homonormativity.[10] As shall be seen in the following chapters, Kohnen's arguments about the screen as both projecting and obscuring, as bringing to light and hiding from sight, are particularly relevant here. For now, it is important to note that even the current influx of queer visibility does not reflect all LGBTQ individuals equally and that there are still media genres which for the most part entirely exclude queer protagonists.[11] Taken together, all of this points towards the specificity of how queers relate to media works and towards the (often oppositional) practices of looking which have often formed a pivotal part of queer media consumption.[12] For authors like Brett Farmer, queerness is thus 'a "difference that makes a difference" in filmic reception', and so he ascribes 'intense, overinvested' qualities of fannish absorption to gay male spectatorship.[13] In the same vein, others have also argued for the particularity of gay male audiences, while audience research on lesbian and LBT audiences emphasizes the importance these groups place on on-screen representation.[14]

Drawing on all of this, I focus here on the relevance of media works to the memory and self-narrativization of the queer subject. How, in other words, do queers tell stories of their past in relation to on-screen representation? What is the place of memories such as McKinnon's, where heteronormative media is repurposed to mirror queer sexualities? How do LGBTQ individuals remember overtly queer media works? And finally, how are these queer media memories represented on-screen? In looking at the interrelationship between memory and film, memory studies researchers have embraced audience memories of the cinema as a valuable field of study, as evidenced by the recent special edition of the *Memory Studies* journal on cinemagoing, film and memory.[15] Researchers have also undertaken numerous studies of audience memories in various national contexts, be it in the UK, Spain, Italy, Mexico or Australia.[16] However, studies of specifically queer audience memories are not as easily found, and so leave unexplored the ways in which LGBTQ media memories differ from their heterosexual counterparts. Such a gap is especially relevant due to the particularity of the queer position in relation to the media that I have described, as well as the possibility of such memories eventually fading, unrecorded and unexamined. As B. Ruby Rich notes when referring to Derek Jarman and the importance he attributed to seeing Pasolini and Visconti films as a young queer: '[S]uch memories need to be exhumed and followed, like the scent of a track gone stale, utilizing the tools that film theory, cultural studies, and the emergent "queer theory" have given us.'[17] While Rich uttered this call more than two decades ago, I echo it here through my focus on how such queer media memories have been represented on-screen. Instead of undertaking a survey of audiences, however, I look here at the ways in which cinema has represented queer audience memories, with the figure of the filmmaker at once standing in for that of the audience member.

In focusing on these issues, I draw in particular on the work of Dijana Jelača, whose concept of dislocated screen memories encapsulates within itself the ways in which on-screen representations both mask and represent the past, at once revealing and obscuring its contours.[18] For Jelača, 'cinema is always an interplay between memory – both reflected and constructed through film – and its role in the present'.[19] She therefore draws on Freud's concept of screen memory to comment on how one memory can serve as a 'screen' for another, more traumatic one. Jelača notes that

> [w]e might deploy Freud's screen memory as an analytic that may illuminate … something about the dynamics of cinematic memories as both revealing and concealing, authentic and inauthentic at the same time. Cinema and the concept of screen memories curiously emerged around the same time … and indeed, the analytical stretch from screen memories to cinematic screens is not difficult to make, particularly when one takes into consideration a prominent aspect of the cultural workings of cinema: cinema is always an interplay between memory – both reflected and constructed through film – and its role in the present.[20]

In her own work on trauma and representations of war, Jelača deploys this concept to comment on how on-screen representations both screen and dislocate the traumatic – in other words, how 'cinematic memory' represents trauma through its 'simultaneous erasure and emergence'.[21] The films Jelača analyses often do this by leaving the traumatic event itself unrepresented and focusing instead on the ways in which trauma's echoes can still be felt in the present. In this section, however, I use the concept of dislocated screen memory not in relation to representations of trauma, but to describe the complex memories LGBTQ people have of the screen and the ways in which it both reflects and obscures their experience.

By adopting Jelača's approach to the screen as a surface which both depicts and conceals the past, I address two distinct aspects of queer spectatorship; on the one hand, I utilize it to describe the ways in which media works both represent and annihilate queer pasts and memories. On the other, perhaps less immediately evident level, I use the concept to address queer dislocated memories *of* the screen – for example, of how McKinnon might remember *Lethal Weapon* as both obscuring and reflecting his desire or how another LGBTQ individual might recall a filmic or televisual work in a similar manner. As Jelača writes, 'the encounter between the spectator and screen [which creates] cinematic memory often takes a hybrid shape of inorganic and organic forms mutually intertwined and informative of one another until they can no longer be fully separated'.[22] In this sense, how a queer individual might remember a work of cinema or film surpasses recollections of what is found on screen and instead encapsulates the entire range of affect and interpretation which the viewer might attach to the work. This process of interpretation is of course not unique to queer people; however, the particular positionality of LGBTQ individuals as both seen and unseen, coupled with the specific history of discriminatory representation to which queers have been subject, shapes queer memories of the media in ways which do not always match those of their straight counterparts. Significantly, such memories can even extend towards media works which the subject has not seen, but nonetheless attaches affective relevance to, as evidenced in McKinnon's example of a gay man he spoke to reminiscing about a famous queer film whose screening he was too afraid to attend.[23]

In the next two chapters, I will therefore look at specific examples of how queer memories of the media have been represented in film. The films I focus on are part of what Rich has termed 'New Queer Cinema', a predominantly American and British period of LGBTQ filmmaking stemming from the early 1990s, which presented a definitive break 'with older humanist approaches and the films and tapes that accompanied identity politics'.[24] New Queer Cinema was characterized by a move away from trying to advocate for the positive perception of LGBTQ people and by 'traces of appropriation, pastiche, and irony, as well as a reworking of history with social constructionism very much in mind'.[25] Such a focus on queering historical narratives was not unprecedented. The filmography of Derek Jarman is particularly significant here with films like *Sebastiane* (1976) and *Caravaggio* (1986) serving as precursors to New Queer Cinema both in terms of style and its focus on historicity.[26] Affectionately nicknamed the movement's grandfather by Rich, Jarman continued to make films that embodied all the descriptors she attached to New Queer Cinema until his death in 1994. Nonetheless, while Jarman's work exemplified the movement, the influx of younger queer filmmakers, as well as the attention they received from the wider film community (best exemplified by their success at film festivals such as Sundance), enables us to consider New Queer Cinema as a distinct period in LGBTQ film development. In looking at contemporary queer representation, I begin with New Queer Cinema precisely because of its pivotal place in the turn towards increased queer cinematic visibility.

In looking at New Queer Cinema, it is necessary to recognize the influence of the AIDS crisis on queer memory projects in general and on the movement in particular. As Elizabeth Lapovsky Kennedy notes, the AIDS crisis brought an 'urgency' to the queer search for history and pushed both grassroots activists and later the academy 'to reclaim a history before its bearers died'.[27] A similar urgency can be recognized in the films of New Queer Cinema, which Michele Aaron correctly describes as defying 'the sanctity of the past, especially the homophobic past'.[28] While often not tackling the AIDS crisis directly, these films nonetheless addressed the various temporalities of queerness. In movies such as Derek Jarman's *Edward II* (1991), which adapts Christopher Marlowe's eponymous play; Christopher Münch's *The Hours and Times* (1991), which focuses on John Lennon's relationship with The Beatles' manager Brian Epstein, famously rumoured to have been in love with Lennon; Tom Kalin's *Swoon* (1992), which recalls both the real story of Leopold and Loeb as well as Alfred Hitchcock's *Rope* (1948), and Isaac Julien's *Looking for Langston* (1989), which reimagines the poet Langston Hughes while also depicting the AIDS crisis, it is thus possible to see an engagement with queer artistic legacies that have come before and a reworking of how these stories have previously been told. Similarly, films such as Barbara Hammer's *Nitrate Kisses* (1992) and Mark Christopher's *The Dead Boys' Club* (1992) also present echoes of the past in the present, either through thematizing pasts such as the aforementioned Motion Picture Production Code (Hammer) or the ghosts of the 1970s pre-AIDS crisis gay scene (Christopher).

Like these films, both of my case studies focus on the interrelationship between past and present by thematizing the links between viewer and screen, and between the LGBTQ fan and the queer artist. The first chapter focuses on Todd Haynes's *Velvet Goldmine* (1998), in which the biography of a fictional glam rock star is presented in conjunction with another character remembering his own infatuation with this same star. Focusing on a queer character's memories of fandom, *Velvet Goldmine* serves as an eloquent commentary on how media events of queer visibility contain the potential to act as 'screen memories' for the affective experience of fans invested in them. I analyse the queer genealogy presented in the film as one which thematizes the creation of queer celebrities as different as Oscar Wilde and David Bowie and the subjective relevance which such figures may play in a queer fan's self-narrativization. The memory of fandom is presented in *Velvet Goldmine* as a transformative experience, and it is for this reason that the chapter focuses on the film.

Chapter 2 examines Cheryl Dunye's *The Watermelon Woman* (1996), a mock-documentary focused on how a queer celebrity is remembered. The film centres on the main character's search for the so-called Watermelon Woman, a Black actor from the 1930s who is also revealed to have been a lesbian. Centring on a mostly forgotten Black lesbian actor, Dunye's film thematizes the ways in which misrepresentation and forgetting shape queer memory and also comments on the (im)possibility of remembering interracial lesbian relationships. In both films, the celebrity at the centre of the story is fictional and serves as a symbol not only for the real stars it echoes, but also for the contexts which produced them and the fan fantasies which find themselves attached to their personae. Through focusing on the relevance of such fantasies (*Velvet*) and the ways in which the celebrity might serve as an embodiment for a *lack* of memory or misremembering the past (*Watermelon*), these films comment on the centrality of queer media to the formation of LGBTQ memories. In other words, they point towards the ways in which queer memory can contain not only the recollections of what occurred in reality, but the memories of what was imagined or experienced through artistic representation.

1

The picture of Arthur Stuart: Todd Haynes's *Velvet Goldmine* and queer fan memory

In a scene from Todd Haynes's *Velvet Goldmine* (1998), a teenager watches television with his parents. Arthur (Christian Bale) sits on the floor of his drab Manchester living room as David Bowie-like glam rock star Brian Slade (Jonathan Rhys Meyers), the sheer opposite to such dull colourlessness, appears on the screen for a press conference. In the background, the boy's parents sit glum and immovable, eyeing their son as Slade responds to a journalist on whether his make-up and glittering clothes are 'likely' to give his fans 'the wrong impression'. When the bisexual Slade announces that this 'wouldn't be the wrong impression in the slightest', the young Arthur jumps to his feet, mirthfully pointing at the television and saying: 'That is me! That is me! That's me, dad, that's me!' In the face of his outburst, however, there is no audible reaction from his parents. Then, as Slade continues to speak of his sexuality, we find that Arthur himself has in fact remained seated in front of the television, glancing warily in the direction of his mother and father (see Figures 1 and 2). Clearly, the moment of confession was a fantasy, but what an important, telling fantasy it was.

This scene illustrates a number of concerns which this chapter will focus on. On the one hand, it points towards the ways in which memory need not relate to literal events or actions but can be formed by imagined experiences and subjective impressions. In this way, the scene establishes the centrality of imagination to the memories of its protagonist and, by extension, to memory itself. On the other hand, it demonstrates how identification with mediated representation shapes the development of the subject in general and the queer subject in particular. This chapter will look at *Velvet Goldmine* with the following questions in mind. How does it comment on the relevance of queer media representations? How does it present the memories of fans? How does it position the role of imagination in the construction of the queer subject, and how does it represent the relevance of fantasy in memory? In focusing on these

Figure 1 Arthur looks furtively at the television.

Figure 2 The fan imagines coming out.

issues, the chapter will look at *Velvet Goldmine* as a text primarily concerned with the issue of fan memory, in which real and imagined experiences coincide, with each carrying an affective relevance that informs the other.

Released in the second half of the 1990s and thus after what Rich describes as the boom of New Queer Cinema, Haynes's film can nonetheless be seen as representative of it. As noted in Introduction to this section, the elements of pastiche, appropriation, irony and a focus on queer history are all visible in

Velvet Goldmine, which follows films like Julien's *Looking for Langston*, Jarman's *Edward II*, Kalin's *Swoon* and Münch's *The Hours and Times* in engaging with earlier artistic representations of queer men. Far from betraying any 'anxiety of influence', the film is self-consciously intertextual, drawing from artists as diverse as Oscar Wilde, David Bowie, Orson Welles and George Orwell to depict the experience of one queer artist as palimpsestuously entwined with that of their precursors. Lines from Oscar Wilde's writing, primarily drawn from *The Picture of Dorian Gray*, appear often within the script with the film also adapting some of the novel's plot points and characters to fit its own narrative. The notion of duality is especially prominent in both texts with the question of 'image' being directly linked within *Velvet Goldmine* to lines from Wilde's novel, as will be addressed in detail later on in this chapter. For now, it is enough to note that the film draws heavily on the book, with instances of this ranging from Brian's lover addressing him with the same words which Dorian's lover Sybil Vane uses in the novel, to the two managers vying for Slade's affection mirroring the characters of Basil Hallward and Henry Wotton.

At the same time, as others have noted, *Velvet Goldmine*'s structure of a journalist looking back at the 'mysterious' persona of a famous man borrows heavily from Orson Welles's *Citizen Kane* (1941).[1] Like *Citizen Kane*, Haynes's film features interviews with people with whom Slade used to be close, each of whom tells us part of the rock star's story. Unlike *Kane*, however, *Velvet* is characterized by scenes of magical realism interspersed in its narrative. These scenes, which often resemble dream sequences, range from moments as diverse as a child walking into what is clearly a painted forest, or Brian's press conference presented as a literal media circus with Slade as its ringmaster. The familiar structure of *Citizen Kane* thus acts as an anchor for both the more exuberant visual moments of the film, as well as its queer temporalities, which often jump from one moment to another in a manner that does not fully disclose the actual course of events or whether certain events are in fact real or imagined.

The film begins in 1984 and revolves around journalist Arthur Stuart (Christian Bale) as he attempts to find out what happened to Brian Slade, a 1970s glam rock superstar whose career was ruined after he faked his own assassination on stage. Visually modelled after David Bowie, Slade (whose surname echoes the eponymous glam rock band) is the film's primary image of androgynous bisexuality. Like Bowie in the early 1970s, Brian is depicted performing in front of disgruntled hippies in a long dress, mimicking the UK cover of *The Man Who Sold the World* (1971), while his subsequent make-up, platform boots, glitter-studded clothes and blazing blue hair mirror Bowie's *Ziggy Stardust* and *Aladdin*

Sane periods. Also like Bowie, Brian's performances are overtly homoerotic, and the film restages moments such as Bowie's infamous onstage fellatio of guitarist Mick Ronson's guitar. Like Bowie's 1971 concept album *Ziggy Stardust and the Spiders from Mars*, Brian's music also tells the story of the rise and fall of a fictional alien, the bisexual rock star Maxwell Demon and his band the Venus in Furs, a name drawn from both the Velvet Underground song and the Leopold von Sacher-Masoch novel which inspired it.

The film thus presents a parallel universe of sorts, with moments and characters mimicking real events. Like Slade, other characters in the film also echo their real-life role models; Brian's wife Mandy Slade (Toni Collette) is based on Angela Bowie, and Slade's lover Curt Wild is visually and musically modelled on Iggy Pop. Scenes in the film also recreate moments which reportedly happened in the lives of Bowie, Pop and Lou Reed. As Bowie reportedly did, Brian first approaches Mandy in a crowded club by saying 'do you jive'.[2] Like Lou Reed, Curt Wild is subjected to electric shock treatment by his family.[3] Through being littered with such references, recognizable to fans of Bowie and Reed, *Velvet Goldmine* presents an alternate reality of sorts – a glam rock puzzle for its viewers to solve.

Through addressing itself most directly to glam rock fans, it thus stresses the figure of the fan as pivotal to its narrative. As numerous critics of the film have noted, such a 'fannish' presentation of the past lacks realism, with even Boy George opining that [he] 'saw *Velvet Goldmine* and thought it was an insult to my youth. I sat in the cinema tutting throughout and thought they got it completely wrong.'[4] What such criticisms of the film's lack of accuracy miss is precisely its deliberate insistence on *unreality* – on impression rather than fact. Like the scene described in the beginning of this chapter, with Arthur watching Slade's appearance on television and imagining his own coming out, the inner experience of bisexual self-awareness is here far more important than the fact that Arthur did not, in reality, come out to his parents yet. Instead of documenting the era of glam rock as it was, the film itself presents a fan's memory of how it *felt*, as well as the great extent to which such feelings are tinged with fantasy, be it sexual or otherwise.

Imagining Brian: Star reflections and fan memories

In attempting to find Slade, Arthur does not represent the impartial journalist. Rather, *Velvet Goldmine* travels from 1984 into Brian's past (told to Arthur by various interviewees who were close to him and shown through flashbacks) and weaves it together with Arthur's memories of being a closeted Slade fan in Manchester. In this way, the assignment of finding Brian acts as a memory journey for Arthur himself, focusing in equal measure on the figure of both the star and the fan. By presenting Arthur not as the objective journalist but as the once-enamoured fan, *Velvet Goldmine* draws another distinction between itself and *Citizen Kane*. In this sense, both the puzzle of Brian's fake assassination and Arthur's initial unwillingness to look back could be read as the film's central mystery. This is particularly evident in the way the film approaches the character of rock singer Curt Wild (Ewan McGregor), whose position as both Brian's lover and the object of Arthur's desire often leaves unclear whether certain interactions between him and Arthur have actually taken place or function symbolically as markers of Arthur's development. Similarly, Arthur is often shown witnessing or noticing events he would have been unlikely to have seen. For example, he is seen in the beginning of the film as attending Brian's final concert and is shown as the only person in the crowd who spots Slade's fake assassin. By singling out Arthur in this way, the film underscores the often-blurred line between imagination and reality in its own narrative and raises the question of how events in its plot function as reflections of Arthur himself.

For Arthur, Brian Slade embodies what Richard Dyer calls a 'star image', which 'function[s] crucially in relation to contradictions within and between ideologies, which they seek variously to "manage" or resolve'.[5] Dyer elaborates 'that certain stars, far from managing contradictions, either expose them or embody an alternative or oppositional ideological position (itself usually contradictory) to dominant ideology'. In this sense, 'the "subversiveness" of these stars can be seen in terms of "radical intervention" (not necessarily conscious) on the part of themselves or others who have used the potential meanings of their image'.[6] Dyer's description is relevant precisely because it highlights not only the 'radical interventions' which star images can enact, but also the potential relevance of star images for others. Both ambiguously gendered and sexually drawn to individuals across the gender continuum, Slade encapsulates what Marjorie Garber describes as 'the two, sometimes apparently conflicting, definitions of bisexuality: having two genders in one body, and being sexually attracted to members of "both" sexes'.[7] His onstage 'assassination' therefore enacts the symbolic death of sexual and gender nonconformity, which the film further underscores by depicting the era of glam rock as one of bright colours and visual opulence, while the 1980s are shot through predominantly dark hues.

In the film, the relationship between its central star and the reporter/fan attempting to find him functions as one of doubling, with Slade's star image acting as a mirror and catalyst for Arthur himself. For example, the moment mentioned in the beginning of this chapter, in which Arthur imagines yelling 'that's me!' while watching Slade come out on television, functions almost as a queering of the Lacanian mirror stage with identification coming not when the subject is faced with the image of themselves but that of another. The set-up of the scene underscores this reading, as most shots of Arthur as he watches the press conference happen in close-up and are focused on his gaze while the lower part of his face remains obscured. In this way, they emphasize the act of looking and self-recognition, while at the same time underscoring his inability to speak through obscuring his lips. In this scene, the only voice Arthur has is Slade's own.

The persona of Brian Slade therefore acts as a stand-in for Arthur, a type of celebrity imago whose manifest bisexuality and gender ambiguity reflect Arthur's desires but not his actions. In this sense, Slade's coming out acts as a screen memory for Arthur's own, functioning both as a mask for and a manifestation of his desires. This idea is reinforced at several other instances, such as a scene showing the teenage Arthur in high school. It depicts him in English class, not paying attention to his teacher as he draws a picture of Slade in his notebook (see Figure 3). As Arthur works on the image, his teacher reads out a passage from *The Picture of Dorian Gray*:

> There were times when it appeared to Dorian Gray that the whole of history was merely a record of his own life, not as he had lived it in act and circumstance, but as his imagination had created it for him, as it had been in his brain and in his passions. He felt that he had known them all, those strange terrible figures that had passed along the stage of life and made sin so marvellous and evil, so full of subtlety. It seemed that in some mysterious way their lives had been his own.

At the end of the passage, the camera zooms in on the lecturer's face as he and Arthur make eye contact, drawing the viewer's attention to the relationship between Arthur and the quoted passage. Wilde's writing is mobilized to present Slade as a mirror for Arthur, a reflection not 'in act and circumstance, but as his imagination had created it for him'. In this way, the 'whole of' glam rock's 'history' is depicted within the film as at once a reflection of Arthur's own desires and of his increasing awareness of his sexuality.

Another moment which invokes the dynamics of doubling comes at the beginning of the film when Arthur is assigned the task of tracking down Slade. The sequence in question echoes *Kane*'s 'News on the March' report (which relates Kane's accomplishments to viewers in Welles's film) and focuses on glam

Figure 3 Fan fantasies – Arthur's drawing of Brian.

rock, Slade and fans coming out as bisexual. Unlike the sequence in *Kane*, *Velvet Goldmine*'s report only partially mimics the style of actual television news reports by featuring interviews and clips from Slade's music videos. It also contains a clip of Arthur himself sitting in a crowded bar, presumably watching this same report as an older man places his hand on his knee. 'Meaning is not in things but in between them,' says a quote from Norman Brown shown on screen. The report ends with a shot of Brian's face on burning celluloid, which dissolves to reveal first a white background and then a close-up of Arthur's eyes as we learn he is watching this report ten years later. The dissolve of Brian's face echoes the burning celluloid seen in Ingmar Bergman's *Persona* (1966), referencing another seminal example of cinematic doubling. Regarding *Persona*'s protagonists, Joel Deshaye reads the relationship between the actor Elisabet (Liv Ullmann) and the nurse Alma (Bibi Andersson) as one between a celebrity and a fan and argues that 'we are often fascinated with' the metaphor of celebrity 'without even thinking of it as metaphor, because the lives of celebrities are (at least in our fantasies) dramatic extensions of our private experiences'.[8] In *Persona*, this metaphor is most clearly illustrated in a scene when the faces of actor and fan merge into one.[9] No such sequence exists in *Velvet Goldmine*, but the film's continuous merging of events from Arthur's own life with that of Slade points towards the interdependence of the experience of Arthur as a fan with Slade as a star.

For Arthur, both the moment of watching Slade's press conference and buying Slade's record is intimately linked with the family setting. He remembers himself as a teenager, opening a copy of *The Musical Express* in his room, its headline announcing that it 'explores the fantasy world of Brian Slade', thus poignantly pointing towards the ways in which Slade functions within the film *as* Arthur's fantasy. The film intermingles this scene of Arthur reading the *Express* with moments from Brian's own life, therein queering the individual and temporal borders of each character's experience. The sequence depicts Slade and Wild's first kiss during a press conference set in an actual circus ring with uniformly tuxedoed male reporters making up the audience while Brian, attired in golden suit and top hat, leads the proceedings. 'Man is least himself when he talks in his own person,' he tells the reporters; 'Give him a mask, and he'll tell you the truth.' As Brian and Curt kiss, Arthur soon opens the paper to see pictures of the couple together, their own desire serving as a clear stand-in for Arthur's own.

A similar dynamic is repeated in subsequent scenes, which bind together several separate and temporally distant developments. One is a public performance of sexuality, as Brian and Curt appear together on stage to perform Brian Eno's 'Baby's on Fire'. Together, they recreate Bowie's onstage fellatio of Mick Ronson's guitar. The scene is interspersed with shots of *The Musical Express* being printed and distributed, and Arthur turns the page of his newspaper to see a picture of the feigned fellatio *before* it can be seen actually taking place. After Slade drops to his knees on stage, thus causing an uproar among both the audience and the media, Arthur is filmed masturbating to the image. Thus, Slade's performance again becomes intimately entangled with the fantasies which crowd Arthur's own sexuality. His identification with Slade mirrors Garber's proposition that a celebrity singer functions as 'the conduit for the doubly identificatory emotions of her, or his, audience. Doubly identificatory because, once again, the object of identification is both the entertainer and the ventriloquized protagonist of the song.'[10] Both Slade and Wild serve as markers of identification in this sequence, as does the image of their desire.

At the same and yet, invariably, different time, Arthur's father is seen angrily stomping up the stairs towards Arthur's room, sick of the loudness of Slade's record. As his father breaks open the door to his bedroom, the crying Arthur is found masturbating by his mother and father. 'You bring shame to this house. You bring shame to your mother and me. It's a shameful, filthy thing you're doing. Do you hear me!?', Arthur's father exclaims. The scene thus links the development of desire between Brian and Curt with Arthur's own sexual development; as the musicians' romance takes shape, Arthur is outed to his parents via the newsmedia consumed during his masturbation. Taken together, these temporally and geographically distant scenes are nonetheless linked by the passage of sexual desire and affect from one scene to another – from queer celebrity to fan. As Brian and Curt's relationship becomes public, Arthur's private act of fantasizing is exposed to the watchful gaze of familial authority figures.

All of this stands in a particular relationship to *Velvet Goldmine*'s focus on fandom. Far from granting Arthur a privileged position as a fan, the film positions such immersion as constitutive of the experience of fandom. Like Haynes's own *Superstar: The Karen Carpenter Story* (1987), which retold the pop star's life by enacting it entirely with Barbie dolls, *Velvet Goldmine* also features a scene of girls playing with Ken dolls, glammed up so as to resemble Brian and Curt (see Figure 4). The camera leaves the girls' identities a mystery by panning from above over the records and dolls that litter the floor of their room, showing only their legs and the dolls to whom they give voice. As the girls play out a romantic scene between the singers, they bring to mind precisely how often the couple's interactions are mediated and seen through the eyes of others. By occluding the girls' identities, the way in which the scene is filmed establishes the primacy of their fantasy. As Stephen N. doCarmo notes, 'in taking as his subject those barely-fictionalized versions of Bowie and Iggy Pop, Haynes is giving us not only fiction but "slash fiction" as well – a type of storytelling that rewrites and reworks mass-market fictions to suit the interests and desires of the people (traditionally women) doing the rewriting'.[11] However, while doCarmo is correct in pointing out the relevance of fanfiction practices in the film, he does not examine this crucial aspect further, as shall be done in the next section.

Figure 4 Curt as a Ken doll.

Glam fanfiction: Poaching through queer utopia

It is useful to go back to the work of Henry Jenkins in looking at *Velvet Goldmine* and see how his pioneering analysis of fans and fanfiction practices draws on Michel de Certeau's concept of 'textual poaching'.¹² As de Certeau argues, the relationship between readers and writers can best be summed up as one of nomadic poaching, as readers approach the text as if they were poachers who take from it what they find pleasurable. In Jenkins's reading of de Certeau, this '"poaching" analogy characterizes the relationship between readers and writers as an ongoing struggle for possession of the text and for control over its meanings'.¹³ Jenkins points out how 'de Certeau's term, "poaching," forcefully reminds us of the potentially conflicting interests of producers and consumers, writers and readers. It recognizes the power differential between the "landowners" and the "poachers".'¹⁴ This emphasizes the unequal power relationship between those who create a media text and those who engage with it. Jenkins goes on to note how 'fans must actively struggle with and against the meanings imposed upon them by their borrowed materials; fans must confront media representations on an unequal terrain'.¹⁵ Emphasizing the active role of fans, Jenkins's analysis contradicts the notion of the fan as mindless, passive consumer. Far from being unthinking, the fan is not only critical but creative and 'poaches' what they like from the text to transform it into a text of their own, i.e. fanfiction.

In *Velvet Goldmine*, Haynes acts not only as a poacher of celebrity and rock star lore, but also as a fan who poaches from an entire lineage of white Anglophone dandyism to construct his filmic fanfiction. The film's very first scene is set almost a century and a half ago and focuses on no less than a flying saucer, carrying within itself the infant Oscar Wilde. The baby is left sleeping peacefully on the doorstep of the Wilde family house; on its white lace blanket, a green pin is attached. From this moment on, the pin will function as a marker of queer genealogy within the film; it will be worn by the school-age Oscar in the next scene, as he proclaims to his serious-faced teacher that he wants to be 'a pop idol' when he grows up, the green pin glistening on his tie. It will be discovered 'a hundred years later' by another queer boy, who finds the pin on the ground as his bullying classmates push him there. Upon finding the pin, Jack is shown entering a veritable fairy tale – a painted forest overlooked by a glistening sun. 'One mysterious day', the voice of a female narrator tells us, 'Jack would discover that there were others quite like him.' The sudden fairy tale setting is thus linked to the discovery of a queer lineage and is followed by the boy looking in the mirror, spreading the blood from his split lip as if it were lipstick and smiling at his own reflection. As we soon find out, the boy will grow up to be Jack Fairy, a proto-glam rocker, and the pin will travel from him to Slade and Wild, only to end up in the hands of Arthur himself in the film's final scenes.

On one level, this trek is a tribute to what Haynes sees as glam rock's obsession 'with the past, … its mission to weave its references into a world that combined nostalgia and futurism'.[16] On another, it acts as emblem for the flow of influence from one queer artist to the other – a trail of breadcrumbs leading viewers to the source of dandyism itself. Queerness, this introductory sequence tells us, *does* indeed have a past, even as the film locates this past within the realm of flying saucers and imagination. As the magical realism of its introductory sequence illustrates, it is the green pin itself which can be seen as the film's real 'Rosebud', to borrow from *Citizen Kane*. Like the green carnation worn by the real-life Oscar Wilde and parts of his inner circle, the pin's repeated reappearance in the film raises questions of its significance. Is it a visual marker of dandyist aesthetics and philosophy? Does it signify gender ambiguity, bisexual and gay inclinations, or rather a specific way in which sexuality and gender identity can be lived? In his reading of the film, Glenn D'Cruz notes the parallels between Wilde's alien status within the film and Foucault's argument that the nineteenth century marks the 'invention' of the homosexual as a 'species'.[17] By so linking the queer and the extraterrestrial, the film's opening sequence can be read as presenting an origin story of sorts for contemporary queer sexuality. Moreover, through pointing towards Wilde's status as a 'pop idol', it signals the star-like visibility ascribed to Wilde by a number of authors, with even his trial being referred to as a 'media spectacle'.[18] His relevance within the film thus spans not only from his writing, which the film's characters frequently quote, or from his function as a symbol of a newly formed homosexual identity, but also from his role as an emblem of queer male visibility. Wilde as a 'pop idol' and the green pin/carnation that he wears thus function as markers not only of the artistic activity of bisexual and gay white men, but also of their public visibility and the mediation of their sexualities.

In exploring the relevance of Wilde as a queer superstar, it is useful to draw on Alan Sinfield, as he attempts to disentangle contemporary assumptions of how queerness can be signified/recognized from those that would have been prevalent in Wilde's own time. As Sinfield argues, prior to Wilde's own trial, his contemporaries 'didn't see queerness in the way we have come to see it. Our interpretation is retroactive; in fact, Wilde and his writings look queer because our stereotypical notion of male homosexuality derives from Wilde, and our ideas about him.'[19] For Sinfield, the crucial difference lies in how 'effeminacy' was regarded at the time – before Wilde's trial, the camp, cultured and effeminate figure of the dandy was not linked in the public consciousness with homosexual identity. After it, the link appeared inextricable. Drawing from this, it is possible to read *Velvet Goldmine*'s introductory sequence as a parable for the birth not of homosexual identity in general, but a specific type of white Anglophone queer identity. This identity, recognizable through its allegiance to art, camp, a dandified, androgynous manner and upper-class pretensions, is traceable from Oscar Wilde to glam rock but means different things at different points in time.

By giving us fanfiction about Wilde, *Velvet Goldmine* not only announces the magical realism which marks its narrative, but also indicates the links between history and fantasy. Prior to the descent of Wilde's flying saucer into Dublin, a narrator's voice proclaims that 'histories, like ancient ruins, are the fictions of empires'. Through linking national histories with fiction and the might of empire, this statement juxtaposes the fiction of flying saucers with the 'truth' of state-sanctioned narratives, finding the former might in fact be more genuine than the latter. The narrator's voice continues that 'everything forgotten hangs in dark dreams of the past, ever threatening to return'. The unfolding, dreamlike development of the film is therefore established as the resurfacing of what was deliberately forgotten by state-sanctioned narratives of history. In turn, by introducing the tale of Oscar Wilde through flying saucers and pop idols, the film presents its own recreation of the past as deliberately and inherently anachronistic. Through its glam rock futurism, Wilde's origin story seems to caution against the belief that the past can ever be known as anything other than a fairy tale. By emphasizing the fantastic and the unlikely, the film points towards the centrality of imagination in any attempt at excavating and engaging with the past. Through pinning together Slade on the one hand and Wilde on the other, *Velvet Goldmine* emphasizes the relevance of queer celebrities such as Wilde and Bowie and establishes a trail of artistic intertextuality and intermediality between them. In the same way that Brian Slade both is and is not David Bowie, the film's pop idol Oscar Wilde is not and could never be the real, historical figure of Wilde but is rather our fanfiction fantasy of him.

In this sense, the film's fanfiction is impossible to disentangle from David Bowie's real coming out as bisexual, as well as his later rejection of the word. As Jenkins notes, 'fandom, after all, is born of a balance between fascination and frustration: if media … didn't frustrate us on some level, there would be no drive to rewrite or remake it'.[20] Having first come out in an interview for *The Melody Maker* in 1972, Bowie's homoerotic lyrics and performances continued to promote queer sexuality as integral to his rock star persona. Music journalist

Jon Savage wrote of Bowie's coming out that 'this really was news. ... Film stars like Montgomery Clift had killed themselves in a previous age trying to deny it, but this was the first time, five years after legalization, that any star came right out and said it.'[21] Similarly, musician Tom Robinson described Bowie's relevance as 'seismic' in its effect on 'gay musicians'.[22] In 1983, however, Bowie appeared on the cover of *Rolling Stone* next to a headline proclaiming simply 'David Bowie Straight'.[23] In the interview (again significantly titled 'Straight Time'), Bowie proclaimed his previous declaration 'the biggest mistake [he] ever made' and explained that he had been both 'young [and] experimenting'.[24]

In *Velvet Goldmine*, this disavowal of the queer community is mirrored not only in Slade's fake onstage assassination, but in Arthur's discovery at the film's end that Slade has become a representative of the very heterosexism he used to oppose. Set in 1984 New York, Arthur's adulthood evokes not only Orwellian narratives of indoctrination and authoritarian control but also takes place a year after Bowie's famed proclamation of heterosexuality. The city is filmed in predominantly dark hues with its inhabitants wearing drab colours and donning masks of the pop star Tommy Stone (Alastair Cumming), therein pointing towards a uniformity of identity. Stone is shown praising the work of President Reynolds and the so-called Committee to Prosper. Although he is not similar to Slade either in casting or in dress, Stone is also visually modelled on David Bowie with platinum hair and white suit echoing Bowie's *Let's Dance* 80s phase.[25] Near the film's end, Arthur is shocked to discover the two are in fact the same person – as Brian's celebrity is revealed as undamaged, his star persona is depicted as unrecognizably altered. While this development can certainly be read as a commentary on Bowie's career trajectory, numerous authors have pointed towards how it criticizes 1980s neoliberal conservatism with the fictional President Reynolds standing in for Ronald Reagan and, through stressing the Orwellian, authoritarian aesthetic of 1980s New York, echoing the AIDS crisis.[26] Through contrasting the bisexual and androgynous exuberance of glam rock with the uniformity which dominates the 1980s, it points towards the havoc wrought on the gay community not only by the AIDS crisis but by political responses to it. At the same time, by renaming Ronald Reagan, the film performs the same fictionalizing operation on the political sphere as it does on that of popular music, therein linking these two aspects of society.

Brian's disavowal of queerness and transformation into Tommy Stone therefore functions as an allegory of social attitudes towards the queer community. The discrepancy between the dystopian 1980s and the magical realism of the 1970s reflects what Christopher Castiglia and Christopher Reed describe as the 'unremembering' of queer sexual liberation. They argue that 'the years following the onset of the AIDS epidemic witnessed a discursive operation that instigated a cultural forgetting of the 1960s and 1970s, installing instead a cleaned-up memory that reconstitutes sanctioned identity out of historical violence'.[27] By demonizing promiscuity and encouraging homonormativity among the queer population, the 1960s and 1970s could be disowned as decades of irresponsibility instead of having a potentially transformative power. Reed and Castiglia thus write that the wider societal response to the AIDS crisis facilitated what they see as an 'assault on gay memory', therein hindering what they see as the transformative potential of communities built on non-normative sexual exchanges.[28] In other words, the loss of memory also minimizes the potential of non-normative behaviour in the future. Through their focus on the memories of gay men, Castiglia and Reed explain the political potency of acts of memory through their ability to 'generate and justify a different sexual consciousness'.[29] For *Velvet Goldmine*, the question of how the past has been buried, as well as how it is beginning to be re-remembered, is of crucial relevance. In this sense, Arthur's search for the past can be read not only as the journey of a fan, but more broadly as a search for the memory of non-normative ways of being.

This search for an affective engagement with memory is particularly pronounced in the film's depiction of Curt Wild, who functions in many ways as a marker of Arthur's development. Early on in the film, the two are shown passing each other in the subway in 1984 and making eye contact. Neither character reacts in recognition and, once on the tube, Arthur hears a young boy reading from the poem 'Antigonish' (1899) by William Hughes Mearns:

> Yesterday upon the stair
> I met a man who wasn't there
> He wasn't there again today
> How I wish he'd go away

Like his imagined coming out a decade later, this interaction with Curt is not real; it is more a metaphor for memory and the willingness to remember than an event in itself. Their next two meetings come in the final quarter of the film and are very different. In the past, Arthur is shown attending the so-called Death of Glitter concert, his hair sprayed blue like Brian's. In so mirroring Brian's image, Arthur is thus seen as finally inhabiting his own/Slade's sexuality on the level of body as well as imagination, a notion which is further underscored as he too, like Slade once did, ends up in a sexual tryst with Curt. As the concert ends, the two men draw nearer to each other and are eventually depicted having sex on the building rooftop. While doing so, they watch as a flying saucer passes above them, glitter falling from the sky. This is the second time the spaceship has appeared in the film, establishing a link between the sex between Arthur the fan and Curt the rock singer and the queer legacy of Oscar Wilde. Once again, the line between fantasy and reality is unclear, pointing towards the broader symbolism of what sex with Curt would signify for Arthur, i.e. his coming out, the merging of fan and star, and the literal manifestation of his once yelling 'this is me' to his parents. All of these things take place simultaneously, wrapped once again in the haze of unreality which marks memory.

Finally, in 1984, Arthur and Curt again meet by chance, this time in a bar after Tommy Stone's performance. While not showing any signs that he knows who Arthur is or that they had once known each other, Curt nonetheless gives Arthur a gift he had received from Brian years ago – a green pin. Barely recognized by Arthur himself at the beginning of the film, Curt is now the one who bequeaths to him a tangible marker of his queerness, thus signalling Arthur's renewed acceptance of it. In giving him the pin, Curt thus stands in for not only the desires of Arthur the teenage fan, but also of Arthur the adult, once again ready to incorporate the memories evoked by Slade and Curt into his identity. In this sense, Curt-the-person-who-might-not-really-be-there, as well as Curt-the-memory, represents what Muñoz sees as the utopian potential of the past, transforming Arthur's perception of the present into one which includes the 'alternative temporal and spatial maps' which memory can provide.[30]

In *Velvet Goldmine*, the utopian potential of the past is drawn from the experiences of fans, with Arthur's interactions with Curt serving as emblems for fannish absorption in the glam rock movement and for the power of fan memory. Far from reprimanding fans for a supposed 'naiveté', the film underscores the transformative potential of such affective immersion. It establishes queer utopian fan memory as potentially liberating and encourages the creation of queer identity through a poaching of the past. While Arthur may have seen Wilde's spaceship in 1974 during his encounter with Curt, it has taken another ten years for this memory to congeal into a marker of proud Wildean sexuality. The very meaning of this past moment is thus transformed, reanimated through the process of remembering with Arthur himself being changed through it. As the green pin travels from Curt to Arthur, it brings together temporally distant moments, awakening the once-buried dreams of the past in the hope of a better, queerer future.

Coda

In this chapter, I have looked at how *Velvet Goldmine* represents the memories of fans and the ways in which queers might imaginatively engage with the past. Focusing on the film's depiction of the star as a screen for the desires of the fan, and on Arthur's journey into the history of glam dandyism as a mirror for his own history, I have highlighted the relevance which the film attributes to fan memories with respect to the formation of queer subjectivity. *Velvet Goldmine*'s depiction of the affective and imaginative potency which memories of queer art and celebrity hold for the queer subject makes it a particularly rich text in this regard. While the film focuses specifically on Anglophone dandyism and glam rock, I read its depiction of queer fandom as surpassing this specific context and as a commentary on the broader utopian possibilities of drawing on the memories of queer fans. Through stressing how the figure of Slade acts both as a cover-up for and a manifestation of Arthur's own sexuality, *Velvet Goldmine* emphasizes the relevance of queer screen memories and how these might be deployed as productive resources in the present.

2

Going on Faith: Cheryl Dunye's *The Watermelon Woman* and the invention of Black lesbian memory

When surveying the notion of queer media memory, the previous chapter centred on representations of LGBTQ fan memory and the formative effects which openly queer artists may have on the self-narrativization of the fan subject. In this chapter, I examine the other side of this equation – on how LGBTQ subjects are misremembered and deliberately forgotten by the media, and how echoes of such discriminatory representations might be found even in queer relationships. Such acts of unremembering and misrepresentation will be examined more closely through an analysis of Cheryl Dunye's mock-documentary *The Watermelon Woman* (1996), which focuses on a character's search for the eponymously nicknamed Black actor. Released only five years after Julie Dash's *Daughters of the Dust* (1991), which was the first feature film in US history directed by a Black woman to receive theatrical distribution, *The Watermelon Woman* marks the first time a film made by a Black lesbian was granted such distribution.[1] Like Dash, Dunye is concerned with the memory of African American women and shares with her the ambition of reimagining their past.

When it was first released in 1996, *The Watermelon Woman* sparked a congressional controversy over its use of government funds for the depiction of 'offensive' and 'pornographic' material.[2] At the time, Michigan Representative Peter Hoekstra was ultimately unsuccessful in persuading his fellow representatives to rescind the funds granted to the film by the National Endowment for the Arts. Today, it still remains one of the rare examples of American cinema to deal with the subject of Black lesbianism. More than 20 years since its release, only Dee Rees's *Pariah* (2011) can be listed as another US feature film made by and about an out Black lesbian to receive comparable praise. Similarly, while African American queer female characters do appear in films such as *Bessie* (2015), *Precious* (2009), *Set It Off* (1996), *The Incredibly True Adventure of Two Girls in Love* (1995), *Daughters of the Dust* (1991) and *The Color Purple* (1985), such works are few and far between. In her reading of the film, Catherine Zimmer correctly identifies this lack as 'a testament to how little has really changed in the power structures of cinematic production [in spite of] the seemingly massive impact of the New Queer Cinema and the culture of Sundance and independent film'.[3] The gender imbalance of New Queer Cinema directors is thus even more relevant when regarding Dunye's work, with her position as a Black queer woman in the film industry being doubly precarious. It is precisely this lack of Black queer female cinematic heritage that Dunye's film thematizes, and so its mockumentary format can be read as itself a comment on the cinematic invisibility of African American queer women.

The Watermelon Woman is a rare cinematic examination of the possibility of reconstructing a queer Black history and also comments on the deliberate silences in which such histories are often enveloped. In *The Queer Limit of Black Memory: Black Lesbian Literature and Irresolution*, Matt Richardson recounts the ways in which Black queers are systematically excluded even from projects which address Black counter-memory.[4] As an example, Richardson describes his visit to the Museum of the African Diaspora in San Francisco, in which he encountered only hetero- and gender-normative representations of Black individuals. 'Institutions like MoAD are created to remember loss,' argues Richardson, 'but even there, Black queers do not figure into the collective memory. The Black queer falls even deeper into the abyss of negation because we are not even part of the memory of loss.' Instead, he notes, their 'claims are rejected as inauthentically Black and "un-African." We are disremembered and unrecognized by our own – negated by the negated, dissociated from Black memory.'[5] Drawing from Richardson, we might speak not only about projects of memory but of active forgetting, a deliberate disremembering of those individuals or parts of the Black past not considered acceptable.

Like Isaac Julien's *Looking for Langston* (1989), which offers an impressionistic take on the Harlem Renaissance as well as the AIDS crisis, and Rodney Evans's *Brother to Brother* (2004), which also draws on Hughes and Ted Nugent in its presentation of queer Black history, *The Watermelon Woman* also functions as a commentary on the forgetting to which such histories are most often consigned. Unlike Julien and Evan's films, however, it constructs its own heroine and creates its own past. As Kobena Mercer wrote of *Looking for Langston*, it enters 'the archive of black cultural life not as a repository of stable facts but as an institution of public memory and social history that is shot through with gaps, absences, and lacunae [and] asks whether the past is ever recoverable'.[6] Like Julien and Evans' films, it is also one of the few queer Black films exhibited in cinemas to deal directly with the complexities of how histories of racist representation influence the past and present of LGBTQ interracial relationships.

It is for these reasons that this chapter focuses specifically on Dunye's film and examines how it contrasts the (overwhelmingly unrecorded) experiences of Black women with the prosthetic memories of Blackness made in cinema. By focusing on filmic archives as well as personal ones, *The Watermelon Woman* comments on the links between the two and on how our personal experiences can be overshadowed and influenced by cinematic representation. In approaching the question of how one fictional Black lesbian actor is remembered, *The Watermelon Woman* uses its subject to provide a broader critique of how both LGBTQ artists and interracial queer relationships have been misrepresented and forgotten, deliberately screened away from memory projects and what are considered 'acceptable' narratives of African American history.

Finding Fae: Faking the documentary, making up memory

The film centres on aspiring filmmaker Cheryl (played by Dunye herself) and her ambition to make a film 'about Black women, because our stories have never been told'. She focuses her research on one actor in particular, the so-called Watermelon Woman (Lisa Marie Bronson) whom she first encounters in a 1930s film about the antebellum South. Initially nameless at the film's beginning except for this nickname (itself a reference not only to the racist history of African American representation, but also to Melvin Van Peebles's *Watermelon Man* (1970)), the figure of the 'Watermelon Woman' reflects Cheryl's 'shock' at the discovery that 'in some of the films, the Black actresses aren't event listed in the credits'. Later revealed as Faith 'Fae' Richards, her initial namelessness thus raises questions of the legibility of African American women in the media, particularly of Black lesbians.

From its opening sequence, *The Watermelon Woman* highlights the ways in which cinematic systems of representation either actively exclude or misrepresent Black women. The film begins with Mozart playing in the background and shows Cheryl and her best friend Tamara in the process of filming a middle-class wedding. In contrast to the music and the guests' polished appearance, Cheryl's camera focuses repeatedly on minutiae not usually seen in wedding videos, such as people frowning, Tamara setting up the reflectors, and Cheryl arranging the family for portrait shots. The sequence ends after Cheryl and Tamara are paid for their work and is followed by Tamara's filming the streets she and Cheryl are riding past. 'What are you shooting?' asks Cheryl. 'Come on, Cheryl, this is the really good stuff,' Tamara replies. 'This is like ... Urban, poverty ... It's very in, it's very new.' Through these tongue-in-cheek sequences, the film offers a commentary on the types of representation available to Cheryl and Tamara as Black female subjects – middle-class heteronormativity on the one hand or 'gritty' urban realism on the other. As evidenced both through the unfocused nature of how the wedding sequence is filmed, and the bickering heard throughout the 'urban' sequence, neither Cheryl nor Tamara is at home in either of these systems of representation.

In stark contrast, the next scene introduces viewers to Cheryl's real project. Cheryl addresses her own camera: 'Hi, I'm Cheryl and I'm a filmmaker. Oh, no, I'm not really a filmmaker, but I have a videotaping business with my friend Tamara and I work at a video store so I'm *working* on being a filmmaker.' By introducing herself and her project about the 'Watermelon Woman' in such a manner, Dunye's filmic alter ego stresses its relevance not only at the level of knowledge (i.e. the project will tell hitherto untold stories of Black women), but also as a personal process of *becoming* a filmmaker through introducing the viewer to the precedent of another Black queer woman in film. In this way, the process of naming and indeed, *creating* Fae, is paralleled with Cheryl claiming the term 'filmmaker' for herself as she does at the film's end by again directly addressing the camera. In the film's beginning, however, her authority as a director ('I'm *working* on being a filmmaker') is deliberately undercut, which emphasizes the uncertain nature of her position as a Black lesbian in American film.

In the next scene, Cheryl introduces us to the 'Watermelon Woman' through a clip from *Plantation Memories*, Dunye's fictional equivalent to big budget old-Hollywood productions such as *Gone with the Wind* (1939). The clip shows a melodramatic exchange between Fae in the role of a Black mammy and her white mistress, with Elsie (played by Fae aka the 'Watermelon Woman') comforting her mistress as she weeps at the absence of her beloved. Featuring a melodramatic soundtrack reminiscent of the Hollywood films of the era and marked by histrionic acting, the scene first depicts Elsie running towards her mistress and then situates the two characters side by side as Elsie caringly wipes away her mistress's tears. In being so set up, it attributes a nostalgic wholesomeness to the mistress/slave relationship and depicts it as one of familiarity and care.

Though critical towards such representations, Cheryl is nonetheless fascinated with them and calls *Plantation Memories* her 'all-time-favourite' film of Fae's. She therefore hints not only towards the past relevance of such cinema, but to its continued capacity to produce what Alison Landsberg has termed 'prosthetic memories'. As noted in Introduction, Landsberg argues that mass-mediated representations of the past have the potential to produce sensuous memories in the viewer. Through naming them prosthetic, Landsberg highlights that they are not the product of one's immediate social context but rather transgress boundaries of ethnicity and experience. At the same time, their prosthetic form highlights their interchangeable and commodified nature, as well as their capacity to produce an affective, bodily experience. Landsberg explains that these prosthetic memories 'are privately felt public memories that develop after an encounter with a mass cultural representation of the past, when new images and ideas come into contact with a person's own archive of experience'.[7] Because of this, she notes they not only 'blur the boundary between individual and collective memory, [but] also complicate the distinction between memory and history'.[8]

With regard to the political potential of such memories, Landsberg writes that 'this new form of memory is neither inherently progressive nor inherently reactionary, but it is powerful. ... Taking on prosthetic memories of traumatic events and the disenfranchisement and loss of privilege that such an experience often necessitates can have a profound effect on our politics.'[9] In the same vein, the opposite experience is also true, and so reactionary prosthetic memories might have long-lasting political effects. Drawing from this, Dunye's presentation of *Plantation Memories* as the source of her fascination with Fae becomes particularly important as it critiques racist representations without denying their potential to nonetheless provoke affect and attachment in the viewer, as they do in sparking Cheryl's search for Fae. In fact, the very title of Fae's film invokes the question of how memories of the plantation are represented, or rather, how visualizations of racist histories live on, and the complex ways in which they affect their viewers. By highlighting this interaction between reactionary cinema and the viewer, the film positions itself not only as a commentary on the cinematic past of African American female representation, but more broadly as a reflection on the possibilities of cinematic veracity with regard to race, gender and sexuality. In this sense, *The Watermelon Woman* presents a dual critique of how cinema creates prosthetic memory, as it questions not only the effect of films such as *Plantation Memories* but of the documentary genre as well.

Through mimicking the documentary format, *The Watermelon Woman* reflects Bill Nichols's view of the 'documentary as a fiction (un)like any other', also highlighting how the legitimacy typically bestowed upon the form transforms the viewer's relationship to the text.[10] Nichols notes 'the status of documentary as *discourse about* the world', thus leading to its own 'rhetorical strategies and stylistic choices [usually going] largely unnoticed'.[11] Drawing from this, it becomes clear how Dunye's film troubles the legitimacy bestowed upon the documentary form as a *document* of the world and brings to light the constructedness of all on-screen representations. Jane Roscoe and Craig Hight's reading of mock-documentaries or mockumentaries is therefore particularly helpful, as they stress the way in which these copy the documentary form in order to 'ask the question "can we really believe what we see?"'[12] In this sense, Dunye's use of the mock-documentary form acts as a powerful critique of institutionalized knowledge and remembrance.

By engaging with films such as *Plantation Memories* and their real-life counterparts, *The Watermelon Woman* criticizes the romanticized visions of slavery present in such racist representations, extending this critique from the documentary genre to American cinema more broadly. It draws a very conscious parallel between the fictionality of its own narrative, that of *Plantation Memories* and of its real-life cinematic counterparts in order to question the relationship between cinema and truth and to present it as historically flawed. The clip from *Plantation Memories* is revisited again later in the film; only Dunye does not focus her camera on it. Instead, she films herself seated next to a television set (visible here only by its borders) and mouths the dialogue in an even more theatrical manner than its performers (see Figure 5). While doing so, Cheryl also wears a scarf on her head similar to the one Fae wears in the 'original', evoking both iconic Aunt Jemima imagery and roles such as that of Hattie McDaniel in *Gone with the Wind*. Dunye's parodic mimicry, complete with her using the scarf at the scene's end to blow her nose, underscores the ridiculousness inherent in films of this type.

Moreover, by showing Cheryl herself as she performs the mammy character, the scene juxtaposes real Black women with racist mammy imagery, at once exposing its falsity and highlighting its continued persistence (both in cinema and the expectations that Black women continue to be met with in life). While often associated with the past of US cinema, Clitha Mason's work demonstrates the persistence of the mammy image in contemporary American film, tracing her presence in films as recent as Tyler Perry's *Madea* series and *The Help* (2011).[13] Within the context of the film, the use of the mammy figure as a

Figure 5 Cheryl mimics Fae's mammy next to a recording of *Plantation Memories*.

controlling image under which real Black women are erased is highlighted through Cheryl's initial struggle to find out what Fae's name is. 'Is "Watermelon Woman" her first name, or her last? I don't know', Cheryl asks the camera in characteristically humorous fashion. In this way, Fae's namelessness reflects how, as Kimberly Wallace-Sanders describes, the '*mammy* is often both [a] title, and the only name' an African American woman has been given in fictionalized representation.[14] More to the point, however, Fae's namelessness also points towards Wallace-Sanders's description of 'the actual African American women whose names were lost when they became "Mammy", often even among the white southern children who describe her as the most influential figure of their childhoods and yet never learned her given name.'[15]

In attempting to excavate such forgotten stories, Dunye's cinematic doppelganger also reflects real-life attempts by Black feminists to unbury the tales of the women who preceded them. Patricia Hill Collins notes the fate of artists such as Zora Neale Hurston, whose grave was left unmarked, or the early nineteenth-century Black feminist Maria Stewart, whose words we are today able to access only through the reports of others. She writes that 'many Maria Stewarts exist, African-American women whose minds and talents have been suppressed ... The shadow obscuring this complex Black women's intellectual tradition is neither accidental nor benign.'[16] As Richardson notes, such erasure is doubly true of queer Black women. He writes that 'while there has been some documentation and discussion of Black gay male history and representation, Black lesbians and transpeople have not received as much academic attention'.[17] Drawing from this, it becomes clear why Fae is never allowed by Dunye to speak for and of herself but rather is to be found only in the telling and re-remembering of those who speak of her. The fact that such discoveries always remain partial and shaped by the perception of others appears here to be precisely Dunye's point.

For example, the first third of the movie passes without audience members learning Fae's real name, and her namelessness acts here to emphasize the many ways in which Fae herself might be illegible to those that speak of her. This is particularly clear in moments such as when Cheryl interviews Camille Paglia, who appears as herself. Unlike all the preceding African American talking heads, whose presence was explained within the film by a personal connection either to Cheryl or the people she knows, Paglia's interview is introduced only by way of a black screen announcing its location, and her presence explained solely through the descriptor 'Camille Paglia Cultural Critic'. This lack of introduction sets Paglia apart from the others Cheryl interviews precisely through her *lack* of connection to the community she is commenting on, emphasizing the absurdity of Paglia's commentary, which refashions the mammy into a positive symbol which reminds Paglia of her own grandmothers and which deliberately dismisses African American scholarship on the subject. The white students Cheryl interviews on campus are not much better, as they inform her they know nothing of Fae as they 'haven't covered women in the blaxploitation movement yet'.

In direct contrast to this, the interview in which we learn Fae's real name is also the one in which we learn of her lesbian identity. Having received information from her mother about a person who used to frequent the clubs Fae sang in, Cheryl goes to interview 'Shirley, *miss* Shirley, never married, worked in a factory most of her life – I think she's in the family.' Upon meeting Shirley (playwright Ira Jeffries), Cheryl is proven to be correct, and so the camera zooms enthusiastically on Shirley's face as she says Fae 'used to sing for all of us stone butches'. The moment in which Fae is given her real name corresponds to the one in which her sexuality is revealed, and it is by linking the two that *The Watermelon Woman* depicts one as unknowable without the other. The scene thus attributes to Shirley, who is a Black queer woman, the ability of 'reading' or recognizing Fae correctly, which is a capacity missing in most of the other talking heads Cheryl interviews. Differently put, it shows Fae as illegible to those unaware of her identity as a Black lesbian, reserving her full name for those privy to her queerness.

Through figures like Shirley, *The Watermelon Woman* contrasts personal, often unacknowledged archives with official ones like the academy or library, as well as with Hollywood's prosthetic memory. In doing so, Dunye points towards the frailty of unrepresented memory, towards its spectral properties, and asks us to consider the many pasts that are invariably lost to us. At the same time, it also depicts the difficulties of breaking free from racist discourses. This is evident in the film's presentation of interracial relationships, with one taking place in the past between Fae and Martha, who also directed *Plantation Memories*, and the other in the present between Cheryl herself and the white Diana (Guinevere Turner). The next section will therefore look more closely at how the film specifically troubles the possibilities of remembering interracial relationships between women and how these relationships are themselves affected by racist histories of representation.

Going on Faith: Interracial relationships, plantation memories

In the case of Cheryl and Diana, Dunye presents their relationship as continually framed by cinematic representations. Their first meeting happens in the video store where Cheryl and Tamara work, and their first conversation revolves around the films Diana considers renting (among the options she mentions, there's *Cleopatra Jones* (1973), a blaxploitation classic featuring a white lesbian adversary, and *Personal Best* (1982), a pivotal early example of white US lesbian representation (see Figure 6)). In the scene where the two have sex for the first time, they do so after watching a film of Fae's that is explicitly concerned with the question of racial passing (see Figure 7). Similarly, in a scene where the two have dinner with Tamara and her girlfriend Stacey, Dunye conspicuously positions Diana in front of a large poster of Isaac Julien's *The Attendant* (1993), a short film that deals precisely with questions of memory and interracial sexuality. In all of these examples, the film points towards the systems of representation that form the paradigmatic background of their interaction and questions the influence of these representations on their relationship.

The connection between cinematic representation and sexuality is also emphasized through the film's other interracial couple. Like much of her life, Fae's relationship with Martha remains for the most part a mystery to us as

50　　　　　　　　　　*Screening Queer Memory*

Figure 6 Diana and Cheryl framed by cinema, in the video store.

Figure 7 Cheryl and Diana watch a film of Fae's before they first have sex.

viewers, as we learn of its existence only through the interviews of others. This lack of information about their relationships is juxtaposed with our knowledge that Martha was not only Fae's lover, but the person who directed *Plantation Memories*. The conjunction of these roles problematizes the imbalance of power between the two, for while both of them are queer women living under a heteropatriarchal system, Martha is the one who *directs* Fae in the mammy role. Thus, while Martha is in this case the one who makes prosthetic memory, Fae is relegated simply to being a nameless performer in it. Dunye utilizes her character to draw and question the link between racist representation and interracial relationships, which is a theme that pervades *The Watermelon Woman*.

The link between Fae's subordinate position and the mammy role she plays is made explicit within the film by June Walker, Fae's lifelong partner after her relationship with Martha. Upon hearing Cheryl is making a film about Fae, June asks her to omit any mention of Martha Page from her life. She asks Cheryl why she would 'even want to include a white woman in a movie on Fae's life? … I think it troubled her soul for the world to see her in those mammy pictures.' June's request for the removal of Martha from a film about Fae's life is here linked with the racist ideology promoted by *Plantation Memories* and similar films. According to June, one is inextricable from the other, and Dunye's film continually questions both the racist and romantic legacies which bind Black and white women together. It is here worth noting that June frames this plea precisely within the context of Black lesbian history and how it will be recorded:

> **June Walker:** She did so much Cheryl, that's what you have to speak about. She paved the way for kids like you to run around making movies about the past and how we lived then. Please Cheryl, make our history before we are all dead and gone, but if you *are* really in the family, you better understand that our family will always only have each other.

As June asks Cheryl not to include Fae's relationship with a white woman into her documentary, the film stresses the question of whether and how we remember interracial relationships. The casting of poet and scholar Cheryl Clarke as June is particularly significant here, as Clarke herself has written on the subject of interracial relationships that the character she plays addresses. In 'Lesbianism: An Act of Resistance', Clarke argues that 'we, as black lesbians, must vehemently resist being bound by the white man's racist, sexist laws, which have endangered potential intimacy of any kind between whites and blacks.'[18] She traces the historical roots of the prohibition against miscegenation and emphasizes its patriarchal, heterosexist bias, positioning interracial lesbianism as an act of resistance against this system. Clarke comments that 'it cannot be presumed that black lesbians involved in love, work and social relationships with white lesbians do so out of self-hate and denial of our racial-cultural heritage, identities and oppression'.[19] In the film, Cheryl and Tamara represent two opposites of this debate, as Tamara berates Cheryl both for her interest in racist cinema, as well as her interest in white women. In reference to Cheryl and Diana's relationship, Tamara comments that 'all I see is that once again you're going out with a white girl acting like she want to be Black, and you're being a Black girl acting like she wants to be white'. In response to this, Cheryl angrily answers that 'who's to say that dating somebody white doesn't make me Black? I mean who's to say anything about who I fuck in the goddamn first place?' This is a view echoed by Clarke herself as she asks why 'a woman's commitment to the struggle [should] be questioned or accepted on the basis of her lover's or comrade's skin color? White lesbians engaged likewise with black lesbians or any lesbians of color cannot be assumed to be acting out of some perverse, guilt-ridden racialist desire.'[20]

She concludes that interracial lesbianism questions and transforms the history of relationships between Black and white women, which is a view in direct contradiction to that proposed by her character within the film. The presence of interracial lesbian relationships therefore raises the question of how these relationships are to be inscribed into both Black and white history and to whom these histories can be said to belong as they are so often deliberately disremembered. This theme is repeatedly underscored; at one point in the film, Martha Page's sister is depicted as vehemently denying both that her sister had been a lesbian and that she had had an interracial relationship, therein pointing towards the ways in which such histories are erased from familial memory. In another scene, Cheryl's visit to a lesbian archive raises questions of archive ownership and the veracity of commemorative projects. When the archive volunteer tells Cheryl that, as the donors wanted the collection to be only about African American lesbians, 'whenever [they] see a picture of a white person in the photos, [they] just cross them out', the difficulties inherent in preserving the memories of relationships deemed less acceptable become clear.

By framing the film around two interracial love stories, Dunye explicitly speaks out against such erasure and instead constructs both a past and a present in which community boundaries present themselves as far more unfixed and permeable than some would like. The film repeatedly places interracial relationships in dialogue with the history of cinematic representations of miscegenation, thus presenting them as influenced by these representations in often unacknowledged ways. In a sequence where Cheryl, Diana, Tamara and her girlfriend Stacey have dinner together, Stacey questions why Cheryl 'always hook[s] up with these typical "white devil" types', and it is significant here that this exchange takes place next to a poster of Isaac Julien's *The Attendant* (1993), in front of which Dunye positions Diana (see Figure 8).

The Attendant is set in the Wilberforce House in Hull, England (the birthplace of abolitionist William Wilberforce), and revolves around a Black security guard's attraction to a white museum visitor. It focuses on the role of race and subordination in sexuality and its artistic representations, beginning first with a close-up of François-Auguste Biar's 'Slaves on the West Coast of Africa' and its depiction of African men whipped or prostrated, only to recreate the scene with live subjects wearing S&M leather collars. The erotic dimensions of racist subordination are underscored through this recreation and are once more emphasized through a highly sexualized scene of whipping between the guard and the visitor, this time set in front of the drawings of Tom of Finland. By bringing the two together, the power exchange depicted in Finland's drawings (one of which centres on a sex scene in which a Black man penetrates a white man he holds on a leash) is transferred into the guard and the visitor and is made manifest

Figure 8 Cheryl and Diana positioned directly in front of a poster of Isaac Julien's *The Attendant*.

as the scene shifts from the guard being depicted as the one being whipped to the one who holds the whip, the white man joyfully prostrated at his feet. For Elizabeth Freeman, the film's focus on sadomasochism serves as an example of erotohistoriography, in this case a reparative deployment of sadomasochism as a method of countering colonial legacies.[21] *The Attendant* encourages such a reading through its emphasis on the historicity of the Black and white body and the ways in which it contrasts contemporary interracial sexual practices with racist histories of sexual subjugation, at once underscoring their echoes in the present. In depicting such interracial coupling, Julien stresses the connection between sexuality, representation and memory, and so the guard is also depicted as singing 'Remember me!' to a nearly empty theatre, its lack of patrons a clear sign that he will in fact be forgotten. Through these scenes, *The Attendant* troubles the role between remembrance, artistic representation and the archive (as emblematized in the museum space), and it is therefore little wonder that Dunye brings it deliberately in dialogue with the debates raised by *The Watermelon Woman*.

With regard to the resonance between the two works, this is nowhere more evident than in Dunye's depiction of the first sex scene between Cheryl and Diana. In the sequence leading up to their lovemaking, Diana has invited Cheryl over to her spacious apartment, and the two watch a video of one of Fae's few 'race' films. The clip features Fae arguing with another African American woman over her attempts to 'pass' as white. As Diana and Cheryl kiss for the first time, Fae slaps her lighter-skinned companion. After this, the sequence focuses on the sex scene between Cheryl and Diana, and the movie is no longer heard in the background. The interaction between them is depicted as both erotic and positive through its focus on the pleasure of the couple and its use of soundtrack (Leslie Winer's *Skin* plays in the background, the lyrics denoting that 'I ain't afraid of where you come from / I ain't afraid of where you been / I ain't afraid of what you're giving in / I ain't afraid of skin'). As Robert Reid-Pharr notes, by juxtaposing 'Cheryl and Diana's exchange with that between Fae and Irene', the sequence 'allows the audience to see the repressed racial antagonism in the one and the suppressed homoeroticism in the other'.[22] In putting these two scenes side by side, Dunye frames the first sex scene between Cheryl and Diana in a context influenced by previous histories of racialized representation, highlighting their inability to exist outside a framework that is always already marked by racist discourses. Like the sexual encounters depicted in *The Attendant*, they are at once a break from the past as well as an unwitting continuation of its legacies.

The film positions Diana herself in a complex relation to race, as she is revealed as having been born in Jamaica (her father is a diplomat), volunteering with underprivileged African American children, having had Black boyfriends, and an aunt who was married to a Black Panther. The last two facts are revealed during a scene in which Cheryl and Diana lie together in post-coital bliss, only for Cheryl to leave abruptly after Diana mentions them. Through her sudden departure, Cheryl's disquiet echoes bell hooks's writing on the sexual consumption of otherness and Diana's potentially fetishizing attitude towards African Americans. Hooks argues that 'when race and ethnicity become commodified as resources for pleasure, the culture of specific groups, as well as the bodies of individuals, can be seen as constituting an alternative playground where members of dominating races, genders, sexual practices affirm their power-over in intimate relations with the Other'.[23] This is what hooks calls 'eating the Other', and it is at the thought of being so consumed that Cheryl rebels. The very title of the film reinforces this notion, as Fae's cinematic nickname highlights the ways in which she, 'The Watermelon Woman', is consumed by others without regards for her own subjectivity.

The film does not present such objectification outside of its historical context but rather utilizes Fae to link it with the past of racist representation to which both Cheryl and Diana have been exposed. In this sense, the objectification and erotic consumption of the Other fall in line with Sara Ahmed's description of the ways in which some emotions 'stick' to certain subjects. Ahmed explains that the saturation of some objects with affect influences our perception of them to a degree that 'the object of feeling is never simply before the subject. How the object impresses (upon) us may depend on histories that remain alive insofar as they have already left their impressions. The object may stand in for other objects, or may be proximate to other objects.'[24] These emotions, the origins of which are most often left unremembered, then 'stick' to objects without the conscious knowledge of the person who feels them of how they were produced. 'In other words', as Ahmed explains, '"feelings" become "fetishes", qualities that seem to reside in objects, only through an erasure of the history of their production and circulation.'[25] In the same way, Dunye's film depicts the circulation of emotions from racist controlling images like the mammy to Fae and Cheryl herself. Most crucially, *The Watermelon Woman* makes plain that, while these images are depicted as focal points of affect, their history is insufficiently documented, as Cheryl's interviews demonstrate.

Similarly, *The Watermelon Woman* highlights the passage from prosthetic memories, as created by films such as *Plantation Memories*, to the creation of fetishes. It juxtaposes its fictionalized cinematic interracial narratives with those of 'real-life' interracial couples such as Cheryl and Diana to comment on their often intangible and inarticulate interdependency. It is significant here that the scene which depicts Cheryl and Diana's falling out does not actually feature any prolonged argument but is characterized by brevity and Cheryl's abrupt departure. While Cheryl believes at that moment that Diana is 'such a mess' and Diana sees Cheryl's project as 'a crutch', the two do not discuss the issue further and Diana is never seen within the film again. While this may suggest an unwillingness to elaborate on the matter, it points also towards the possibility that they may be *unable* to speak of it. In this sense, both the fear and rejection of being fetishized, and the possibility that one fetishizes another are presented as something beyond Cheryl and Diana's articulation, and it is relevant that the film follows its revelation of their break-up with Cheryl's rejection of June Walker's request that she keep the relationship between Fae and Martha unmentioned. 'The moments she shared with [June], the life she had with Martha on and off the screen, those are precious moments, and no one can change that', Cheryl tells the camera. In doing so, she does not deny the histories of racial fetishism in these relationships but hints towards the fact that this dynamic may in fact be reinforced precisely by the silences which often deliberately veil such relationships from remembrance. Cheryl tells the camera at the film's end:

> **Cheryl:** What [Fae] means to me, a twenty-five-year-old Black woman, means something else. It means hope, it means inspiration, it means possibility. It means history. And most importantly, what I understand, is that I'm going to be the one who says – I am a Black lesbian filmmaker. Who's just beginning. But I'm gonna say a lot more, and have a lot more work to do.

Cheryl's final address to the camera thus highlights the importance of finding a precedent for oneself, of tracing one's Black lesbian lineage to those who came before. Dunye thus positions a memory project like Cheryl's as one which can bring hope and inspiration to other queer women of colour and can enable their own artistic activity. In this way, questions of memory and forgetting are presented not merely as issues of how we think about the past, but what we believe to be possible or achievable in the present.

Coda

More than twenty years after *The Watermelon Woman* was released, Black queer history still remains largely unrepresented. For example, in Raoul Peck's *I Am Not Your Negro* (2016), the writings and interviews of James Baldwin are juxtaposed with a variety of recordings, some of them from Baldwin's lifetime, while others are as recent as the Black Lives Matter protests. By bringing these two timelines together, the documentary presents Baldwin's words as equally relevant today as they once were and challenges notions of a 'post-racial' US by showing the continued persistence of discrimination and racist violence. In stark contrast to the sensitivity with which his writings on racism are cinematically deployed, however, Peck's film omits Baldwin's queerness, quoting only an FBI report which terms Baldwin a 'suspected homosexual' and never his own words on the matter. As Dagmawi Woubshet points out, 'the apparent desire to represent Baldwin as the quintessential Race Man – a public spokesman and leader of African Americans with ostensibly straight bonafides – goes against not only the principles of Baldwin's work, but also the reality of his fraught position in the civil-rights movement as a queer black man'.[26] The film therefore performs two acts of separation: the first by disarticulating Baldwin's sexuality from his ability to speak of it himself, as well as dividing his experiences as a Black man from his experiences as a *queer* Black man.

A similar silence on LGBTQ Black experiences can be found in the abundance of recent historical films dealing with Black histories, as exemplified by *I Am Not Your Negro*, *Hidden Figures* (2016), *The Birth of a Nation* (2016), *Selma* (2014), *Twelve Years a Slave* (2013) and *The Butler* (2013), all of which testify to a preoccupation with how Black pasts are remembered. Of these films, it is notable that all save for *Hidden Figures* centre on (heterosexual) male protagonists, while only one of them is a female-led project (*Selma*, directed by Ava DuVernay), thus highlighting both whose story is more likely to be told and *who* is most likely to tell it. On television screens, the ground-breaking release of Ryan Murphy's *Pose* (FX, 2017–) and its depiction of African American ballroom communities during the 1980s and 1990s serves as a thus far unprecedented depiction of BAME American queer history. *Pose* notwithstanding, the tendency in contemporary US cinema and television towards heteronormative retellings of the Black past continues to hide stories such as Fae's from view and to exclude viewers such as Cheryl from the histories they present. As *The Watermelon Woman* demonstrates, such exclusions do not come without a cost but instead allow for a plethora of misconceptions about the past, leaving Black lesbians unmoored from all that preceded them.

Conclusion

In both films analysed in this section, a scene appears in which the central characters find themselves mirrored by the television screen. In *Velvet Goldmine*,

Brian's highly publicized coming out serves as an important moment of self-recognition and psychic self-proclamation for the young Arthur. In contrast to this, *The Watermelon Woman* positions Cheryl herself next to a television as she mouths Fae's mammy monologue in a histrionic manner, thereby emphasizing its ridiculousness and contrasting the complexity of real Black women with the ways in which they are represented on screen. Unlike Arthur, who attaches great relevance to the televised declaration he is observing, Cheryl is both critical of the scene in question and drawn to the woman she sees behind the mammy character. Thus, while *Velvet Goldmine* uses its cinematic mirroring scene to depict a character's coming to sexual self-awareness, *The Watermelon Woman* contrasts established practices of cinematic and televisual representation with a more ambivalent account of both attachment and criticism. Taken together, both scenes and, by extension, both films represent two sides of queer media memory. While one points to the ways in which queer media might act as a screen for our own desires, the other highlights the erasure which still often engulfs queer pasts, particularly those of already marginalized subjects. Like Arthur and Cheryl, queers have found themselves simultaneously seen and unseen, represented and forgotten in media works and celebrity figures.

Since the period in which these films were shot, there has been a notable influx of LGBTQ representation, with queer media memories recently being mobilized by reboots of iconic LGBTQ works like *Will & Grace* (NBC, 1998–2005, 2017–20), *The L Word* (Showtime, 2004–9), *Tales of the City* (PBS, 1993; Netflix, 2019) and *Queer Eye* (Bravo, 2003–7; Netflix, 2018–). While these reboots are of course part of a broader tendency towards televisual and cinematic nostalgia which has seen works as different as *Ghostbusters* (2016) and *Fuller House* (Netflix, 2016–20) being remade, they nonetheless address themselves particularly to queer fans, mobilizing their memories of these shows in what can easily be interpreted as an effort to also repeat the ratings these series used to attract. In this sense, it is interesting that these shows at once mimic and update their predecessors, for example through the greater inclusion of BAME and trans protagonists in *The L Word: Generation Q* (Showtime, 2019–), which was noted by many critics as setting it apart from the original series.[27] Such mobilizations of fan memory thus serve as both nostalgic addresses towards the viewers who had once watched these series (or had discovered them at a later point via streaming platforms such as Netflix), while at the same time addressing themselves to new audiences.

Another recent example of queer media memories being mobilized comes from Netflix's *Hollywood* (2020), which reimagines what the history of Tinseltown may have looked like if minority communities had been represented on the silver screen. The show envisions events such as Rock Hudson coming out as gay and revealing he is in an interracial relationship during the 1940s, a development which paradoxically ends up neither endangering him nor his Black partner, nor even damaging their careers. While this absurdly rose-tinted vision of the past ignores the life-threatening levels of discrimination to which both queer and African American communities were subject at the time and still continue to endure in many circumstances, I mention *Hollywood* here precisely due to the ways in which it acts as a sort of fanfiction on the past of US cinema – a wish fulfilment of sorts in which figures like Hudson, whose cinematic image was once decidedly heteronormative, can be transformed into an overtly queer figure decades before his homosexuality was revealed to the public. Like Dunye's *The Watermelon Woman*, the Hudson seen in *Hollywood* and his fictional lover are both embodiments of precisely the types of queers that old Tinseltown was so proficient at erasing, therein forcing audiences to contend only with racist and heteronormative representation.

Taken together, these nostalgic interventions into both queer and heteronormative media point towards the broader significance of memory in our enjoyment of television and film, as well as the affective relevance of media which intervenes in these memories. For queer people, this relevance is intimately tied with the complex interplay of visibility and obfuscation which has marked both the past and the present of on-screen representation and has as such determined the LGBTQ viewer's relationship with the screen as one of both recognition and absence; of memory, and a deliberate forgetting. While such forgetting is becoming less and less commonplace in contemporary on-screen representation, the relationship between an LGBTQ viewer and the screen is nonetheless still not the same as that of their heterosexual counterparts. As such, a deeper understanding of how queer people remember the media, as well as the place these memories have in the self-narrativization of the LGBTQ subject, is sorely needed. In this section of the book, I have looked at Haynes's and Dunye's work with precisely this goal in mind, analysing how these films have commented on queer fan memory. In the next section, I will look at issues of intergenerational memory transfer within the LGBTQ community more broadly, as well as the significant role this has granted to film and television in the process of queer memory creation.

Part Two

Queer memory, intergenerationality and television

In an episode of the recent revival of NBC's *Will & Grace* (NBC, 2017–20), we see the now middle-aged Will (Eric McCormack) on a date with the 23-year-old Blake (Ben Platt). As the two men converse in Will's apartment, both recount their coming-out stories. For Will, his own was 'pretty typical. My mom cried, my dad drank' ('Who's Your Daddy', 2017). For the younger Blake, however, this was not the case. 'I told my parents I was gay when I was eight,' Blake recounts. 'They were divorced. They both threw me a coming-out party on the same weekend. That was hard.' Will is stunned by this. 'Is this the new gay?', he enquires. 'How is it supposed to get better if it was always fine?' Through these two characters, the episode constructs and contrasts two generational versions of queerness. On the one hand, there are gay men like Will, who have encountered homophobia. On the other, there is what Will calls 'the new gay', who come out as children and are met with nothing but acceptance and support. While Will is initially willing to overlook these and other differences between them, he eventually forgoes sex with Blake when the younger man proclaims he 'knows all about Stonehenge'. 'Do you mean Stonewall?', a furious Will asks and proceeds to teach him the details of gay history. In this way, the episode presents the battle for gay rights as a thing of the past, so remote the young Blake has no practical reason to learn more about it. The scene is premised on Will and Blake being too different to properly understand each other – of gay rights having advanced so dramatically that their ages make a relationship between them untenable. Will tells the young Blake that 'it's great that [he has] no shame' but warns him that 'you guys can never forget the struggle that came before you – the people that fought and loved and died so that you could walk down the street in skinny jeans with rights you never even knew you never had. The minute we forget what we went through to get here is the minute it could all be taken away.'

While the show's humour in these scenes is characteristically hyperbolic, its portrayal of the interaction between the two men nonetheless exemplifies a number of issues crucial to the mediation of both the queer present and the queer past. On the one hand, it paints a misleading and idealized picture of the United States as a land free from discrimination – a particularly ironic feat considering the fact that anti-LGBT employment discrimination was only declared illegal in the United States in 2020 and that only nineteen US states and the District of Columbia prohibit discrimination against LGBTQ people in areas such as housing.[1] On the other, even projects such as 'It Gets Better', which began as recently as 2010 after a number of suicides committed by teenagers due to homophobic bullying, are presented as part of the distant past, while younger LGBTQ people are depicted as politically inactive and wilfully ignorant of queer history.[2] In spite of such misrepresentation, *Will & Grace*'s characteristically flippant approach to these issues nonetheless serves as a good introduction to precisely the issues on which Part Two of this book is centred – namely the question of queer intergenerational contact and how the experiences of one generation of LGBTQ people are, or are not, passed on to their younger counterparts.

As I have noted in Introduction to this book, the question of whether and how queer memory is transferred from one generation to another is a complex one. Unlike other minority communities, the family is often not a safe space for queer individuals and so is also less likely to be a locus in which queer legacies are passed on.[3] While LGBTQ families do present exceptions to this, it is nonetheless necessary to take into account the many queer pasts that remain unshared within one's family, particularly in the case of closeted individuals.[4] Outside the family, intergenerational contact among queer people is also limited, again leading to a lack of postmemory transfers.[5] A similar sentiment has been expressed by LGBTQ people outside the academic context – for example, director David Weissman, whose documentary *We Were Here* (2010) chronicles the US AIDS crisis, has argued that 'in families and in ethnic groups, history is passed on from generation to generation … we don't have that as queers, we don't have any direct lineage from older queers to younger queers'.[6] At the same time, the effects of such generational segregation have been worsened by the AIDS crisis, which has led to the loss of innumerable queer lives, therein also influencing the ways in which queer postmemory is passed on.[7]

This lack of intergenerational contact has serious implications for the creation of queer memory and yet has rarely been a topic of academic analysis.[8] In order to address this gap, I draw here on Marianne Hirsch's concept of postmemory, which Hirsch uses to describe the passing of memory from one generation to another.[9] For Hirsch, 'memory signals an affective link to the past, a sense precisely of an embodied "living connection"' with the past of another person, usually a member of one's family or social group.[10] Hirsch highlights the profound effects postmemory can have and how such adopted memories become crucial facets of a younger generation's identity. Crucially, the formation of postmemory can therefore happen through contact with a cultural manifestation, as well as through a work of art, be it a photograph or a written text. As Hirsch argues, a 'postmemorial work … strives to reactivate and reembody more distant social/national and archival/cultural memorial structures by reinvesting them with resonant individual and familial forms of mediation and aesthetic expression'.[11] Like Landsberg's notion of 'prosthetic memories', mediated postmemories can also be transferred outside of the familial unit and beyond the borders of one's immediate experience. Both cinema and television play crucial roles in the formation of our perception of the past – a role of particular relevance for the queer community.

In this sense, this part of the book focuses in detail on how queer film and television have both served as a substitute for intergenerational contact and the passing on of postmemory, while also looking at how contemporary queer television has addressed matters of queer (inter)generationality. In depicting different generations of queers, recent examples of queer television have also addressed the issue of LGBTQ ageing, which research has shown carries different challenges for LGBTQ elders than for their heterosexual counterparts. From higher rates of growing old alone to homophobic treatment in retirement homes and a subsequent need to go back into the closet out of fear, queer ageing is intimately tied with discrimination.[12] While groups such as 'Opening Doors' in London or the US 'Prime Timers' offer older queer people the chance of socializing with others their age and younger members of the community, such organizations are few and far between and are more easily found in large urban centres. It is thus pivotal to note the ways in which the invisibility of older queer people has been further exacerbated by the media, with decades of queer representation being marked by a focus on white, youthful and normatively attractive protagonists.

Moreover, while older LGBTQ individuals face specific challenges, the ways in which they perceive the world will also differ from that of younger queers. As Ken Plummer writes, different 'generations may also come to develop distinctive ways of seeing and inhabit different symbolic worlds; [a set of what he terms] generational sexualities'.[13] Plummer writes that 'the stories we tell of social life are usually bound up with the generations we live in – we tell *generational narratives*. These can be seen as perspectives or standpoints on social worlds. Such stories we tell and the standpoints we take are deeply connected to how we organize and structure our memory worlds.'[14] This does not mean that all generational perspectives are the same or that intersectional differences do not mark individuals who are part of the same generation. Rather, it points towards the ways in which generationality might shape our perspective – of how shared experiences and cultural works might influence the outlook of a generation. For older LGBTQ people, the shared experiences of discrimination under very different circumstances might lead to a notably different perspective from that of younger community members, for example with respect to the reappropriation of the word 'queer' as a term of self-signification.[15]

For much of the 1990s and 2000s, such generational differences in perception and experience were nowhere to be seen on cinema and television screens, with much queer-oriented media focusing predominantly on white, youthful protagonists. Exceptions to this can be found in films such as *A Man of No Importance* (1994), *Love and Death on Long Island* (1998) and *Gods and Monsters* (1998), all of which explore the position of an older gay man through centring on his friendship with and desire for a much younger man. All of these films feature a gay man growing old in solitary circumstances, mostly disconnected to anything that might be termed a gay 'community' and depict his desire as futile in the face of the younger man's heterosexuality. The films thus juxtapose different temporal experiences; the presumed promise of youth and sexual normativity is contrasted with the solitary old age of the queer character, meant at least in part to provoke sympathy in the viewer for the older queer man's plight. A similar model of contrasting the experiences of a younger straight man and an older gay man can also be seen in the more recent *Beginners* (2010), which focuses on a father-and-son relationship, and in *Grandma* (2015), which brings together the perspectives of an older lesbian character with her straight teenage granddaughter. However, these films subvert the older model of an ageing queer protagonist's thwarted lust for a younger person, as both older LGBTQ individuals (Christopher Plummer in *Beginners* and Lily Tomlin in *Grandma*) enjoy relationships with younger queer people who return their desire. Other examples of filmic intergenerationality include *Brother to Brother* (2004), mentioned in Chapter 2 due to its portrayal of the Harlem Renaissance, which viewers learn of through the friendship of an older and younger gay man, and *Love Is Strange* (2014), which portrays an older gay couple forced to move in with younger relatives after one is fired by a homophobic employer. While these films portray older queer men, *Cloudburst* (2011) depicts the unlikely companionship between an old lesbian couple struggling to remain independent and a young straight man.

On television, the so-called gay boom of the 1990s also led to a majority of youthful white protagonists such as those found in *Ellen* (ABC, 1994–8), *Will & Grace* (NBC, 1998–2005) and the UK version of *Queer as Folk* (Channel 4, 1999–2000). With respect to the representation of older gay men, Michael Johnson Jr. correctly argues that 'the abject invisibility of gay men as "elders/seniors" … has permeated the televisual landscape'.[16] As Johnson comments, 'this invisibility' renders the queer 'middle-aged or elders as inconsequential through their conspicuous absence [and operates] to exacerbate existing stigmatization' of older LGBTQ people.[17] While such trends largely continued in the 2000s, exceptions could sometimes be found in secondary characters, for example on the US *Queer as Folk* (Showtime, 2000–5), in which the older queer population was represented through Vic Grassi (Jack Wetherall), the HIV-positive uncle of one of the show's central protagonists. More recently, however, television series in both the United States and the UK have started to grant more prominence to intersectional LGBTQ representation, including older and middle-aged queer characters taking centre stage in shows such as *Transparent* (Amazon Prime, 2014–19), *London Spy* (BBC, 2015), *Cucumber* (Channel 4, 2015), *Vicious* (ITV, 2013–16), *When We Rise* (ABC, 2017) and the recent reboot of *Will & Grace*. What unites all of these series is not only the screen time granted to older and middle-aged LGBTQ protagonists, but also their focus on intergenerational contact, which is sometimes depicted as the subject of single episodes (for example, in *Will & Grace*) and sometimes serves as the bases for the entire series (as seen in *Transparent*, *London Spy*, *Cucumber*, and *Vicious*). While *Vicious* depicts such contact as taking place between an old gay couple and a younger heterosexual man, the other series mentioned here depict intergenerational contact between LGBTQ people, be it within the context of activism (*When We Rise*), friendship (*London Spy*), and family (*Transparent*).

Drawing on all of this, the following chapters focus on two specific televisual examples of LGBTQ intergenerationality and postmemory. Chapter 3 analyses Joey Soloway's *Transparent* by looking at its depiction of queer memory within the family and the ethical potential of fantasy. The series unsettles common televisual tropes by depicting its central transgender protagonist not in opposition to a heteronormative family, but rather as part of a familial unit populated by several generations of LGBTQ women. I thus approach the series by looking at how it presents the passage of memory within the family, and among transgender and cisgender queer women. I analyse how *Transparent* presents its central characters as haunted by the erasure of transgender memory and focus on its depiction of the affective cost of such haunting. At the same time, I also look at how the show portrays the influence of both pain and privilege on memory and argue that it depicts postmemory as a potentially productive vehicle for the development of empathy between individuals and across opposed social groups.

After looking at *Transparent*'s depiction of transgender memory, Chapter 4 focuses on Tom Rob Smith's miniseries *London Spy* and its portrayal of postmemory in an intergenerational friendship between two gay men. I look at how the series utilizes this intergenerational relationship to contextualize contemporary homophobia and to track the continuities between the past and present of discrimination. *London Spy* uses the character of the elder gay man Scottie (Jim Broadbent) to locate its plot within wider narratives of queer history, therein functioning as a queer postmemorial work. The chapter also analyses the show's depiction of HIV and the ways in which it draws on cinematic AIDS archives, specifically Derek Jarman's film *Blue* (1993), to depict the AIDS crisis and seropositive memories. In thematizing the figure of the gay spy, and bringing it together with issues such as seropositivity and homophobia, the series offers a commentary on the nature of queer citizenship and emphasizes the connections between then and now.

Both Chapters 3 and 4 look at televisual works which depict the affective afterlives of pivotal events in twentieth-century history on queer individuals, starting from how *Transparent* portrays familial postmemories of the Holocaust, to how the AIDS crisis is remembered in *London Spy*. In both chapters, my focus on depictions of queer memory within the family (*Transparent*) and among friends (*London Spy*) addresses broader questions of how postmemory is or is not passed on among LGBTQ people. In tackling these mediated depictions of queer postmemory, both chapters make clear not only that the flow of memory from one generation of LGBTQ people is rarely even or uninterrupted, but also the relevance of postmemory in recognizing and addressing the continuities between past and present. In other words, they argue that postmemory is – whether passed on through interpersonal contact or on-screen representation – a vital resource for moving beyond the confines of our own experience and surpassing discrimination both towards and within the LGBTQ community.

3

Haunting and queer histories: Representing postmemory in Joey Soloway's *Transparent*

In each episode of Joey Soloway's widely acclaimed TV series *Transparent* (2014), the opening credits present a montage of grainy old family videos. We see sights as common as a woman blowing out candles or a large group of people swaying in a dance hall. Intercut with such scenes, however, are the belles of Frank Simmon's documentary *The Queen* (1968), which tracked the contestants of a drag queen beauty pageant in New York. The recordings blend seamlessly one into the other – it is only after one learns where some of them are from that the presumed discrepancy becomes notable. At the end of the sequence, a date appears, marking the final recording on screen as stemming from 1 January 1994, the year in which the show's transgender main character (Jeffrey Tambor) first started addressing herself as Maura instead of Mort.[1] As Stephen Vider points out, when 'taken together [these] clips could [easily] be the introduction to a gender studies course: What does it mean for the bar mitzvah boy to "become a man," and the drag queen to "become a woman"?'[2] In this way, they serve as an apt introduction to a TV series dealing with a transgender woman who is also a father coming out as trans to her family. However, while the opening credits do point towards the constructed nature of gender and subjectivity, their focus on how the past has been documented and (mis)remembered also highlights the temporal aspects of this construction. By putting together recordings of the heteronormative family and of gender nonconformity, they comment on how these seemingly separate temporalities exist not only at the same time, but within the same person.

Drawing on this, this chapter looks at seasons one to four of *Transparent* by focusing on its presentation of transgender memory, both in relation to the family and with respect to larger narratives of sexology and feminist history. The series revolves around Maura Pfefferman, whose coming out as transgender is framed within the show not only in present terms, but also in terms of the past. Like its opening credits, the series utilizes otherwise common formats such as flashbacks to depict transgender, lesbian and bisexual pasts. Through these flashbacks, it both historicizes transgender identity and exposes the hidden transgender histories of the Pfefferman family, thus raising questions of memory and temporality. As Maura starts to come out to her children, the affective cost of silence and unacknowledged trauma is thematized through the ways in which past events still permeate the present. The question of transgender memory takes centre stage, as what has previously been concealed from the family history begins to come to light. In all of this, the travel of unvoiced trauma from generation to generation of Pfefferman women plays a central role, and the series emphasizes the role of haunting in our perception of the present.

I focus on *Transparent* due to a number of key reasons; firstly, the show's significance as one of the few US televisual works to feature a transgender central protagonist cannot be overstated. Like *Orange Is the New Black* (2013–19), *Sense8* (2015–18) and *Pose* (2018–), *Transparent* represents a change from the vast majority of US transgender representation, which had for decades relied on negative stereotypes.[3] In positively depicting both the transgender individual and the trans community, the series transcends the ridicule and vilification on which transgender representation was usually based, and what GLAAD's (2012) survey of a decade of trans TV representation (2002–12) has shown as the all-too typical portrayal of transgender people as either victims or villains.[4] Moreover, *Transparent* eschews expectations by depicting its main character not as a lone queer individual in an otherwise heterosexual family, but rather by showing several generations of LGBTQ-identified women within the same familial unit. Produced by Soloway's company Topple, short for 'Topple the Patriarchy' (which Soloway yelled out on stage upon winning an Emmy award), the link between *Transparent* and feminism was also established early on.[5]

Nonetheless, its status as an 'exemplary' transfeminist text has also been called into question multiple times, initially due to the highly contentious casting of the cisgendered Jeffrey Tambor as its lead character, which many have argued contributes to the misrepresentation of trans women as merely 'pretending' to be women.[6] In 2018, Tambor was fired from the show after an internal investigation had been conducted surrounding accusations of sexual harassment by *Transparent* actor Trace Lysette and Tambor's former assistant Van Barnes.[7] Moreover, it is imperative to note that Tambor's dismissal only took place after showrunner Joey Solloway urged Lysette not to make her accusations public, later using their memoir to compare Lysette's actions to those of the character Fredo in the film *Godfather 2*, famous for his betrayal of Michael

Corleone.⁸ Drawing from this, it is thus of the utmost importance here to take into account the transmisogynist abuse which can be found even on what was once lauded as feminist and LGBTQ-filled set.⁹ The discrepancy between such media visibility and the inadequate state of transgender rights is also of pivotal relevance here – as transgender individuals continue to suffer from staggering levels of transphobic violence and discrimination, it becomes necessary to ask who profits from transgender stories and how.¹⁰ In this context, it is indicative that *Transparent* as a series ended soon after Tambor's firing with the fifth season being transformed into a feature-length finale, consequently raising questions about the precarity of trans artists and trans-focused projects, no matter how successful.

By focusing on *Transparent*, this chapter interrogates the contribution made by the show to transgender and queer feminist on-screen representation. It analyses how *Transparent* situates its characters not only with regard to their familial memories, but in relation to broader issues of how transgender and feminist pasts are remembered. In particular, its focus on transgender memory aims to tackle the following questions: how does the series comment on the passing of memory from one generation to another? How does it present the influence of both pain and privilege on how we remember the past? And finally, how does the show's presentation of memory relate to notions of shared heritage and community among LGBTQ people, specifically between transgender and cisgender queer women? Such issues are not abstract. Instead, they are integral to the possibility of connection, of understanding which moves past borders of cis- and transgender, or between the generations of one's own family.

Looking forward, looking back: Trauma and transtemporality

The series revolves around the Pfeffermans, a Los Angeles–based, upper middle class, Jewish family, and begins when Maura Pfefferman starts coming out to her children as transgender. In presenting her coming out, *Transparent* focuses in particular on how this relates to past events and her children's perception of the past. Like Maura herself, each member of the family is marked by events which have for long been unvoiced. For her son Josh (Jay Duplass), the conflict between past and present is most clearly located in his once-romantic relationship with his babysitter Rita (played in the present by Brett Paesel), which others around him describe as abuse and he refuses to accept as such. For her eldest daughter Sarah (Amy Landecker), the past is embodied in her ex-girlfriend Tammy (Melora

Hardin), whose sudden appearance prompts Sarah to break off her marriage. For Ali (Gaby Hoffmann), Maura's youngest child, flashbacks centre around the week of her failed bat mitzvah, thus raising the question of how and whether she has 'become a woman'. As later seasons reveal, Maura's ex-wife Shelly is suffering from a far deeper trauma and keeps hidden that she was sexually abused as a child. Finally, in the case of Maura herself, decades of hiding her gender identity are also revealed through flashbacks and reflect what Jack Halberstam describes as the central 'dilemma [of] the transgender character [; namely, that of creating] an alternate future while rewriting history'.[11]

More precisely, Halberstam writes that 'the transgender film' and, as I argue here, the transgender TV series, 'confronts powerfully the way that transgenderism is constituted as a paradox made up in equal parts of visibility and temporality'.[12] As Halberstam notes, 'whenever the transgender character is seen to be transgendered, then he/she is … threatening to expose a rupture between the distinct temporal registers of past, present, and future'.[13] Such ruptures are not, as Halberstam is aware, unique to the transgender character but are made clear through how other characters react to them within the narrative. In *Transparent*, Maura's coming out prompts just such a reaction from her children, as they re-examine their own relationship to the past. In one scene, for example, Josh wonders aloud:

Josh: Okay, so what does this mean? Everything dad has said and done before this moment is a sham? He was just acting the whole time?
Sarah: No.
Ali: It just means we all have to start over. ('The Wilderness')

The dialogue here makes plain how the show's characters perceive Maura's coming out as an impetus for personal change; on the one hand, Josh questions the relationship of the past to his present reality. On the other, Ali sees Maura's coming out as a motivator for a new beginning. However different these responses are, they point towards a conscious breaking with the past, a temporal shift enabled by a change in how the past is narrativized. Nonetheless, while Ali attempts to create herself anew in the face of the past, the emphasis on flashbacks throughout the series points towards the ways in which the past remains present.

In the show's first season, these flashbacks focus mainly on the furtive beginnings of Maura's transition and on Ali's failed bat mitzvah. The second season moves even further into the family's history, going back to Nazi Germany and Maura's transgender aunt Gittel's (Hari Nef) involvement in the Magnus Hirschfeld Institute for Sexual Research. In this way, *Transparent* uses the figure of Hirschfeld as an emblem for broader histories of sexology and the development of transgender rights, and presents the family's private past as inextricable from them. The third season follows the family after Gittel's death and depicts Maura and her ex-wife Shelly's childhood in the United States during the Cold War, while the fourth season shows us the period surrounding Ali's birth and again depicts developments in sexology through the character of Maura's psychiatrist, who attempts to convince her that she is in reality a gay man.

Taken together, the mixing of these various individual and familial temporalities can be read in light of Carla Freccero's assertion that 'haunting, ghostly apparition, reminds us that the past and the present are neither discrete nor sequential' and that 'the borderline between then and now wavers, wobbles, and does not hold still'.[14] Freccero utilizes Derrida's concept of spectrality so as to describe how it 'invokes collectivity, a collectivity of unknown or known, "uncanny" (both familiar and yet not) strangers who arrive to frequent us. To speak of ghosts is to speak of the social.'[15] Thus, the notion of haunting becomes particularly relevant for our analysis of *Transparent*, both in terms of its depiction of the Pfefferman family members as defined by their familial past and through the ways that the series more generally comments on the existence of different temporalities within the same moment.

For example, the presence of haunting is stressed within the show not only through repeated flashbacks, but through the casting of several actors in more than one role. In season one, Bradley Whitford appears as Maura's friend Mark (drag name Macy), one of the first people to whom Maura reveals her identity. In the second season, he embodies Magnus Hirschfeld himself and, in so doing, serves as a pivotal figure in the life of Maura's aunt Gittel. In the same vein, Trace Lysette plays both Maura's younger friend Shea and appears in flashbacks taking place in the 1980s as a ballroom performer. While there are several other similar examples, the most significant instance of such doubling comes from the casting of Gaby Hoffmann and Emily Robinson as both Maura's mother Rose and her child Ali (with Hoffmann appearing as the adult version of the characters, and Robinson as their younger selves). The merging of these two characters subverts the notion of a linear flow of events, and so we are as viewers met with the paradoxical conflation of, on the one hand, Ali's resentment over Maura's failures as a parent ('Why Do We Cover Mirrors?') while, on the other hand, also witnessing young Maura's childhood abandonment by her mother ('If I Were a Bell').

Moreover, while these characters often appear separately, it is relevant to note that a scene in the show's second season brings their timelines together and allows them to interact. Within this storyline, Ali is depicted as an onlooker during one of the family's most traumatic memories – the Nazi burning of Hirschfeld's library and rounding up of Gittel and the institute's other queer members, which is a moment I shall return to later. For now, it is sufficient to note that, by showing Robinson and Hoffmann exchange glances in the scene, *Transparent* undermines the distinction between the past and the present as separate and distinct conceptual categories, consequently making clear that it is not only Maura but the entire Pfefferman family that remains bound to and defined by the past. The series makes this theme verbally explicit through Ali's comments on 'inherited trauma in [one's] DNA' ('Cherry Blossoms'), thus indicating the ways in which temporal borders are not only unclear and uncertain but permeate from the past of one individual into the present of another.

In turn, such a transfer of memory is reminiscent of the work of John Stratton, who describes the circulation of unvoiced trauma and affect in his own family following the Holocaust. Stratton writes of the inability to speak of what had happened, and how a knowledge of the past was passed down 'not strictly [as] postmemory [but rather as a] reaction, expressing an emotional complex made up of fear, anger, perhaps sadness and other emotions. All these passed on without realisation, a legacy composed of affect.'[16] It is precisely this notion of 'a legacy of affect' travelling between family members that is so relevant in *Transparent*, as the series presents the afterlife of trauma as shaping not only its sufferer, but the family as a whole. The lack of familial postmemory depicted in the series is especially prominent in its reimagining of the Holocaust, which Soloway retells through focusing on its transgender victims. While the Pfeffermans are a Jewish family, Gittel is separated from her mother and sister through her refusal to leave Germany and the institute. Unwilling to abandon the acceptance she feels there as a transgender woman, she is eventually murdered by the SS, while her family manages to emigrate to the United States. After her death, the rest of the family omits the details of Gittel's life from Maura and the subsequent generations of the family.

Such deliberate forgetting mirrors the experiences of the real queer victims of the Holocaust, whose persecution under the Nazi regime did not become a part of even LGBTQ activist memory until the late 1960s.[17] As Erik N. Jensen notes, one of the reasons behind this silence lay in the continued illegality of queerness even after the Nazi camps had been abolished, which left few able to speak of what they had been through. In *Transparent*, it is not Gittel but her family that refuses to be honest about her death, an omission most clearly manifested in the young Maura's mistaken impression that Gittel was the wife of her uncle Gershon, instead of the name she took upon coming out as trans.

When knowledge of the past is passed on in the family, it is wielded as a weapon against Maura's transgenderism. In a particularly distressing flashback in the show's third season, her grandfather threatens Maura with Gittel's fate after discovering her wearing her mother's clothes. While beckoning the child closer, he yells at her: 'You wanna know what happened to your uncle Gershon, do you? Morton, you want to know!? He burned to death in the oven. You want to know why!? Because your mother and your grandmother let him run around in a skirt!' ('If I Were a Bell').

These developments portray with precision the destruction to which transgender postmemory is subjected in innumerable families. Like Stratton's notion of affective legacies, they also highlight how such omissions continue to be present as affect – as a series of reactions which may seem inexplicable to the uninformed. By focusing on the question of familial history, the series thus comments on the very possibility of transgender memory within a heteronormative context and exposes the ruptures between what is said and what is left untold. It stresses the present dimension of the past through its impact on future generations and highlights the ways in which this past continues to haunt them.

Into the woods: Constructing gender, remembering the past

In presenting this passage of affect, *Transparent* draws particular links between Maura and Ali and utilizes these characters to examine the ways in which gender is constructed. In the first season, a large number of flashbacks revolve around the weekend of Ali's cancelled bat mitzvah, which Maura spends away from the family at the cross-dressing Camp Camellia ('Best New Girl'). While seemingly unrelated, both events mark a failed or thwarted attempt at acquiring 'womanhood'. For Maura, the experience of Camp Camellia seems at first a welcome seclusion from the demands of gender normativity, but this illusion is progressively shattered as the weekend goes on. Firstly, a seemingly idyllic scene which begins as Maura and Mark/Macy (the aforementioned Whitford) cycle through the woods is transformed when the two stop to make a phone call. While speaking to his son, Mark urges the boy to 'man up,' and his performance of hegemonic masculinity makes plain the rift between the Camp and the outside world. After this, Maura learns that both the camp's patrons and Mark are vocally critical of men who not only dress, but identify, as women. This exchange thus exposes the transphobia which litters Camp Camellia and positions Maura's retreat from gender normativity as anything but a repose from it.

In parallel to this, Ali is depicted as having refused to partake in the Jewish ritual meant to mark her transition from girl to woman and is left alone at the house by her family. We watch her go to the beach, drink beer and make advances towards a man who appears to be in his twenties, but part of her experience is left unrevealed to the viewer, and so we never learn what happened after she kissed him. The episode therefore leaves unanswered whether heteronormative notions of her sexually 'becoming a woman' can be applied to this exchange and marks such notions as themselves lacking. Taken together, the coinciding of these two plotlines queries the meaning of femininity and of belonging to a certain gender. It raises the question of whether one is ever fully initiated into a certain category of personhood, be it that of an adult or a woman, therein echoing Judith Butler's conception of gender as 'a kind of imitation for which there is no original'.[18]

This stands in a particular relationship to the show's exploration of different transgender and radical feminist counter-memories in its second season. The season's opening credits foreshadow this central theme by combining clips seen in the season one opening with scenes such as black and white recordings of female couples and technicolour clips from lesbian women's marches, therein evoking the rarely represented history of queer women in general and of lesbian feminism specifically. By bringing together recordings such as an early twentieth-century marriage ceremony between women, and shots of two women looking at the Statue of Liberty, they raise the question of how these pasts should be thought of with respect to US national memory (see Figures 9 and 10). The credit sequence thus indicates the patriarchal and heteronormative nature of how the past is typically remembered and presents an alternative through its focus on lesbian feminist counter-memories.

Figure 9 The season two opening credits and lesbian counter-memory.

Figure 10 National memory – a female couple looks at the Statue of Liberty.

Again drawing a close connection between Ali and Maura, the topic of lesbian counter-memory is first brought to the fore in an episode when Maura, herself a former university lecturer, offers to introduce Ali to some of her former colleagues ('New World Coming'). Once at the university, they encounter Leslie Mackinaw (Cherry Jones), a lecturer and poet who works at the gender studies department ('Woman is a dirty word around here,' quips Leslie). Leslie's introduction to Ali does not go as planned, however, as she accuses Maura of having blocked her application to *Perspectives on Politics*, the journal she had been editor of. As they speak, the question of the accuracy and validity of memory is directly addressed several times:

> **Leslie:** I applied for the editorial board. And you blocked me. I applied every year for ten years. Me and my sisters-in-arms and I applied, and applied, applied, and applied. And you took only men. Oh, and one chick who had these huge, huge tits that you – you couldn't keep your eyes off of, if – if I remember correctly.
>
> **Maura:** Oh, my God, you were part of that group.
>
> **Leslie:** (*laughing*) Well, it's very nice of you to remember. (turning to Ali) The Berkeley Seven. We were the scourge of the administration. We drove out a provost.
>
> **Ali:** What is a provost?
>
> **Leslie:** Exactly.
>
> **Maura:** Leslie, I just want to say this. I don't stand behind what I – what I did back then, all right? And I profoundly apologize if that does – if that does you any good. I actually don't – I don't remember much of it.
>
> **Leslie:** Well, why would you remember it? ('New World Coming')

The episode, significantly titled 'New World Coming', thus marks Maura's first confrontation with her own past misogyny. The dialogue highlights the gaps in her memory so as to illuminate precisely the gendered 'technologies of memory' and 'frames of interpretation' which Marianne Hirsch and Valerie Smith note as crucial in the transmission of patriarchal collective memory.[19] It contrasts the private pain which we as viewers know Maura has for decades suffered with the public privilege she had also been granted while being thought of as Mort. The continued flagging up of memory within the conversation ('If I remember correctly / It's nice of you to remember / I don't remember much of it / Why would you remember it') points towards its focus not only on Maura's past actions, but how those actions are recalled and narrativized. In other words, it points towards the ways in which patriarchal privilege may be so commonplace as to be forgotten, to be omitted from memory entirely – as Leslie asks, 'Why would you remember it?' In a later scene within the same episode, Maura comments on the exchange to her trans support group:

> **Maura:** I met somebody today ... I knew back in the day. We were at Berkley and um ... She was part of this radical feminist group, they were called the Berkeley Seven. They burned effigies of us. They thought that we were holding them back. And we did, we held them back, that's the truth. I mean ... I hurt people.

In response to her admission, the group offers only silence. Nonetheless, while this silence highlights the gravity of the misogyny Maura speaks of, her confession also emphasizes the ways in which Maura's own memory of her actions has been altered. Leslie's lesbian counter-memory is thus here depicted as having a transformative effect on Maura's perception of the past and the patriarchal blind spots of her own recollection. At the same time, Leslie is established as having an influence on not only Maura, but Ali as well. Following their first meeting, the episode depicts Ali's learning about the counter-memory of Leslie's radical feminism and sexually evocative writing as a turning point in her own development (Leslie 'would,' exclaims a friend of Ali's, 'be like Jack Kerouac or Allen Ginsberg, if we didn't grow up in a patriarchy'). While at a queer women's bowling event, Ali surveys the room while her voiceover reads Leslie's poetry. Taken from the work of Eileen Myles, Ali's voice announces: 'I always put my lover's cunt on the crest of a wave/Like a flag that I can pledge my allegiance to/ This is my country.' Shot in warm colours, the camera stands in for Ali's gaze in the beginning of her monologue and focuses on the physicality of the women who surround her – queer women moving closer to each other, the naked thighs of one woman, the kiss experienced by another. In the background, Leslie's poetry is not heard in silence but is transposed onto the indie rock band Django Django's song 'Found You,' the rhythm of which adds a further intensity to the scene. As Ali draws closer to her friend Syd (Carrie Brownstein), shots continue to focus on the intimacy between women but this time revolve on small touches between the two. This episode is the first in which Ali becomes ready to manifest her attraction towards women, thus linking Leslie's artistic and political legacy with Ali's personal and sexual present.

It is not, however, only the prejudice of patriarchal privilege that the series questions, but also the reasoning and implications behind the transphobia present in parts of the cisgender radical feminist community. In the season's penultimate episode ('Man on the Land'), Ali takes Maura and Sarah along with her to the Idyllwild Wimmin's Music Festival, unaware that it has banned the entry of transgender women, thus echoing the controversial policies of real-life festivals such as the Michigan Womyn's Music Festival and Australia's Seven Sisters Festival.[20] Set in woods similar to the first season's Camp Camellia, the festival's animosity towards transgender women mirrors that expressed by the men at Camellia and also overtly raises the question of the reasoning behind the construction of gendered 'safe spaces'. In a conversation between Leslie and Ali, both women comment on the perceived liberty of being in such a space, with Leslie exclaiming that she had 'never felt totally free until [her] first summer [there] walking around buck naked in the woods', to which Ali affirms:

> That's so true. It's so nice here. So comfortable. No predators. … God, it's awful that every woman is just walking around all the time in the real world with this low-grade anxiety of being raped or maimed. ('Man on the Land')

Through this and similar exchanges, the episode locates the need for the construction of women-only spaces in gender-based suffering, while at the same time questioning the reasoning behind the exclusion of transgender women from these spaces. In the same scene, the conversation continues when Maura joins the group and argues with some of the women there about the meaning behind the festival's 'women born women' policy. The concern, Leslie's friend Sandy (Sandy Martin) stipulates, is not about Maura's biological sex, but in what she perceives as her inability to sympathize with gender-based oppression:

Sandy: Look, I drove the plough. I cleared these woods and we did it with one thing in mind; that we women could have one goddamn safe space in the world.

Maura: No one's trying to take your woods away from you. I just feel that I have a right to be here too as a transgender woman.

Sandy: See, this is where it gets really weird, because you know suddenly the conversation is all around you and all of us are trying to make you comfortable.

Maura: You're trying to make me comfortable? …

Sandy: And I don't give a shit about your goddamn penis. It's about the privilege.

Maura: What privilege are you talking about? I was in way too much pain to experience what you're calling privilege.

Leslie: Your pain and your privilege are separate. And Berkeley was a great example of that.

Ali: Right, even though… even though you were suffering privately, which of course you were, you were still compensated as a man, and you owned the house. You had your name on the house. I mean, Mom was the one that had to leave. It's not unreasonable.

Maura: That's what this is about? The house? And Mom?

Ali: No.

Maura: (*getting up*) I'm going. I have to go. ('Man on the Land')

There are two primary concerns raised within the scene. On the one hand, Leslie's proposal that 'pain and privilege' exist as two 'separate' but, as implied by her and Maura's history at Berkeley, in practice indistinguishable categories warrants serious consideration in our study of both *Transparent* in particular and of the construction of memory in general. On the other, the scene also raises the question of how it is that we remember and narrativize our respective histories of pain and privilege and whether our personal investment in the former blinds us from comprehending the implications of the latter. As is made plain from the ways in which the show's first season mirrors its second through Camp Camellia and the Idyllwild Festival, each of these oppressed groups is depicted as themselves contributing towards the oppression of others, which is a notion further underscored in the following sequence as Ali attempts to find Maura.

Like the opening credits which bring together divergent histories, the sequence merges two separate plotlines. In one, Ali searches for Maura in the present day. In the other, the SS descends on Hirschfeld's Institute while Gittel and Rose are there. As they proceed to drag out the institute's members, Ali is shown as herself walking into the hidden history of her family. The sequence is shot in low-key lighting and is marked by elements of magical realism; instead of on Berlin streets, the event is suddenly located in the Festival woods. As Ali surveys the bonfire of Hirschfeld's books, we see a woman playing the violin beside it. In the background, Alice Bowman's 'Waiting' can be heard, its melancholic melody and lyrics ('Are you coming back? / Are you coming back? / I'm waiting') underscoring not only the affective intensity of the scene, but also the ways in which it is removed from reality. Crucially, Ali is herself depicted not as an unnoticed witness but makes eye contact with her young grandmother Rose and holds her hand as Gittel looks back at them both (see Figures 11 and 12). Together, the two witness as Gittel is taken away by the SS, never to be heard from again by the family.

Figure 11 Ali and the young grandma Rose hold hands.

Figure 12 The terrified Gittel looks back through time at her family.

Taken together, the impossible elements of this scene highlight the fundamental impossibility of representing trauma accurately and, through magical realist aesthetics, emphasize the invaluable role which imagination plays in making someone else's memory our own. In doing so, they point towards another element of haunting which Freccero describes as crucial – namely that of fantasy. Freccero elaborates that 'spectrality also acknowledges fantasy's constitutive relation to experience. It suggests that fantasy is the mode of our experiential existence, that it mediates how we live our desire in the world.'[21] Drawing from this, I argue that *Transparent* stresses the relevance of fantasy as crucial to the creation of postmemory and presents it as a powerful tool for bridging the gap between ourselves and the other. It allows Ali access into the secret pain of others in a way which stresses not the historicity of the event she is witnessing, but the correlation of imagination and affect necessary for us to 'remember' that which we did not ourselves experience.

At the same time, by placing this scene in an episode focused on transgender exclusion from a women-only space, the episode forces two divergent counter-memories to coincide and highlights the ways in which marginalized groups might themselves continue to inflict pain on others. While it is presented as liberating for cisgendered women, the Idyllwild Festival is depicted as not only painful for women like Maura, but as reflecting a larger historical continuity of suffering embodied in the flashback featuring Gittel. Through enabling Ali's entrance into this legacy of discrimination, the episode stresses what Hirsch describes as the 'ethical' potential of postmemory. Hirsch argues that postmemory is not merely a family matter, but rather promotes 'an ethical relation to the oppressed or persecuted other for which postmemory can serve as a model: as I can "remember" my parents' memories, I can also "remember" the suffering of others'.[22] Ali is thus positioned as representative of such memory – of abandoning the limits of our own experience so as to inhabit that of another. As the sequence stresses, we cannot imagine another's trauma accurately. Nonetheless, we *can* imagine it, and the relevance of empathetic affect which imagination creates can alter how we perceive the experience of others. In presenting such an experience of postmemory, *Transparent* stresses its potential to transform the relationships between individuals, be it a member of our family (Ali and Maura) or of a different social group (the conflict between anti-transgender radical feminists and transgender women). In this sense, postmemory can function as an affective resource with the potential to lessen the divide between oneself and the other, and for surpassing the limits of one's own past.

Coda

This chapter approaches *Transparent* through looking at its presentation of postmemory in the family and among transgender and cisgender women. It focuses on these two seemingly unlinked aspects of the series to ascertain how they comment on the possibility of identification and empathy between individuals and across generational lines. This is particularly relevant in our current moment, with anti-transgender sentiments rife both in the media and in certain feminist circles.[23] In this sense, memory should not be thought of merely in relation to the past, but with regard to the type of futurity it serves as the base for. As Jose Esteban Muñoz notes, 'the past has a performative nature, which is to say that rather than being static or fixed, the past does things'.[24] In *Transparent*, examples of this range from the lack of transgender postmemory which marks the Pfefferman family, as well as Ali's entrance into the family history, both of which point towards the influence memory has on shaping our relations to others. *Transparent* thus offers a broader commentary on the passage of affect and memory from one generation to the other, as well as on the ethical potential of imagining the experiences of others.

4

New spies, old tricks: Intergenerational narratives and memories of the AIDS crisis in *London Spy*

In August 2010, the British media reported the death of mathematician Gareth Williams. The deceased was by no means a famous figure – in fact, his employment at MI6 meant it was part of his job not to be. Instead, it was the manner of his death that the press was quick to sensationalize; his body was found in a locked padlock bag with the deceased having suffocated within it. For years afterwards, media outlets continued to speculate on how this had occurred and continued to present both Williams's life and death in sensationalist, scandalous terms, with news reports ranging from his supposed penchant for male escorts to his presumed love of cross-dressing.[1] In headlines such as 'Murdered spy a regular at gay bar near MI6 HQ' in *The Times*, 'Our murdered spy son was not gay – this is a smear, says his family' in the *Express*, and 'The spy in the bag: Did MI6 agent's kinky sex games lead to his death?' in *The Scotsman*, the mediation of queerness as deviant and Williams himself as an infamous figure is clearly visible.[2] Five years after his death, Williams's passing was even echoed in a BBC miniseries, Tom Rob Smith's *London Spy* (2015), which tracked the fictional Danny (Ben Whishaw) as he attempts to find out who committed the murder of his lover Alex (Edward Holcroft), whose body he finds suffocated in a locked box. While not directly mentioning Williams himself, the parallels between *London Spy* and his death were not lost on many, prompting *The Guardian*'s Boris Starling to wonder whether '*London Spy* [has] gone too far?'[3]

Building on this connection, this chapter looks at how *London Spy* has echoed and adapted not only Williams's death, but precisely the media sensationalism which responded to it. First aired on BBC2 in 2015, *London Spy* was nominated for the BAFTA TV Award in the categories of best miniseries and best leading actor, its first episode seen by 2.5 million viewers and its last by almost 1.6 million.[4] The series is as an atypical addition to televisual incarnations of the spy genre, both by virtue of privileging a queer love story as its focal point, and through its focus on the mediation and memory of homophobia. While its plot hinges on a tragic love story between two younger men, it instead spends most of its duration tracking the friendship between its younger central character (the aforementioned Whishaw) and the significantly older Scottie (Jim Broadbent), whose own experiences of homophobia serve to contextualize the show's central plot within broader narratives of LGBTQ history. Through focusing on an intergenerational friendship between gay men, *London Spy* thus approaches larger issues of how generational experiences of queerness have or have not changed in contemporary Britain and of how queer memory is mediated and passed on. In doing so, it exemplifies broader trends in the development of contemporary queer television, which has historically tended to favour younger, often affluent gay white men as its central protagonists but now displays a marked interest in intergenerationality and queer memory.[5] In commenting on these issues, *London Spy* thus presents a relevant addition to the landscape of British queer television, and yet its contribution here has not yet garnered academic attention, with the exception of a single case study which does not examine these issues.[6]

Moreover, a focus on generational experiences of queerness also raises the issue of queer postmemory – of how and whether it is passed on among different generations of queers and what role media such as film and television have in its creation. In *London Spy*, this issue is approached not only through the intergenerational friendship mentioned above, but through the series self-consciously situating itself within a distinctly queer cinematic heritage, specifically by echoing Derek Jarman's film *Blue* (1993). In mobilizing *Blue*, *London Spy* comments on the potential of queer art to act as a cinematic 'archive of feeling', therein countering the deliberate erasure of queer memory from the public sphere and serving instead as an affective resource in its creation. Taken together, I draw on the commentary presented within the series in order to further examine the connection between on-screen mediations of queerness, queer memory and generational experiences of sexuality. As the example of Gareth Williams makes clear, queerness still continues to be mediated as scandalous and deviant in spite of the progress made with respect to LGBTQ rights. In historicizing such media representations, *London Spy* offers a productive gateway not only into how the media misrepresent and rewrite queer lives and histories, but also into the potential of queer television and cinema to act as alternative forms of memory and, in so doing, to counter such rewriting.

Retelling the queer spy: Media representation and institutional homophobia

The series begins with Danny (Ben Whishaw), a young working-class queer, going to a gay bar to the sound of Donna Summer's 'I Feel Love' on his headphones, a hint towards the impending romance which is to follow. Initially seen striding past a queue of men, his bearing self-confident and nonchalant, Danny is shown in the following scene stumbling out of the same bar at dawn, drunk and alone. Clearly upset, he calls an unidentified person on his mobile but receives no answer. He staggers down Vauxhall Bridge and, upon again receiving no answer from whoever he was calling, throws the phone on the pavement, smashing it into pieces. As he stumbles to the floor to pick them up, another pair of hands is there to help him. This is Alex, who had just been jogging past, and who asks Danny with genuine interest whether he is alright. Their exchange lasts no more than a few sentences, but in the following days, Danny remains interested in Alex and rises each morning at 5 a.m. in the hope of running into him. Soon enough, the two meet again, and in spite of their many differences – Danny is out and Alex is closeted; Alex is a visibly wealthy banker, Danny works at a warehouse; Danny has had a number of partners, while Alex has never had either a relationship or sex with another person – they fall in love. For months, their relationship appears idyllic, and yet the cold tonal palate in which the series is shot, as well as its ominous music, creates an uneasy atmosphere. At the end of the first episode, the romance is tragically cut short as Danny finds Alex dead, suffocated in a wooden box inside his attic. Danny is taken into police questioning, where he is told Alex was not in fact Alex at all, but rather Alastair Turner, a mathematician who worked for MI6. While shocked at these revelations, Danny nonetheless resolves to find out what happened and spends the show's remaining four episodes searching for the truth behind his murder.

As noted earlier, *London Spy* draws direct parallels between Alex's fictional murder and Williams's very real death. Significantly, the series also mimics this media reaction and shows the UK press continually depicting Alex and Danny's relationship as lurid and shocking instead of loving. 'I took drugs', says a headline of Danny. 'I never knew his name', says another (see Figure 13). Danny's attempts at telling his story are granted no sympathy – instead, he is reduced to a drug-using sex-fiend and is promptly dismissed from his warehouse job because of these headlines. In light of these similarities, *London Spy*'s mobilization of Williams's death and its subsequent mediation can be read as a broader commentary on the position of LGBTQ individuals in British society and of

Figure 13 The salacious media treatment of Alex's death and his relationship with Danny.

the persistence of homophobic discrimination. By directly mirroring both Williams's death and the ways in which it was mediated, the series addresses itself specifically to viewers familiar with the case and draws on their memories of it in order to comment on homophobia in the UK.

It is here significant to note how the show's own depiction of the media bears many similarities to how *London Spy* was itself received by parts of the British press, especially with regard to its depiction of sex between men. Following the broadcast of its first episode, *The Sun* falsely reported that Ofcom was starting an investigation into the series due to complaints about its 'explicit' sex scene, while the *Daily Mail* also falsely reported Ofcom investigating the complaints of 13 'shocked' viewers.[7] While it was later established that Ofcom had received only a single complaint and decided not to investigate this report due to the show being screened after 9 p.m., one needed to look no further than the show's reviews to find instances of homophobic reactions to it.[8] In a review succinctly titled 'James Delingpole cringes at *London Spy*'s gay sex scenes', the eponymous *Spectator* columnist complained that 'the main problem with being a TV critic, I've noticed over the years, is that you have to watch so much TV' and that he found himself 'cringing at pert male arses heaving up and down in a sensitive gay love scene in some moody new BBC spy drama'.[9] In a clear demonstration of his homophobia, Delingpole elaborates that he finds 'straight sex enough of an embarrassment but watching two men going at it – even pretty ones like the stars of *London Spy* (BBC1, Mondays) Ben Whishaw and Edward Holcroft – really is an ordeal too far' and that he will not be watching more, in spite of the 'happy ending' which saw one of the central gay characters dead.[10]

Similar sentiments were expressed by the *Daily Mail*'s Christopher Stevens, who complained in his one-star review of the show that 'believe it or not, BBC execs reckon there is not enough gay drama on the Beeb. You might think that it's become impossible to switch the telly on without seeing two men locked in a naked clinch, or in drag, or snogging. … But apparently not. According to Auntie, viewers are starved of shows with homosexual lead characters.'[11] While other news outlets such as *The Huffington Post* reported on the reader backlash which Stevens's review inspired, such 'backlash' extended only to online comments.[12] In this way, both the homophobia and critical praise (expressed, for example, through the BAFTA nominations it earned) which greeted *London Spy* upon its release attest to the paradoxical position occupied by queer media works within the UK televisual landscape, and it is with this in mind that I return to the show's own thematizing of LGBTQ rights and (in)equality.

Through utilizing the figure of Williams in particular, and the queer spy in general, *London Spy* draws on what Allan Hepburn describes in his analysis of literary representations of espionage as the perception of 'homosexuality [itself] as a species of treason'.[13] In *Intrigue: Espionage and Culture* (2014), Hepburn examines the perceived connection between queerness and subterfuge and traces its prevalence in both British and US culture during the twentieth century from the Second World War onwards. He describes the 'semiotic slide between communist and homosexual' which became 'endemic to the period' and promoted the belief that 'duplicity is thought to be grounded in sexual behaviour'.[14] Consequently, the removal of homosexuals from governmental positions in both the UK and the United States; the McCarthy Witch Hunts in which, as Sidney Blumenthal writes, it was 'easier to confess to being a spy than to confess to being a homosexual', all serve as proof of the assumed weakness of character ascribed to queer men at the time.[15] It should perhaps be no surprise that one finds the remnants of such attitudes in the above-noted articles about Gareth Williams or in similarly sensationalistic pieces such as a 2016 article from *The Independent*, imaginatively titled 'British spy exposed by wife over secret gay sex near MI6 HQ'.[16] As its title suggests, the article dealt with the marital issues of an unnamed man possibly associated with the country's Secret Intelligence Service and his spouse's discovery that he had frequented gay dating websites and had sex with men near the SIS headquarters. It mentions that his wife 'raised fears he would be susceptible to blackmail by hostile intelligence services' were these encounters to be revealed, adding in this way not only to the scandalous tone of the piece, but the presumed link between homosexuality and improper or 'faulty' citizenship.

In UK and US on-screen representation, the link between queer espionage and duplicity has also appeared. Sometimes, it has been critically examined, as is the case in Marek Kanievska's 1984 adaptation of Julian Mitchell's *Another Country*, which positions institutional homophobia as the central reason for its protagonist's departure from the UK and eventual career as a Russian spy. At other occasions, this link is portrayed more uncritically, as is for example the case in *The Imitation Game* (2014), which reimagines Alan Turing's (Benedict Cumberbatch) life through focusing mostly on his work at Bletchley Park. In spite of there being no indication in Turing's biography to substantiate this, its hero is depicted as successfully blackmailed for part of the movie by a Soviet spy on account of his homosexuality. While this betrayal occupies only a minor portion of the film, it has nonetheless been rightfully noted and criticized by *The Guardian* columnist Alex Von Tunzelmann, who argued that 'creative license is one thing, but slandering a great man's reputation – while buying into the nasty 1950s prejudice that gay men automatically constituted a security risk – is quite another'.[17] Thus, both the current news media and on-screen portrayals of spies should be viewed as indicative of larger societal attitudes for, as Rosie White writes, 'in fiction and in fact, espionage makes apparent the link between knowledge and power. Spy fictions in print, on film and television may thus be understood as a means of examining the operations of hegemonic discourse'.[18] Through focusing on the media fetishization of Alex and Danny's relationship and sexuality, the series depicts the ways in which non-normative versions of queerness continue to be vilified.

Both visually and through its plot, *London Spy* depicts the unequal relationship between LGBTQ people and the state, with the media vilification Danny endures paralleled by the treatment he receives from institutions meant to ensure his safety (MI6 and the police). The show's very beginning juxtaposes Danny's dishevelled exit from a gay bar with the MI6 headquarters building, which occupies the background for most of the scene, therein signalling the breaking down of barriers between the 'private' and the state. The presence of governmental control in the supposedly separate realm of the private is also notable as Danny and Alex's romance develops in shots depicting them not through the eyes of each other, but through a CCTV camera, or through an extreme long shot which juxtaposes them, tiny in size as they walk along the Thames bank, with the towering presence of MI6 in the background. The flimsy barriers between public and private are visually reinforced through shots of Danny looking out through his apartment window at the activities of his neighbours in a manner resembling Alfred Hitchcock's *Rear Window* (1954), with their private moments as exposed to him as, by analogy, his own are to whoever wants to look.

Crucially, the series does not reserve such shots only for depictions of the influence of state surveillance on the individual but also portrays the effects of other institutions in an equally oppressive manner. For example, Danny's job as a warehouse worker is shot in predominantly black and blue tones, and his irrelevance as an employee there is doubly emphasized through high-angle shots framing his small figure as trapped between two seemingly unending walls filled with boxes, the height of which surpasses that of the frame (see Figure 14). When Danny attempts to make his side of the story public after Alex's death, similar visual methods are used to denote his lack of authority. For instance, his entrance into the building where he is to meet the journalists is filmed from the perspective of a high-angle shot that conveys the overwhelming size of the structure he is attempting to sway. In the same vein, when he is questioned by police as a suspect in Alex's murder, the presence of surveillance is foregrounded by the double framing of the scene (see Figure 15). The monolithic institutional opposition faced by the show's main character depicts the disparity between Danny's position as a working-class queer and the ways in which organizations meant to promote his safety and civil rights (the police and MI6), freedom

Figure 14 Danny at the warehouse.

Figure 15 Danny during his encounter with the police.

of speech (the media) and economic security (the warehouse) all serve to subordinate and control him.

London Spy thus appears at a peculiar moment in time when, on the one hand, rainbow flags can be seen flying from MI6 headquarters (with MI6 itself being hailed as a very gay-friendly employer) while, at the same time, the potential queerness of one of its employees continues to captivate both the public and the media.[19] Consequently, it is through emphasizing all the ways in which Danny is discounted as a young working-class queer man that *London Spy* offers a commentary on the current state of queer rights in the UK. In presenting Danny as a factory worker who lacks the resources to fight such overwhelming discrimination, including his own dismissal from work, the series echoes criticisms which claim that it is precisely such individuals who are excluded from notions of equality and who still continue to bear the brunt of homophobic discrimination.[20] For now, it is relevant to note that the series utilizes the character of Danny's older best friend Scottie (Jim Broadbent) to contextualize such treatment within broader narratives of queer ageing, history and remembrance, therein signalling its relevance as a symptom of queer positionality within the public sphere. By bringing together two gay men from different generations, *London Spy* highlights the continuities between homophobia experienced in the past, and the discrimination that still persists, as well as drawing attention to perspectives too often forgotten in on-screen representation – namely those of ageing LGBTQ people.

Representing queer postmemory: Scottie, *Blue* and archives of feeling

From its beginning, *London Spy* depicts Danny and Alex's relationship in conjunction with Danny's friendship with the older Scottie. In 'Strangers' (episode 2), Scottie is revealed to have himself been a spy once, and he recounts to Danny the tale of his own eventual banishment from MI6. Initially recruited while at Cambridge, Scottie was later contacted by Soviet operatives who had gathered proof of his sexuality. Faced with the choice of being marked as a traitor and 'deviant', Scottie tells Danny of how he had initially determined to kill himself rather than being blackmailed. In the end, however, the older man decided death was not his only option and went to speak with his employers. 'You told your bosses you were gay,' Danny says, to which Scottie laughs: 'That's a wonderful wrong answer, however the option did not yet exist.' Rather, he tells Danny:

> **Scottie:** I admitted that I'd made a mistake, with a man, and that the operative probably had evidence of that mistake. But it was only once. An act of disgusting madness. 'I'm not a homosexual, and I'm not a traitor!' I proposed, preposterously, that they employ someone to follow me for the rest of my life, photograph my every move. I would never touch another man. I didn't discover until later that it hadn't been a Soviet operative, it had been an internal investigation. You've heard of a mole hunt? Well, this was a fag hunt, which they saw as more or less the same thing. Her Majesty's Secret Service had had its fingers burnt by one too many queer spies, but my prompt confession saved my life. I was moved from MI6 into what was then named the Ministry for Transport, where I was little more than a pen pusher, whispered about by those in the know. Out of gratitude and fear, I kept my end of the bargain. And for 11 years, I did not touch another man. ('Strangers')

Scottie's story serves both to illuminate how the effects of government surveillance become transformed into self-surveillance, and as an almost didactic embodiment of the ways in which the position of queer men has either changed or remained the same across the years. When the two hide from MI6 in an attempt to uncover the cause behind Alex's murder, Scottie recounts his closeted years at Oxford during the 1960s. When it is revealed that the government had hired a male prostitute to attempt to blackmail Alex, Scottie comments that 'sex has always been a means of control' ('I Know'). When Danny is left uninvited to Alex's funeral by his family, Scottie speaks of the myriad of men he has seen in the same situation throughout his years. In all of these situations, his character provides a counterpoint for Danny's and contextualizes his experiences in reference to his own. Through him, *London Spy* allows for queer memory to be passed on not simply to Danny but to the viewer, and for its story to be contextualized within a long history of homophobic discrimination. In this sense, Danny and Scottie's relationship serves at once to provide the historical context for Danny's experiences, as well as enabling the show to comment on the realities of depression, homophobia and isolation experienced by older LGBTQ individuals.

Moreover, the character of Scottie functions not only as an emblem for the specific problems faced by older LGBTQ people but also points towards the specific issues plaguing queer communities more broadly, irrespectively of age. It is significant that Scottie is depicted as suffering from depression, a disease still found in greater proportion within the queer population, and has a history of alcoholism, again more likely among LGBTQ people.[21] The character is also linked to suicide within the show's narrative. In 'Strangers' (episode 2), he recounts once considering suicide as a response to being blackmailed. At the end of 'I Know' (episode 4), the show's penultimate episode, Scottie is murdered by being forced to perform this very same act – an act twice as likely to be attempted by LGBTQ people in Britain than their heterosexual counterparts.[22] From this, it becomes clear that Scottie needs to be read not as a reminder of a time of homophobia long gone, but as a personification of its ongoing effects and continued permutations.

Drawing from this, it becomes clear that *London Spy* rejects what Heather Love has termed the 'compulsory happiness' of contemporary queerness, favouring a different approach which acknowledges the often-ignored presences and continuities between the 'dark' past of discrimination and 'rosy' present of queer rights.[23] The series presents the character of Scottie not as a mere contrast for its more liberated younger protagonist, but rather frames both characters as shaped in varied ways by the same institutions, highlighting the similarities in their oppression. In this sense, it questions the presumed equality attained by queer people in contemporary Britain and highlights the homophobic oppression that continues to operate across generational lines. In doing so, it mirrors Love's reasoning in *Feeling Backward: Loss and the Politics of Queer History* (2007), where she argues that 'such an emphasis is particularly important now, when the burdens of social exclusion are being significantly reduced. ... Attending to the specific histories of homophobic exclusion and violence – as well as their effects – can help us see structures of inequality in the present.'[24] In regarding the progress achieved by LGBTQ activists, she therefore cautions against a deliberate forgetting of grimmer histories. Love comments that as long as discrimination continues to structure 'queer life, we cannot afford to turn away from the past; instead, we have to risk the turn backward, even if it means opening ourselves to social and psychic realities we would rather forget'.[25]

While Love aims this call for 'feeling backward' at queer theory more generally and anchors her own analysis in early-twentieth-century novels, I draw on her impetus here due to the ways in which it is reflected both in *London Spy* and in contemporary queer television more broadly, which has demonstrated a marked interest in looking back and reimagining queer histories. In *London Spy*, the concern with queer memory and how the past is passed on is visible not only through the show's situating of Danny's story within Scottie's broader narration of queer history, but also through a particular focus on the AIDS crisis and how it has been represented. In doing so, the series traces a direct link between cinematic and televisual representations of HIV, and presents such on-screen representation as an affective resource with which the misrepresentation and deliberate forgetting of LGBTQ lives can be countered. Most strikingly, it does so through mobilizing Derek Jarman's *Blue* and through presenting HIV itself as a weapon of governmental violence against LGBTQ people.

The show's first mention of HIV comes in 'Lullaby', its very first episode, when Danny recounts to Alex the shame he feels due to a night of unprotected and drug-fuelled sex with multiple partners in his youth, after which he was lucky enough not to have contracted HIV. For Danny, the experience was a formative one – he is now 'always safe. Always' ('Lullaby'). This emphasis on protected sex is particularly relevant for the ensuing narrative, as the show's third episode again focuses on HIV, but this time positions the virus as the weapon of choice used by MI6 to silence Danny into submission. Namely after refusing to be deterred by the salacious media coverage of his relationship, as well as rejecting all warnings and threats to let the matter of Alex's death rest, Danny is confronted by his puzzled flatmate Sara (Zrinka Cvitesic), who has stumbled upon the antiretroviral drug Truvada among his things. 'Why didn't you tell me?', she asks, as the realization begins to dawn on Danny that this is another message from MI6. What follows is an eight-minute-long sequence which depicts, nearly in real time, Danny's visit to an STI clinic and the two HIV tests he undergoes there, both showing he tests positive for the virus. Apart from the exchanges between Danny and his doctor, the sequence is intimate and largely focused on Whishaw's wordless reactions, which highlight the disbelief and suffering the character is experiencing.

Once the repeated tests prove he is seropositive, Danny is shown at Scottie's house, begging him to believe this was done by MI6. Once again, the older character's reaction serves as a broader commentary on LGBTQ positionality within the public sphere and the ways in which HIV positive queers are treated. Scottie comments:

> **Scottie:** I believe you. I believe they deliberately infected you. Not to kill you, obviously. With medication, you'll live a long and normal life. They did it to discredit you. They'll say you took risks with your own health. That you were reckless and irresponsible. Perhaps they'll even say you infected Alex.
> **Danny:** No, he, he was –
> **Scottie:** Negative. Yes. But what will the tests say? The story of you two has been written. It was written many months ago. A sordid tale, the details of which will leak out into the public sphere. People will recoil. Many will think you got what you deserved. No one will campaign for answers. No one will demand justice. ('Blue')

It is worth pausing on the dialogue in this scene, as it addresses a number of issues central to this chapter. As Scottie notes, it is now possible to live a long life while being HIV positive, provided one has access to medication. However, seropositivity can still be used as a tool to discredit those whose HIV status is revealed – to take away their credibility due to a proposed recklessness with their own and others' health. Scottie overtly references the public sphere, as well as activism ('No one will campaign for answers. No one will demand justice') to show the ways in which both privilege seronegative bodies. Returning for a moment to the real story of Gareth Williams, it is relevant that the mathematician's own appearance in the press did not include any mention of either HIV or AIDS. Through adding HIV to the narrative, *London Spy* thus links the treatment afforded to Williams by the media with the long history of media vilification to which queer HIV and AIDS sufferers have been subjected by the press.[26] To name but one example of this during the height of the AIDS crisis, the press coverage surrounding Rock Hudson's death is especially illustrative. Upon reporting that Hudson was terminally ill, *The Sun* referred to his home as the 'plague palace', while the *Daily Mail* described the way he looked prior to his death as the 'two faces of Hollywood', with Hudson representing its 'dissipated, corrupt, decadent' side.[27] In response to such coverage, Simon Watney argued:

> British TV and press coverage is locked into an agenda which blocks out any approach to the subject which does not conform in advance to the values and

language of a profoundly homophobic culture – a culture, that is, which does not regard gay men as fully or properly human. No distinction obtains for this agenda between 'quality' and 'tabloid' newspaper, or between 'popular' and 'serious' television.[28]

In *London Spy*, the history of news media homophobia which depicts gay men as 'not fully or properly human' is reflected through Danny's contact with both the press and the state. Upon hearing of Danny's HIV positive status, Scottie comments that 'the story of you two has been written. It was written many months ago', emphasizing the link between media discrimination in the past with that of contemporary media outlets. When considered in conjunction with the show depicting MI6 literally deploying HIV as a weapon against Danny, the parallels between *London Spy*'s narrative and 1980s/1990s activist rhetoric become startling. Namely, it was during the height of the AIDS crisis that activists such as those in ACT UP looked at governmental inaction as a form of attack, conceptualizing state negligence not merely as a form of 'accidental' passivity, but rather as a homophobic assault that caused a staggering number of deaths.[29] In *London Spy*, this history is invoked not through a depiction of government negligence, but rather the active deployment of HIV as a tool against queers like Danny, who behave in what it considers an unacceptable manner and lack the resources to fight back.

Crucial to the series' depiction of this is its presentation of historical continuity and of permutations of homophobia which travels from then to now. As Watney argues, the demonization of men who have sex with men during the AIDS crisis cannot be regarded without taking into account the history of how homophobia has been medicalized. He writes that it is 'unhelpful to think of AIDS commentary as a moral panic which somehow makes gay men into monsters, since this is an intrinsic effect of the medicalisation of morality which accompanied the emergence of the modern categories of sexuality in the course of the last 200 years'.[30] In *London Spy*, this medicalization of morality is clearly echoed in the show's HIV plotline and the ways in which it is used to discredit Danny, to make him a witness the general public is unlikely to believe or even sympathize with. Drawing from this, *London Spy*'s depiction of how Danny's history of promiscuity, drug use and later seropositive status are all used to discredit him can be read as a criticism of the contemporary state of queer rights in the UK and of the notions of LGBTQ equality having been achieved. In showing how some queer people, be they seropositive, working class, or sexually promiscuous, are deemed less deserving than others, the series points towards what Erik O. Clarke has described as 'a punitive vision of rights', which punishes those whose behaviour does not live up to homonormative proscriptions.[31] As Clarke argues, the pathologizing of those who do not subscribe to heteronormative notions of behaviour presents particular dangers for LGBTQ people, with value only being ascribed to individuals considered morally worthy, while queers like Danny are excluded from the dominant system, deemed undeserving due to their sexual behaviour. As Scottie says during his 'Blue' monologue, 'People will recoil. Many will think you got what you deserved. No one will campaign for answers. No one will demand justice.'

As the scene continues, Scottie recalls the AIDS crisis through remembering a partner who died from the virus. 'Back then', Scottie recounts of 1983, 'it didn't even have a name. There was no information, no leaflets. No warnings, no answers. You'd watch the news and hear no mention of it – a secret plague.' For informed viewers, references to HIV being referred to as a 'gay plague' are clearly recognizable here, as is the period before it was given the name AIDS and was instead referred to as GRID (gay-related immune deficiency).[32] As Scottie recalls this time, we see a flashback in which the camera stands in for Scottie and passes through his partner's apartment, unremarkable except for the bedroom, which is covered floor to ceiling in blue paint. In its centre, there is a light installation also covered in blue and, on the bed, an immobile blue body (see Figure 16). A paper bag filled with oranges drops from Scottie's hands, and the camera moves closer to the man, whose eyes finally open, revealing he is in fact alive. Scottie explains that 'back then, mysticism and magic stood in for medicine'

Figure 16 The 'Blue' room and Scottie's partner on the bed.

and so the idea of 'blue' had occurred to his partner, who was an aspiring artist, after he had been gifted a book on colour therapy. 'In it', Scottie says, 'blue was described as having healing properties. Blue ... blue alone, was able to fight infections. Blue ... blue alone, could save him. Blue. No doubt the idea appealed to his artistic sensibilities.'

Like the episode's eponymous title, Scottie's rhythmic repetition of the word 'blue' as well as the visual prominence of the colour invoke numerous associations; on the one hand, blue is the colour of Truvada, the famed HIV drug found by Danny in his flat, and is also prominent during the scene depicting Danny's HIV test: the light blue hospital curtain in the background, the blue waiting room, as well as the two blue dots shown to Danny by the nurse on his HIV test as a sign of seropositivity. Most importantly, it is also the title of Derek Jarman's pivotal work of AIDS queer cinema, the 1993 film *Blue*. Through invoking Jarman's work in this way, the episode contextualizes the suffering depicted on screen not solely in terms of queer social and medical history, but also via the legacy of queer cinema. Made by Jarman at the height of his own struggle with HIV, during which he had become partially blind, the film consists entirely of a single shot of monochromatic blue and is narrated by several speakers. In contrast to this visual austerity, *London Spy* pays tribute to Jarman's film through both repeated verbal references to the colour, as well as through what are arguably the series' most lavish shots, in which the colour is prominent. Through doing so, the series draws a deliberate connection between Jarman's *Blue* and the episode, drawing links between the past of queer cinema and itself as a contemporary work also concerned with seropositivity and homophobia. At the same time, its continuous invocation of the colour points towards the connection between those like Danny, who have been newly infected with HIV in the present, and those who were some of its first victims.

In drawing a link between itself and *Blue*, the series presents an overall concern with how the AIDS crisis is represented and remembered, as well as the role of on-screen representation in such commemoration. In their responses to the crisis, activists and artists have created countless hours of video work, as well as invented entirely new strategies for commemorating loss, such as the AIDS Memorial Quilt, which today encompasses 48,000 individual panels, each sewn in memory of a loved one lost to AIDS.[33] However, it is worth keeping in mind the specificity of the commemorative challenge presented by the AIDS crisis, which for years existed as a largely unrecognized issue disproportionately affecting the queer community. When depicted in the media, AIDS sufferers were stigmatized, their pain sensationalized in the construction of what Watney calls the 'spectacle of AIDS'.³⁴ In the same vein, Robert Hallas describes the ways in which, during the 1980s AIDS crisis, 'homosexual bodies were put on display as a traumatizing threat to the general public, while traumatized queer lives were discounted'.³⁵ While activists have since succeeded in changing attitudes towards seropositive individuals and HIV more broadly, questions have since been raised about how their own work is being remembered. For example, Sarah Schulman has noted the ways in which the legacies of AIDS activist groups such ACT UP have been forgotten in the US context, their history substituted with rosier narratives of a gradual acceptance towards AIDS victims naturally occurring.³⁶ Similarly, Christopher Castiglia and Christopher Reed comment that 'among the historical disasters addressed by trauma theory (the Holocaust, the Vietnam War, 9/11), AIDS has rarely been taken up as one of the most significant cultural traumas of the late twentieth century, and the cultural aftershock of reinvigorated assaults on gay lifeways has attracted even less attention as a site of trauma worthy of study'.³⁷ Taken together, such misremembering of the crisis can be heavily influenced by its mediated afterlives, and so it is important to consider *London Spy*'s depiction of HIV not only with respect to the show's principal storyline, but with regard to larger questions of queer seropositive memory.

Through visually and verbally referencing Jarman's film, the series can thus be read as a commentary on how visual works (be they cinematic or otherwise) function as what Ann Cvetkovich calls 'archives of feeling', which take on for queer people the role of memory in 'the absence of institutional documentation or in opposition to official histories'.³⁸ While Cvetkovich is herself not referring to cinema, I borrow here from her description in order to identify the complex ways in which films and television act as affective memory resources. In *London Spy*, Scottie's own story is depicted through a language of filmic intertextuality, thus pointing towards the ways in which queer memory itself cannot be thought of without reference to the screen – without, in other words, considering how one's conception of the LGBTQ past is shaped by how it has been represented in both homophobic media, as well as in queer cinema. It is here significant that *London Spy* thematizes *Blue* in particular, as it points to the very irrepresentability of pain and trauma which marks the AIDS crisis, as well as the frequent erasure of its victims.³⁹ Through echoing Jarman's work, it also brings to mind the visions of the past presented in his broader opus, which defies the idea of film as a 'record' or accurate representation of history. Instead, what can be found in Jarman's work is an affective and imaginative engagement with notions of history, a 'remembering' that is neither factual nor literal, but that nonetheless presents the queerness of the past.⁴⁰ As a televisual work, the ways in which

London Spy situates itself with respect to such cinematic precedents is especially interesting considering the series' overarching concern with the notion of truth and the dangers of misrepresentation. While Danny constantly battles with his and Alex's relationship being trivialized and misrepresented, as well as his own life being presented inaccurately, Scottie's 'Blue' monologue instead functions as an anchor, locating Danny's experience in the veracity of the cinematic.

While *London Spy* is unique in addressing the AIDS crisis through referencing Jarman, its focus on queer histories, legacies and intergenerational contact is illustrative of broader trends in the current development of queer television. In this sense, it is indicative that *London Spy* is also not alone in drawing on cinematic precedents in how it approaches queer history. As mentioned earlier, *Transparent* traces a lineage between its own mediation of transgender identity and previous on-screen representations of trans women by incorporating clips from the 1968 documentary *The Queen* in its season one credits. In a similar vein, Ryan Murphy's *Pose* itself echoes Jenny Livingston's famed New Queer Cinema documentary *Paris Is Burning* (1990), which tracked BAME 'ballroom' communities during the 1980s. In *Hollywood* (Netflix, 2020), Murphy has gone a step further, deliberately rewriting the hidden queer history of the silver screen by depicting an alternate version of Rock Hudson as one of his central protagonists. While the above-mentioned works vary greatly from each other, their emphasis on establishing a lineage between cinematic and televisual queer representation while also thematizing issues of LGBTQ history points towards precisely the ways in which queer memory cannot be thought of without how it has been both shaped and rewritten by the screen.

In echoing *Blue*, *London Spy* thus signals both the fundamentally prosthetic nature of queer memory, as well as pointing towards precisely the frequent rewriting and erasure of LGBTQ life that so often happens in the process of mediation. Through depicting both the character's bedroom and his body as covered with the same blue paint, the sequence echoes the questions raised by Jarman's monochromatic blue screen – questions of the lives and experiences hidden beneath it, masked by the uniformity of phrases such as AIDS 'sufferers' or 'victims' which render men like Scottie's partner nameless and unseen. In this sense, it is no accident that Scottie's deceased partner is described as an aspiring artist, as it foregrounds the generation of queer artistic voices, Jarman included, who have been lost to us due to government inaction during the crisis.

In the next scene, Scottie's lover is shown in a bathtub, the paint from his body dyeing the water blue. The notion of identities obscured by AIDS is again reinforced through the ways in which the scene is filmed, either through high-angle shots of the character submerging himself in the coloured water or through being filmed from behind, his face hidden or partially obscured by the combination of lighting, paint and positioning, only his eyes once more meeting with the camera. As the paint slips from his back into the water, innumerable lesions become visible. In the present, the water once visible in the flashback is echoed on Scottie's face, as he is filmed through a window at night, the shadows of raindrops visible on his skin as if they were there and not on the glass surface (see Figure 17). In the final flashback scene, we are once again back inside his partner's bedroom, all but the blue art installation attached to its centre now white again, flecks of blue paint falling from it onto the empty mattress. Like the man himself, his traces are removed by the new whiteness of the room, again echoing the unremembering of AIDS.

Perhaps surprisingly, the sequence ends by showing Danny and Scottie swimming freely in the translucent blue water of a swimming pool, their movements easy and unfettered (see Figure 18). Visually reminiscent of David Hockney's California swimming pool series, the scene comes after both characters have agreed to keep on fighting and thus resignifies the colour blue from a symbol of futility (as it had been in the scene depicting Scottie's deceased lover) to one of perseverance and hope. The immersion of all three characters, Scottie's partner, Scottie and Danny, in the colour is significant, as it establishes a connection between past and present by bringing together different generations of HIV positive men and those who loved them. Through borrowing from

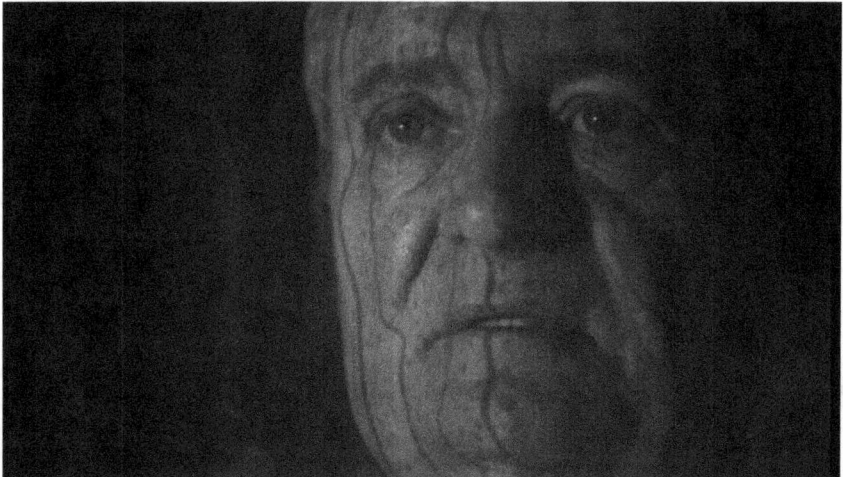

Figure 17 Scottie recounts his partner's illness.

Figure 18 Danny swims in blue.

Jarman and Hockney, *London Spy* builds on a specifically queer visual language and points towards the recuperative power of these artistic legacies. By utilizing the colour blue in order to draw links between seropositivity in the past and the present, Danny's newly infected body stands in for the LGBTQ men who have fallen prey to the virus before him. Like theirs, his seropositivity is incomprehensible without the role which the state has played in it and reflects the governmental influence on queer lives. The flashback and Scottie's 'blue' monologue therefore function to reposition both Danny and the viewer with respect to memories of AIDS. Taken together, the differences between how blue is presented in the flashback and how it is seen in the pool scene demonstrates not only the persistence of the past and its memory within the present, but also the potential for archives of feelings to be transformed by those who inherit them. While blue was once the colour of pain and death for Scottie's partner, it is now the colour of defiance and strength for Danny and Scottie. Through being linked in this way to the histories of the LGBTQ men who have lived with and died of HIV, Danny emerges from the pool refusing to disavow such legacies.

Coda

Like many AIDS-related works, *London Spy* is at its most basic a story of a gay man going up against governmental institutions much bigger than him, attempting in this way to fight for what is left of his partner's legacy. While not a work directly concerned with activism, it is nonetheless important to recognize the ways in which the series mirrors such works and how it comments on the links between queerness, seropositive status and institutional neglect/control. Danny's attempts at finding the cause of Alex's death can thus be read as an allegory for broader issues of how queerness is mediated in Britain – of how it is misrepresented and twisted even in the contemporary press – and how its traumatic memories are often left unacknowledged, as Danny's are of Alex or Scottie's are of his partner. Like countless men before him, Scottie's partner is made nameless by the AIDS crisis, just as Danny's memories of Alex are dismissed by the media, with even Alex's name altered, and are instead replaced by salacious misrepresentations of their relationship. In both of these examples, the question of whether or not representation reflects reality is raised, and it is therefore significant that *London Spy* depicts institutions like the media and the government as duplicitous and corrupt, while at the same time paying homage to works such as Jarman's *Blue*. In evoking works like Jarman's film, it represents them as potent archives of queer feeling – as more eloquent and honest representations of the queer past and of queer pain than can be found in the press. At the same time, through using Scottie as a 'guide' through queer history, it not only contextualizes its own plot within the wider context of the LGBTQ past but also reminds us of the many queers not often seen on screen – the Scotties who remain unheard and nameless, their pain too often unrecognized and deliberately unremembered.

Conclusion

In the introduction to this section, I wrote of a marked focus on LGBTQ intergenerational contact in a number of recent television series including *Transparent, Pose, Cucumber* and *Vicious*. This focus on queer intergenerationality represents a relevant development in the landscape of contemporary queer television, countering the near-constant focus on white youthful gay characters which had preceded it. Apart from leaving older LGBTQ people unrepresented, this focus on youth also left viewers with a dehistoricized vision of queerness, disarticulating it not only from matters such as ageing, but also from questions of historical continuity and memory. In Chapter 4, I analysed how *London Spy* undermines such visions of queerness by contextualizing its own plot not only with respect to viewer memories of the mediation of Gareth Williams's death, but also with respect to broader histories of homophobia. The series thus utilizes Scottie not only to comment on the development of gay rights in the UK, but also to comment on the position of older gay men, whose specific perspectives are seldom depicted on television. As Chapter 3 shows, such invisibility also engulfs transgender individuals, whose suffering and experiences are often conveniently forgotten even by those closest to them. In light of this, *Transparent*'s depiction of Maura's coming out in old age, as well as its focus on the family as a locus of queer memory, is exceedingly important. Through focusing on both hidden transgender legacies, as well as conflicts within the LGBTQ community, the chapter highlights the show's emphasis on the subjective nature of remembering and on how privilege can blind us to the suffering of others.

Both shows thus represent important developments in British and American television, not only with respect to depicting older characters and events which are seldom granted televisual representation, but also through offering rare examples of the crucial value of queer postmemory. The focus in both series on intergenerationality, as well as their depiction of memory passing from one generation to another, is especially relevant, as they provide an on-screen space for the development of queer postmemories which many LGBTQ people do not have in real life. Consequently, this section highlights the role which on-screen representation plays in bridging the gap between those who inhabit different generations and whose perspectives are often forgotten in favour of a unitary and youthful vision of queerness. Through highlighting the silence which often envelops LGBTQ histories, as well as the ways in which even members of the LGBTQ community can remain blind to and even participate in discriminating against others who fall under the same rainbow umbrella, both chapters point towards the profound relevance of queer postmemory and how it is mediated and created by the screen.

Part Three

Remembering queer activism

In March 2017, *The Huffington Post* published an article by transgender actor Alexandra Billings titled 'When We Rose, I Was There'.[1] In a clear reference to the recently released ABC historical drama *When We Rise*, the article questioned the historical accuracy of the series, pointing towards the absence of transgender protagonists in the show's depiction of the AIDS crisis. While recounting her own experiences as a seropositive trans woman and AIDS activist, Billings commented on the larger significance of on-screen representations of the trans past. She argued that 'when history is rewritten and shown as entertainment for the masses, … and when the public sees that we are absent from the plague that took us by force, fiction then becomes fact'.[2] In this way, her assessment of the series' shortcomings highlights a number of issues crucial to this chapter. On the one hand, it raises the question of *whose* past is being depicted – of which story is deemed as 'relevant' enough to stand as representative of the LGBTQ movement more broadly. On the other, it highlights the potential effects which mediations of LGBTQ activism might have on the viewer, therein emphasizing the dangers in representing only select perspectives on the past. While Billings's critique of *When We Rise* presents an especially eloquent illustration of this issue, a similar approach to on-screen representations of queer history can be seen in the boycott against Roland Emmerich's film *Stonewall*, which has already been mentioned in Introduction to this book. In both cases, the critique of these media works stems from the belief that an inaccurate or incomplete vision of history not only influences how we think of the past of the queer movement, but also shapes the state of its present.

In Part Three of this book, I will look at the ways in which the history of LGBTQ activism has been commemorated and recreated in fiction film and television. Within the field of memory studies, the focus on war, trauma and genocide has often meant that memories of non-violent activism remain less examined, while the impact of memories on social movements has also not been much analysed.[3] While this applies more broadly to the study of activist memory, the question of how we remember and commemorate the past of queer activism is of particular relevance at the present moment, seeing as a number of contemporary Anglo-American LGBTQ activist organizations face criticism for embracing neoliberal politics, homonormativity, and homonationalism.[4] As recent examples of such criticism, we need to look no further than the controversy surrounding the Human Rights Campaign (HRC) granting the agrochemical corporation Monsanto a perfect score (for the eighth year in a row) in its 2018 Corporate Equality Index, prioritizing thus the rights it affords LGBTQ employees while disregarding the company's unethical actions in other areas.[5] In the same vein, a number of Pride-related events have been repeatedly critiqued for charging admission fees and therefore excluding low-income people, as was the case with London Pride and New York Pride.[6] Compounded with the negative effects which austerity cuts have had on LGBTQ organizations, these developments are symptomatic of the effects of neoliberalism on the LGBTQ movement.[7] One of the key issues in how queer activism is commemorated on-screen therefore becomes whether the history of LGBTQ activism which battled economic inequality risks being forgotten, and the movement itself remembered as inherently neoliberal.

At the same time, the question of how the history of the queer movement is remembered can influence not only how we conceive of its past, but also how we imagine its future. This is what numerous authors refer to as memory's 'normative power' which, as Ross Poole elaborates, stems from the ways in which it 'sets the moral agenda of the present, [informing] us of the obligations and responsibilities we have acquired' from the past.[8] This does not mean that the future of any activist movement is inescapably determined by the ways in which it remembers its past, but rather, that the limits of what it considers both achievable and most significant can in part be determined by memory. Cinematic and televisual representations of activism are here of particular relevance, as they are both affectively powerful and more widely accessible than (academic) literature on the subject. As Red Chidgey argues in her recent work on feminist memory, media representations of activism can extend 'the temporality of the protest act, which sees new versions and imaginings of diffuse protest pasts circulating through the public realm'.[9] This is a vital effect of such mediation for, as Chidgey puts it, 'activist histories are restless' and can influence present activism by providing transformed glimpses of the past.[10]

Moreover, the emphasis placed on certain parts of activist history, as well as on certain activists themselves, can influence not only how a movement is conceived of, but also of *to whom* it is thought to belong. As I have written earlier, the examples of the boycott against *Stonewall* and Billings's own criticism of *When We Rise* point towards a concern with whose histories are being represented and to whose expense this is being done. To take the example of Emmerich's *Stonewall* for a moment, its focus on a white male protagonist at the expense of its BAME transgender characters cannot be considered without also taking into consideration the virulent anti-transgender rhetoric that still pervades the United States, as well as the ways in which (as Susan Stryker's path-breaking work has shown) transgender activism has routinely been excluded from retellings of the LGBTQ past.[11] When viewed with these facts in mind, the deliberate emphasis placed in the film on the activism of a fictional white man at the expense of BAME trans women needs to be seen as a cinematic statement as to the relative importance the film attributes to these two groups. As the coming chapter will show, representations of queer activist history as a white, male, monosexual and cisgendered endeavour risk obfuscating the ways in which women, transgender men, and people of other races and ethnicities have shaped LGBTQ history, therein relegating them to a secondary role in the movement's present as well as its past.

The issue of which types of protagonists are represented and whose activism is forgotten also points towards the question of how individual and collective political action can be represented on-screen, as well as the relationship between the two. As Foucault wondered in an interview on the interrelationship between film and popular memory, is it possible to 'make a film about a struggle without going through the traditional process of creating heroes'?[12] How, in other words, can a film depict a social movement composed of many people without glorifying a particular individual? And, if it does go through the process of making 'heroes', which individuals, types of people or groups will it choose to canonize? While researching this book, I encountered this exact question while in the archive of the Manchester People's History Museum. As I was reading through the museum's file on the activist group Lesbians and Gays Support the Miners, the research on which informs Chapter 5, I was approached by an archivist who wanted to tell me they also have files on other local LGBTQ activist groups. 'Since *Pride* came out, everyone who visits wants to read about LGSM, but no one wants to hear about anything else,' he lamented. In this way, on-screen representation can be seen as a double-edged sword, at once capable of pulling groups such as LGSM out of obscurity, while also shaping the narrative of the

LGBTQ rights movement in a way that inevitably draws attention away from other groups and actions.

Taken together, all of these questions point towards the stakes involved in mediating queer activist history and, in this way, in creating new narratives of how LGBTQ political action evolved. By focusing on representations of activism in particular, I draw here on Anna Reading and Tamar Katriel's suggestion that memory needs to be understood 'not [only] in terms of trauma, and the repression and working through of violent pasts, but in terms of the value of remembering human agency and the resilience with which individuals and societies continue to articulate memories of nonviolent struggles for human dignity, human equality, human freedom'.[13] This is of particular relevance for the development of queer memory, as conceptualizations of queerness have sometimes focused on its negative potentiality, a move emblematic of the so-called anti-social turn in queer theory or, in the view of Michael Snediker, of 'queer pessimism'.[14] In surveying this anti-social turn, I am more inclined to side with authors like Simon Watney, who argues that an academic focus on anti-relationality risks denying 'the validity or authenticity of any kind of communitarian or collective lesbian or gay culture or politics'.[15] Moreover, the proposition that queers might simply embrace negative potentiality and the death drive seems dangerously disconnected to issues such as LGBTQ homelessness rates, the prevalence of hate crimes and the rates of suicide in the community. In this sense, even the theoretical rejection of futurity presupposes that one is in a position privileged enough to do so – a privilege not often afforded to many LGBTQ people.

Thus, while it is indeed worth embracing the fierce criticism which authors like Lee Edelman level at the organization of politics around the notion of the heteronormative family, I focus instead on how queerness allows for new types of world-building and alliances which cross borders of race, of class or, indeed, of one's biological family. The question of how the queer past is represented is intimately tied with such world-building, as it in part shapes not only what we believe has been achieved so far but, to an extent, what we believe *can* be accomplished. To give but an example of how past activism can motivate and influence the activism undertaken in the present, we can look at the UK-based activist group Lesbians and Gays Support the Migrants. In both name and their intersectional approach, LGSMigrants mimics Lesbians and Gays Support the Miners, themselves explaining that their goal is to 'build on a proud history of queer solidarity to say: *no one is illegal*'.[16] This is precisely the utopian potentiality Jose Muñoz attributes in queer memory, and it is with this in mind that I approach films like *Pride*, which popularized LGSM's story, transforming it from a tale which even the film's own screenwriter was doubtful of, into a much-beloved work of LGBTQ cinema, screened repeatedly for years since its release.[17]

In the coming chapter, my analysis of *Pride* will first look at the film's presentation of gender and sexuality through focusing specifically on its depiction of lesbian activism. Through doing so, it is also my aim to analyse more broadly how activist and politically transformative action is depicted on screen as gendered and how this gendering differs depending on whether it pertains to queer or heterosexual women. After this, I will examine the film's presentation of the connection between gay rights and the socio-economic systems within which these rights are contained. In particular, I am here interested in whether questions of labour rights and economic policies are presented as either interlinked with, or external to, the past of the queer civil rights struggle, as well as whether and how divisions within the gay community are portrayed. After this, the following section will provide a comparative analysis of other dramatizations of LGBTQ history and will look at works as different as *Milk* and *When We Rise* in order to assess the narrative trends which both bring them together and set them apart. As noted earlier, my analysis of *Pride* is informed not only by the film itself, but also by the research I have undertaken in the archive of Manchester's People History Museum, which hosts an extensive collection of materials related to LGSM. The materials in this archive range from the minutes of meetings to newspaper clippings about LGSM and are thus an extremely useful resource for examining how Warchus's film chooses to remember the group's activism and which aspects it has decided to omit. As I have noted earlier in this book, I draw on archival research not due to the conviction that historical drama must be absolutely factually accurate. Instead, it is due to an interest in how the past of not only LGSM, but the LGBTQ rights movement is being narrated and in the ideological implications of this narration.

5

Reimagining LGSM: Gendered activism and neoliberalism in Matthew Warchus's *Pride*

In May 2018, Durham's fifth Pride parade marched through the city. It was led by a rainbow-coloured Mini Cooper displaying the sign 'Police with Pride', followed by a marching band, and numerous people waving flags and banners. Among the signs, the large banner of the Durham Miners' Association stood out, inscribed with the words 'Men of Merit' and 'The History of Loyalty'. Afterwards, the association's chairman Joe Whitworth made a speech in front of the marchers.[1] He acknowledged that the mining community had not always sympathized with LGBTQ people but talked of how they have learned to embrace difference. He spoke of the 'strong political link' formed between the LGBTQ people and the National Union of Miners during the 1984–5 Miners' Strike and of the support provided to the miners by queer activists. To illustrate his points, Whitworth mentioned two films: Stephen Daldry's *Billy Elliot* (2000) and Matthew Warchus's *Pride* (2014), which I will soon look at in detail. The mention of *Pride* was greeted with loud approval from audience members, many of whom were clearly too young to have experienced the Miners' Strike, and yet displayed an audible affection for the film and its presentation of the activist group Lesbians and Gays Support the Miners (LGSM). In this way, both Whitworth's speech and the audience reaction to it brought to the fore some of the ways in which cinema shapes community memory, be it for those who have themselves experienced an event or for later generations. While *Billy Elliot* and *Pride* both address the period of strike while simultaneously thematizing queer sexuality, it is worth noting here that only the former is actually set in County Durham, while the latter focuses on the experience of Welsh Miners in the distant Dulais Valley. Nonetheless, the reaction of Durham Pride-goers to Whitworth's mention of these films indicates how they have been embraced as markers of heritage extending far beyond Wales and the London base from which LGSM stems.

Founded in 1984, LGSM was the first and most successful LG-only organization to start collecting funds for striking miners.² LGSM members viewed their work as a vital intervention into Tory economic and civil rights policies and argued that questions of LG rights and workers' rights were interrelated. Like other miners' support groups during the strike, LGSM also chose a specific mining community which it would support (so-called twining) and thus formed a close connection with the Dulais Valley community. In 1985, the Dulais Valley Lodge joined the London Pride march in support of LGSM and the two groups, once considered unlikely allies, ended up leading the parade. In the same year, the National Union of Mineworkers (NUM) also pledged its support for gay rights at the Labour Conference, and the motion of adding gay rights to the Labour Party Constitution was passed for the first time. The NUM also later supported the campaign against Section 28, which banned the use of government funds for the 'promotion' of homosexuality in England, Scotland and Wales.³ In 2015, the thirtieth anniversary of the 1985 Pride march was commemorated in London by LGSM and a number of miners' groups – a development influenced by the popularity of Warchus's film. The Mark Ashton Red Ribbon Fund was also founded in honour of the prominent LGSM activist Mark Ashton, who died of AIDS at only 26 years old in 1987, and has so far succeeded in raising almost £40,000 for the Terrence Higgins Trust.⁴

While *Pride* can be credited with popularizing LGSM's legacy, Warchus's film owes its existence at least in part to the willingness of LGSM members themselves to preserve and mediate their own history. In spite of the fact that as many as eleven other queer organizations around the UK followed in its footsteps, the majority of these groups have unfortunately fallen into anonymity. Diarmaid Kelliher attributes the preservation of LGSM's legacy to several factors: the fact that the group was the first of its sort, that it had collected the most money for the miners and, finally, that it documented its own activities, thus creating its own historical archive.⁵ Additionally, while the mainstream media ignored LGSM during the time it was active, their activities were reported on in a number of smaller newspapers, most notably in London's *Capital Gay* magazine and numerous left-wing papers in the UK and abroad. LGSM members preserved a number of these clippings and also produced an almost twenty-five–minute documentary, which was initially made as part of a broader effort to document miners' support groups. The documentary, titled *All Out! Dancing in Dulais*, featured interviews both with LGSM members and with Dulais residents and soon became part of an exhibition prepared by the group on the subject of their activism. As LGSM activist Mike Jackson explained, their goal in putting together an exhibition was 'to inform people of the links that were made, the common problems of media distortion, police harassment and state oppression of both the mining communities and lesbians and gays'.[6] While LGSM struggled to find funding for the exhibition and received refusals from some venues to host it, the exhibition nonetheless did tour a number of smaller galleries, including the independent Tyneside Cinema in Newcastle upon Tyne, Bristol Student Union, Westminster NALGO, Derbyshire Council Labour Group and Brixton Art Solidarity and Sexuality Gallery. In 1991, the exhibition and other materials were donated to the archive of what is now the People's History Museum in Manchester. The materials collected in this archive significantly inform this research, as it not only contains detailed records of the group's meetings and the rationale behind their work, but also traces the mediation of it in a variety of news sources. In this way, it serves as a useful companion to Warchus's film and to questions of how LGSM's work and its context are represented.

Pride begins in 1984 when a group of lesbian and gay activists start collecting money for striking miners. It takes place within the span of a year and depicts the evolving relationship between the activist group and the Welsh village of Onllwyn, for which they are raising funds. Both the film's beginning and its end are bracketed by a Pride march; during the first demonstration, the activists begin collecting money for the miners while, at the film's end, the miners join LGSM in leading the 1985 London Pride march. Described by its director as 'a classic romantic comedy', the film positions these two communities as 'opposites who somehow overcome the obstacles between them' and presents their story through a mixture of humorous interactions and melodrama.[7] As Mike Jackson recounted at the 2018 Durham Miners' Hall screening of the film, Warchus made clear to them that he wanted to make a commercial film which would have the broadest possible appeal.[8] It is arguable that he at least partially achieved this goal; while the film earned a modest sum of almost $17 million worldwide, it was nonetheless awarded the BAFTA for best debut feature and was nominated for best comedy feature film at the Golden Globes and at the GLAAD awards.[9] Four years since its release, it is still being screened, whether by various LGBTQ groups or in miners' halls such as the one in Durham. At the 2018 Durham Miners' Hall screening which I attended, LGSM activists Jackson and Dave Lewis were greeted by a standing ovation after the film finished. This testament of the audience's appreciation speaks to the importance attached to LGSM's story both by older viewers, some of them miners themselves or members of the mining community, and some of them much younger and coming from outside of County Durham, possibly acquainted with these events primarily through the movie. It is precisely this cross-generational and cross-community appeal which makes *Pride* such a relevant filmic text about queer activism, and it is with this in mind that I approach the film. I therefore begin by looking at the gendered narratives of activism in *Pride* and at the ways in which the film highlights the labour of some activists at the expense of others.

The apparitional activist: Remembering the lesbian in *Pride*

While depictions of gay activism in cinema are rarely seen, it is even less often that the activism of lesbian or bisexual women is depicted. This trend is linked to a broader lack of films depicting women's activism, irrespectively of their sexual orientation. As Jennifer L. Borda argues in her study of cinematic representations of women's labour activism, Hollywood in particular presents its fictional heroines through a neoliberal post-feminist perspective and not through one emphasizing collective activism.[10] Similarly, in reflecting on her own journey towards making the film *Suffragette* (2015), director Sarah Gavron describes a nearly total lack of films about women's suffrage preceding her own.[11] Gavron writes of the importance of this lack and recounts how her own education also omitted information about feminism, which had initially left her with misconceptions about the development of women's suffrage. Martha Lott's analysis of media representations of African American women in the civil rights movement points in the same direction.[12] Lott traces the lack of media coverage and negative representations of women during the Civil Rights period, and argues that contemporary filmic representations of Black activism continue to leave unacknowledged the roles which women have played. Consequently, it is necessary to survey *Pride*'s representation of women's and particularly lesbian activism while taking into consideration the broader issues of how active political roles are usually attributed to male characters in film.

Pride focuses on LGSM, which was a predominantly white and male organization. LGSM's membership rose to about sixty at its highest, but no more than a few women were present at meetings. The film illustrates this gender ratio by focusing on eleven LGSM activists and paying particular attention to five characters from the group, one of whom is a woman (the character of Stephanie Chambers, played by Faye Marsay). In contrast to the largely male-dominated make-up of the organization, the film stresses the importance of women in Dulais. The older Hefina Headon (Imelda Staunton) and younger Sian James (Jessica Gunning) are shown as particularly supportive of LGSM, while the main source of opposition towards the group is embodied in the character of the widow Maureen (Lisa Palfrey) and her sons. As Ben Walters notes in his review for *Sight & Sound*, the mining town is essentially depicted as a matriarchy, and its women are shown as having significant sway over public attitudes.[13]

In contrast to this, the activist decisions of LGSM are mostly depicted as originating from the young activist Mark Ashton (Ben Schnetzer) and afterwards being accepted by the group. The film itself begins first with clips of the strike set to Ralph Chaplin's 'Solidarity Forever', only to settle on an apartment whose window proudly displays a banner emblazoned with 'THATCHER OUT'. Inside, Ashton is making tea until the voice of NUM president Arthur Scargill quickly distracts him. 'You can look back in ten years,' says Scargill, 'and you can say; I was proud and privileged to be a party to the greatest struggle on Earth.' In the background, a young man Ashton has spent the night with attempts to catch his attention, telling him he has left his number, and yet Mark's focus on the television remains absolute. As the ignored man can eventually be heard leaving in the background, the close-up of Ashton's face sees a smile beginning to form. He moves quickly, searching for buckets in his cupboard, then going down the stairs and out of the building. As soon as he has shot into action, upbeat music begins playing in the background. This is a technique used numerous times within the film; a close-up of Ashton's face often precedes his coming up with an idea which will determine LGSM's actions, and as soon as the idea does come, Ashton is shown quickly on his feet. Sequences depicting activist action are also often set to music in the film (with 1980s bands such as Bronski Beat, The Smiths and King featuring prominently) and are composed of a number of short scenes, the combination of which functions to convey a sense of urgency, enthusiasm and fast movement. In this particular sequence, Ashton's journey to the Pride march is broken down into several short scenes in which neighbours add buckets to his collection, while an elderly man criticizes his 'deviant parties'. The word 'pride' is mentioned three times in the short sequence: once by Scargill himself, the second time by an interviewed striking miner, and finally by the film's title, which appears as Ashton makes his way to the London Pride march.

By the time Ashton is there, the action of collecting funds for the miners has already begun, and the character of Stephanie is introduced to the viewers with her own bucket already in hand. In the same scene, Ashton and fellow activist Mike Jackson argue about what to do with the large banner they had brought to the march before the idea of collecting money occurred to them. 'Give it to the lesbians,' Ashton says, 'they love a banner.' This is the first indicator that lesbians will be positioned primarily as a source of background humour within the film; for example, the joke that all lesbians are vegetarians is raised in three separate scenes. This emphasis on humour also pervades the film's depiction of conflicts within LGSM, which culminate with the formation of a separate organization called Lesbians against Pit Closures (LAPC). In reference to the real LAPC, an activist in *All Out! Dancing in Dulais* recounted the reasoning behind its formation:

> When I first went along to a Lesbians and Gays Support the Miners meeting, initially I was the only woman there, although some other women did turn up for that meeting. And what became clear is that the reason that not many women were involved in the group was partly because there was a core of men who were all actively involved in party politics and were all trying to push their party line and make that the line of the group. And that intimidated and bored a lot of women who weren't involved in politics in that way, so they stopped coming to meetings. So what some of the women in the group and I did was formed a separate lesbian group called Lesbians against Pit Closures, which we saw as being part of the nation-wide network of women that were working on the strike.[14]

The decision to form a separate group was not embraced by everyone. The real Stephanie Chambers believed that 'the realities of the divisions between lesbians and gay men were reflected in LGSM. It is as important for us to break down these barriers within our community as it is to challenge sexism in society as a whole', which was a view echoed regarding the LAPC by women in the Socialist Workers Party.[15] In contrast to this, other members argued for different perspectives; for example, LGSM activist Paul Canning blamed the group's lack of women and Black people on the leadership's lack of interest in diversity, while activists Wendy Caldon and Colin Crews emphasized the desire of LAPC women to work with women in mining communities in a manner that went beyond fundraising.[16] As Kelliher points out, the split between the two groups mirrors similar divisions in the Gay Liberation Front and the increasing role of lesbians in the feminist movement. While the 1970s have been portrayed as the decade of divisions between lesbians and gay men, in contrast to the ways in which the two groups were brought together during the 1980s due to the AIDS crisis and the ensuing rise of homophobia, Kelliher is right to argue that the rift between LGSM and LAPC shows that such divisions remained during the 1980s as well.[17]

The film marginalizes such divisions in the service of telling the story of the gradual coming-to-unity between the mining community of Dulais and LGSM. Of the three lesbian activists to join LGSM over the course of the film, one has only two spoken lines apart from singing during a scene. Her partner Stella (Karina Fernandez) is positioned within the film as the lone lesbian character embodying the separatist impulse, although her motivation is never fully explained. The problematics of gender within LGSM are repeatedly presented as a peripheral problem, addressed in short scenes which are part of larger sequences centring on other issues. For example, Stella's character is shown raising the issue of a women's group during LGSM's second visit to Dulais at the midpoint of the film, in a scene which emphasizes the dramatically worsening conditions in the village. Families are shown living without electricity during wintertime, the miners' bus has broken down, and a lack in food supplies is emphasized through the community hall bingo game being played for 'prizes' like a tin of beef. As Ashton comments on the adversities facing the village, Stella interrupts him to raise the issue of a women's group:

> **Mark:** That bus is a lifeline. It takes the men to the picket, it takes the food parcels to the remotest villages. Without it –
> **Bingo Caller:** All the fours, forty-four.
> **Mark:** We need to start thinking in larger chunks of money. Because without it they're going to fail. It's as simple as that.
> **Stella:** I'm sorry, but when are you going to address my question about a women's group?
> **Mark:** Stella, this is important.
> **Stella:** I know. But this group has absolutely no democratic process –
> **Mark:** What do you need a women's group for anyway?
> **Stella:** To address the women's issues. Singly. And in a safe environment.
> **Mike:** What's unsafe about this environment?
> **Stella:** I'm a woman, Mike. Okay? I'm also a lesbian. And a feminist –
> **Old Lady:** Listen, love. I don't care if you're Arthur Scargill. Don't talk during the bingo. (*Mark and Mike break out in laughter, unable to contain themselves*)

Within a sequence emphasizing the decline of the Dulais Valley and Ashton's concern for its inhabitants, the brief treatment of Stella's request positions it as incongruous to the seriousness of the situation. The interruption of the unnamed old lady, whose seriousness regarding bingo and mention of Arthur Scargill is clearly designed to produce comedic effect, at once works to paint Stella's concern as not only unnecessary but also frivolous. It is worth noting that this is only the fourth scene in the film in which Stella is shown speaking, which positions her viewpoint as marginal to that of Ashton, on whom the film and therefore the audience have thus far been heavily focused. The scene also contrasts two types of femininity: on the one hand, the role embodied by the unnamed but noticeably no-nonsense rural old woman, as opposed to the implicitly overly sensitive urban lesbian feminist. This is the only scene in the film where the word 'feminist' is uttered. Taken together, the sequence can therefore be read as representing lesbian and separatist feminism as counterproductive and misguided, while simultaneously minimizing Stella's concerns by focusing the rest of the sequence on other matters.

The issue is once again raised almost twenty-five minutes later in the film, during a sequence depicting the fundraising concert 'Pits and Perverts' which LGSM organizes to raise funds for Dulais. While Bronski Beat perform in the background, the sequence is again composed of comedic vignettes illustrating the going-ons of the concert. Immediately before it, we see two young miners, who have learned to dance from one of LGSM's male members and have just met two attractive women. This is followed by LGSM member Joe (George MacKay) taking a picture of a drag queen dressed as 'Martha Scargill', at which point Stephanie approaches him, asking him to hide her from Stella (see Figure 19). Stella hands Joe a leaflet for her and leaves, at which point Steph explains, 'They want me to join their breakaway group, Lesbians against Pit Closures. Strictly women-only. Don't think I can trust myself, do you?' With that, Steph leaves, and a handsome man asks Joe to take his picture. Once again, the film foregoes the opportunity for further discussion, and the matter of LAPC is consigned only to comedic effect.

Figure 19 Stella squeezes between 'Martha' Scargill and Joe to tell a displeased Steph about LAPC.

While generally expressing delight at the film, LGSM member Dave Lewis used his review of *Pride* to criticize this aspect of it, pointing towards its mocking depiction of LAPC. Lewis writes:

> If I have one criticism of the film, it is the way that the women in LGSM who split off to form Lesbians Against Pit Closures (LAPC) are depicted. Whilst I didn't agree with their decision at the time and still don't, the film does not treat their views with respect and gets dangerously near to ridicule. I feel this is unfair and unwarranted, given the rise of feminist ideology in the 70s and 80s. This development merely reflects what was happening within large sections of the political left at the time.[18]

The ways in which the women of both LAPC and LGSM are depicted thus raise particular questions about how the role of lesbian activists is remembered, be it as part of the political left or the (sometimes overlapping) LGBTQ rights movement. The film's depiction of lesbian activism thus mirrors Terry Castle's notion of the lesbian as 'apparitional', consigned to invisibility in records of Western culture.[19] Castle argues that the lesbian is either a figure left unrepresented and unnoticed or that she is equated with gay men and subsumed into the same category. This argument is particularly relevant when regarding *Pride*, as its parodic dismissal of separatist impulses implies that the lesbian can and should be submerged into the general category of male gayness. The film's marginalization of lesbian activist memory serves as a troubling indicator of the ways in which both queer and Labour history is narrated as essentially unrelated to issues of lesbian feminism. In both cases, what is at stake in *Pride*'s representation of LGBTQ history is precisely the specificity of queer women's activism. Moreover, when regarding the differences between *Pride*'s presentation of heterosexual women's community action and its depiction of lesbian activism, it becomes clear that the film emphasizes the role of the former group while obscuring the latter's involvement.

Pride does not extend its marginalizing approach to the heterosexual miners' wives of Dulais, which is especially notable in its depiction of the tough but lovable town matriarch Hefina Headon and of the younger but equally authoritative character of Sian James. The end of the film informs us of the fate of only three specific characters, one of whom is Sian. It tells us that she enrolled at university after the strike and became a member of parliament for Swansea East in 2005, the first woman ever to be elected in that constituency. Given James's unprecedented achievement, it is ironic that the film never depicts her discussing her own role as a woman in Dulais with one of the feminist activists of LGSM. The film's choice to present heterosexual and lesbian activism as unrelated to each other is especially peculiar considering the shared activist past between the real Sian James and Stephanie Chambers, as both women were part of the Greenham Common Women's Peace Camp.[20] During their stays at the camp, which was established so as to protest nuclear weapons being placed there, both women reported being vilified by the police and by the locals. 'The good people of Greenham and Newbury', recounts James, 'were quite aggressive and we were always referred to as "those dirty women".'[21] James notes that women were not allowed into local shops at the time and that the men they were with would not be served at pubs if they were with them. In the same vein, Chambers describes how 'the police and the US Army were definitely abusive and called us "dirty dykes"'.[22] She recounts how women would be arrested for protesting and taken off site for two or three days, detained at the police station without charges being pressed. Chambers emphasizes the ways in which the experience transformed her: 'It changed my attitudes, politically: it opened my eyes. Because those Greenham women … did so much to get the American bombs out of Britain. But you never hear about it: it's women's history and that doesn't get talked about.'[23]

Drawing on this, it is significant that the film presents Sian's character as learning in particular from the male activist Jonathan Blake (Dominic West), who is twice depicted as spurring her into action. In the first instance, Jonathan is shown instructing the people from Onllwyn on the laws surrounding police harassment after a group of miners is unlawfully taken into police custody. This prompts Sian's trip to the police station, where her confrontation with the police leads to the miners being released. In the second instance, Jonathan is depicted as urging Sian not to 'waste her first class mind'. This is also the first and only scene within the film in which Jonathan discusses his HIV-positive status with her, with the scene's dialogue bringing together his experiences as a seropositive man with Sian's experiences as a heterosexual woman in Dulais. Jonathan's words to Sian highlight life's transience:

> **Jonathan:** What are you going to do now?
> **Sian:** Make you some soup. Drive back to Wales.
> **Jonathan:** No, I mean with your life?
> **Sian:** I'm a wife and mother, love. My life goes back to normal now.
> **Jonathan:** Well, it shouldn't. You have a first class mind. You should do something. Go to college. Don't waste it, Sian. There are young people dying every day now. Good people. Clever. Promising. Don't you dare waste it.

Having once been 'an ordinary wife and mother', Sian is here motivated to seek out other roles. While her proposed ordinariness is certainly part of what Elise Nakhnikian describes as the film's broader strategy of presenting the Dulais mining community 'salt-of-the-earth townspeople' to be contrasted with 'gay city slickers', this 'ordinariness' carries certain gendered implications.[24]

Sian is depicted as a figure whose political consciousness and perception of herself are altered by Jonathan and LGSM in particular, and by the strike more generally. This depiction matches the rhetoric surrounding the National Women against Pit Closures (NWAPC) movement at the time, whose members were often portrayed as having been spurred to political consciousness by the strike.[25] While such a movement towards political activism was doubtlessly experienced by many women, it is worth noting that a number of women involved in the NWAPC and similar local organizations had also already been politically engaged, whether it be during the 1972 and 1974 miners strikes, the women's movement or a number of political parties. Florence Sutcliffe-Braithwaite and Natalie Thomlinson argue that the image of the NWAPC 'as a group of politically naive miners' wives was carefully constructed for political reasons' and note examples of prominent activists downplaying their own political experience during public appearances.[26] Similarly, while Sian James herself describes being content as solely a wife and mother before the strike, her involvement in the Greenham Peace Camp paints a more complex picture.[27] Drawing on similar examples, Sutcliffe-Braithwaite and Thomlinson argue:

> The extent to which many of these women sought to legitimise their political activities through a rhetorical strategy of 'ordinariness' (constructed as non-political) is striking. The 'authentic' working-class woman was supposed to be non-political, in contrast to male strikers and supporters. The 'working class', a category often implicitly gendered as male (for example, by some trade unions), had room for political activism. But for working-class women to gain legitimacy, they had to disavow an explicitly political identity.[28]

It is here worth taking into consideration how *Pride* mimics this same rhetoric and how it valorizes the supposed 'ordinariness' of Sian and Hefina, while parodying lesbian activists like Stella. The work of the National Women against Pit Closures movement is never mentioned directly in the film, though the women of Dulais are shown having meetings and performing numerous organizational tasks. The film also draws no parallels between the development of women's organizations during the strike and the work of lesbian feminists at the time. It therefore renders the political consciousness of heterosexual women as dependant predominantly on the political actions of either heterosexual or homosexual men. At the same time, it never allows for even such budding activism to become disassociated from the gendered practice of caregiving; throughout the film, Hefina, Sian and the elderly Gwen (Menna Trussler) are depicted as either preparing or offering food, as well as providing similar types of gendered support. In the moment when the long-closeted Cliff (Bill Nighy) finally comes out to Hefina, they are both depicted as cutting sandwiches, and his admission is prefaced by her advice on how to do this properly; similarly, in the scene where Jonathan urges Sian to make use of her 'first class mind', she has promised to make him soup. It is through its sympathetic depiction of these characters that the film valorizes such caregiving practices and explicitly privileges the women who provide them (Hefina, Sian and Gwen) at the expense of those who do not, such as the lesbian separatist Stella. The political labour of heterosexual women is thus valorized at the expense of the activism of queer women, but this valorization also comes at a price and entails the continuation of patriarchal gendered practices.

It is worth noting here that the film does not reserve clichés about gender and sexuality only for its female protagonists but also depicts the gay male characters as often embodying stereotypical tropes. A very prominent example of this can be found in a sequence depicting LGSM's first visit to Dulais, in which they are first greeted by complete silence by the many patrons of its community hall. As animosity between the two groups begins to dwindle, LGSM member Jonathan breaks the ice between the groups the following night with an elaborate dance routine. In keeping with common tropes about gay men, Jonathan is depicted as a skilled dancer and is soon joined on the dance floor by the many women of Onllwyn whose husbands refuse to dance. Soon, he is even asked for lessons by two young miners who want to attract women. Thus, while lesbians are depicted as humourless vegetarians, gay men are portrayed as disco-loving dancers. Nonetheless, the men are also depicted as the leaders of their activist group and retain this 'masculine' position in spite of their queerness.

The film's treatment of both lesbian and heterosexual women points towards the ways in which the past of women's activism is misremembered and is narrated in terms which subordinate their work to that of their male activist counterparts. Through parodying lesbian separatist impulses, *Pride* obfuscates the reasoning behind them and renders them unworthy of commemoration. In the same vein, by valorizing the specific type of femininity embodied by its depiction of the authoritative but caring figures of Hefina and Sian, the film subsumes the activism of heterosexual women into their roles as caregivers and renders it apolitical. Within the context of queer political activism, such depoliticizing of women's activist labour is particularly notable, considering the ways in which the film itself critiques the depoliticizing tendencies of the contemporary LGBTQ rights movement. These aspects of the film, as well as its presentation of political solidarity in general, will be dealt with in the next section.

Remembering pride: Representing the movement

One of the ways in which the film furthers its message of solidarity and cooperation among diverse groups is through the image of a handshake as a visual symbol of solidarity. The image is initially introduced during LGSM's first visit to Dulais, when miner Dai Donovan tells Mark Ashton about the banner depicting it. In this scene, the film explicitly explains the meaning behind this visual motif:

> **Mark:** I grew up in Northern Ireland, I know all about what happens when people don't talk to each other. That's why I've never understood what's the point of supporting gay rights but nobody else's rights. You know? Or – workers' rights but not women's rights – it's – I don't know – illogical.
>
> **Dai:** There's a lodge banner down in the welfare. Over a hundred years old. We bring it out for special occasions, you know. I'll show it to you one day. It's a symbol like this, right? (*they join hands*) Two hands. That's what the labour movement means. Should mean. You support me and I support you. Whoever you are. Wherever you come from. Shoulder to shoulder. Hand in hand.

By bringing together diverse issues such as the conflict in Northern Ireland, women's and workers' rights, the scene positions conflict as a necessary result of groups fighting only for their own welfare. Certainly one of the film's most didactic moments, this is also the film's only overt reference to the Labour movement. The handshake is visually repeated a few scenes later, this time between Ashton and a miner who has recently been released from police custody due to LGSM's help. This moment marks the beginning of cooperation between the Onllwyn and LGSM and is followed by Phil Collins's 'You Can't Hurry Love', the song serving as background to the slow thawing of animosity on the part of the town's inhabitants. Later in the film, the banner is mentioned again as Dai delivers a speech at the 'Pits and Perverts' benefit, but the camera focuses instead on Joe's hand in the audience, as he is pulled by another man into his first kiss. As the two men kiss, their silhouettes occupy the majority of the screen, and Dai's voice announces to a silent room: 'You've worn our badge, "Cole not Dole", and when the time comes, you have my word on this, we will wear yours.' To this, the audience erupts in screams of support, and yet the camera still stays focused on the kiss as Dai proclaims, 'shoulder to shoulder, hand in hand!' In this way, the film directly foregrounds the connection between queer sexuality and political solidarity and depicts one as inextricable from the other.

The motif of the handshake also appears during a scene in which Joe and Steph are depicted as sharing a bed. 'If we were normal, this is when we'd kiss,' Steph says, to which both characters break out in laughter. No further words are said between them, as Joe offers his hand and Steph takes it. While the scene offers the opportunity to simply be read as a mark of friendship, it is also nonetheless significant considering the film's presentation of lesbian separatism as problematic and therefore can also be seen as pointing towards the value of cooperation between lesbians and gay men. This is verbally reinforced minutes later at the 1985 Pride march, as Joe advocates during a conflict between LGSM and LAPC that 'the important thing is that we march together. All of us. That's what this thing has been about from the beginning, and that is absolutely how it is going to end. Together. Us. United.' This is the moment before the miners arrive, and Joe's words can therefore be read as advocating both cooperation between LGBTQ subgroups and queer cooperation with others.

Taken together, these verbal and visual messages of solidarity and unity represent the film's main message, which presents lack of solidarity among groups as a source of conflict and advocates for empathy across group lines. While this is an extremely relevant and vital message, it nonetheless oversimplifies both the political situation at the time and the debates in the gay community surrounding LGSM's own role. Documents in the People's History Museum archive provide a wealth of evidence not only of this debate, but of the awareness LGSM members had of its significance.[29] In particular, the so-called free page of London's *Capital Gay* newspaper enabled the public expression of contrary viewpoints, with LGSM's actions meeting diverse reactions as to the question of whether or not gay rights were an isolated issue. When announcing themselves as a newly formed organization, LGSM members (1984) wrote in *Capital Gay*:

> We believe the miners are at the forefront of the struggle by working people and oppressed groups against the Tories and state repression. ... The outcome of this struggle will set the political climate for a long time to come. ... A defeat for the miners would bring on a new tide of repression from a stronger and more arrogant Tory Government. This strike is not just about pit closures and jobs – it is about the quality of life and aspirations of whole sections of society. That's why we, as lesbians and gay men, have a vested interest in the miners' victory. Many will say that the miners are notoriously anti-gay, but if they see us actively supporting them, showing solidarity with them, their attitudes will change. ... Miners are struggling against the real enemy of lesbian and gay liberation ... the police force and the state.[30]

Prompted by this article, as well as the noticeable presence of LGSM activists at numerous gay and lesbian venues in London, the pages of *Capital Gay* soon became fertile ground for the clash of disparate views on the nature of gay liberation. 'Would the miners support us?', asked a reader, advocating that gay money should be 'spent on better, more needed, causes, such as our gay defences, our gay old and lonely, our AIDS victims'.[31] Other readers similarly argued that 'the miners will never identify with us' and wrote that the issues of gay liberation and the strike were fundamentally separate.[32] Voices of derision against socialist and communist politics were also raised, for example through a letter arguing that the newspaper would 'soon have to change [its] name … to "The Red Flag"' and should 'stick to what [it is] good at – reporting gay events'.[33] Gay support for the Tories was also voiced, as a reader argued that 'one reason [he] voted for Mrs Thatcher was to protect the freedom we have in this country from people who would dictate to us how we should think'.[34] The efforts of the opposing Conservative Group for Homosexual Equality (CGHE) should also be noted as the group made a point of raising £25 for miners who were not on strike.[35]

In response to all of this, letters were sent to the newspaper by both members of LGSM and by the broader queer community. 'This vicious government,' wrote a reader, 'would see a defeat for the miners as a green light for an unprecedented attack on all forms of civil liberties, from which lesbians and gays would certainly not be immune.'[36] *Capital Gay* columnist Stephen Gee argued that connections should be made between the police oppression of the miners and that of lesbians and gays, and also put forth the notion that a defeat for the miners would ultimately make the situation worse for LG people.[37] 'The enemy is strong and powerful,' another reader wrote, 'and it grows stronger knowing the opposition is divided, consisting of different minority groups fighting for their own survival in isolation,'[38] LGSM's responses addressed other criticisms as well:

> In forming the group and supporting the Miners' strike we have never claimed that all Miners were pro-gay or non-sexist, just as in using the word 'gay' we know some gay men are fascist, racist and sexist. We believe that in supporting the Miners openly as lesbians and gay men, we are creating the conditions in which change is possible. … We have made gains either way, we have made no losses, we have nothing, NOTHING, to lose.[39]

In another LGSM press report, Ashton argued that the group existed 'to point out to homosexual people the reasons why a victory for the miners will be a victory for us as well'.[40] LGSM members recognized the significance of the publicity afforded by the paper to this debate and commented that 'we've gotten the political arguments across to at least ten percent of the population in London', as *Capital Gay*'s circulation at the time was 50,000 and the newspaper would be passed from one reader to the other.[41] With respect to criticism due to the fact that the money was not being raised for AIDS victims, they argued that VD clinics and the NHS would be run down should Thatcher's economic policies continue. 'You've got a lot of gay people,' LGSM's Brett Haran argued, 'who have obviously got a sense of identity about being gay, but they don't make the connections, they don't really see what it means to be gay in the wider kind of society.'[42] If they noticed these links, Haran said, they'd see the numerous ways in which the government was oppressing them. In the same vein, Ashton argued that 'it's working class lesbians and gay men who get queer bashed because you can't afford a taxi back home, you don't have your own transport or live in nice Belgravia-like areas'.[43]

We can thus see in LGSM and their supporters a belief in the link between class oppression and gay rights, which they argued could not be separated. In the film, part of this rhetoric is reproduced in scenes such as Jonathan instructing Sian on the illegality of police harassment, therein drawing attention to their shared experience of police violence. Nonetheless, while the film and its characters highlight the similarities of the repression faced by both groups, primarily embodied by police and media animosity, *Pride* does not present these issues as the effects of a wider, class-based system of oppression. Similarly, while the real LGSM invoked an increase in police harassment against LG people, the use of police entrapment (so-called *agent provocateurs* or pretty police) and events such as the raid on the Gay's the Word bookstore as proof 'of a determined effort to smash and isolate our community and drive us back into invisibility', very little background is given in *Pride* about this or about the strike itself.[44] Apart from the appearance of both Thatcher and Scargill in the film's opening sequence, specific contextual or political facts are largely absent. This omission is particularly notable at the beginning of the film, when LGSM attempts to contact the NUM in order to give to them the funds that they have raised. In these scenes, the NUM is depicted as deliberately refusing to take LGSM's calls and as ignoring their donations, which eventually prompts LGSM into directly contacting the Dulais miners in an attempt to evade NUM homophobia. In reality, however, LGSM's decision to 'twin' with the Dulais Valley community did not spring from any resistance on the part of the NUM; rather, it came from a justified suspicion that NUM funds would eventually be sequestered by the state, as indeed turned out to be the case later on in the strike.[45] Thus, while

LGSM did argue that face-to-face contact carried with it the greatest chance of altering attitudes, their decision was also prompted by reasoning shared by a number of other support groups, all of which are left undepicted by the film.

In the same vein, the impetus behind LGSM members helping the miners is depicted in *Pride* as simply the product of sympathy towards their plight which, while true, at once obfuscates any sort of economic and political reasoning from the group's motives. Rather, their belief that the strike was the 'most important industrial and political dispute since 1926 – affecting millions of people' is not addressed by the film.[46] In focusing in more detail on the character of Mark Ashton, *Pride* also leaves unmentioned his work as an organizer for the Young Communist League and the London Communist Party and only references this through moments such as Steph calling him 'comrade', a heckler in a gay bar audience calling him a 'commie!', or the lapel of his jacket featuring two red stars. At the same time, the idea that members of LGSM were consciously trying to change the attitudes of the communities for which they were raising money is also left unmentioned and is depicted only as an effect of their activism and not one of its goals.

Taken together, such political and factual omissions are relevant not because of a purist belief that historical film need conform absolutely to its source material, but rather due to the larger commentary about the gay rights movement and questions of economic inequality which the film offers. In particular, the question of whether the past of queer activism will be remembered as inherently separate or as interlinked with questions of class inequality is complicated by the film, as it at once depicts an organization which focused heavily on workers rights while, at the same time, divorcing LGSM's activities from any broader analysis of political or economic structures. As such, its invocation of solidarity nonetheless risks presenting the causes of LG people and the miners as fundamentally different and unrelated. In this sense, questions of sexuality or gender identity are depicted as unaffected by matters of economic policy and neoliberal politics. While this does not reflect the tenets of LGSM as an organization, it also speaks to the larger issue of whether gay activism is to be commemorated as an essentially neoliberal or as a socially and economically progressive movement. As evidenced by the debates in *Capital Gay* at the time, queer people certainly fell on both the socialist and the conservative side of this spectrum, and while the film omits issues of economic policy, it does address concerns over the commodification of the LGBTQ rights movement.

As previously noted, *Pride* both begins and ends with a Pride march, thus foregrounding its engagement with queer politics. The presentation of these two marches differs greatly and reflects not only the real differences between the 1984 and 1985 marches, which shall be discussed later, but also the film's larger attitudes towards queer activism. During the course of the first march, future members of LGSM start collecting funds for the miners, and we are also shown explicit instances of homophobic harassment: a group of young skinheads throwing a can at LGSM member Joe, a young mother calling the march 'disgusting' and an old woman holding a placard which reads 'Burn in Hell'. When Joe first arrives at the march, it is depicted as already in motion, bracketed on each side with the buildings of an unnamed street, and filmed through close-ups and medium shots. While these visual setting and manner of shooting are unremarkable in itself, they contrast sharply with the way in which the film's closing Pride march is presented, as both the march's beginning (on a sunlit meadow in Hyde Park) and its progression (across Westminster Bridge) happen in wide and open spaces and are presented through wide-angle shots.

In particular, shots encompassing both the march and the Houses of Parliament emphasize the political relevance of the cooperation between LGSM and the Dulais miners, which the film's intertitles inform us was vital to gaining the NUM's support and changing the Labour Party Constitution. The use of music throughout the second Pride march also differs dramatically from the first; while the first march takes place with little background music, the second Pride is backed by Billy Bragg's 'There Is Power in the Union'. Bragg's lyrics ('The Union forever defending our rights / Down with the blackleg, all workers unite / With our brothers and our sisters from many far off lands / There is power in a union') also underscore a sense of possibility and positive change. As viewers are informed that the NUM's unanimous vote of support proved to be one of the key factors in the Labour Party passing the vote to include lesbian and gay rights into their statute, the camera zooms onto a lodge banner on which a handshake features prominently, embossed atop a depiction of Earth encircled with olive branches (see Figure 20). This is the last time this motif of the handshake is seen in the film and is also its very last frame. The banner visually underscores the film's overall message of political cooperation and solidarity; through unity, the banner seems to say, the world can be changed.

In contrast to such a positive depiction of the march itself, it is significant that the film does not depict it as starting off smoothly. Rather, as people are shown gathering for the march in Hyde Park, the scene focuses on a conflict

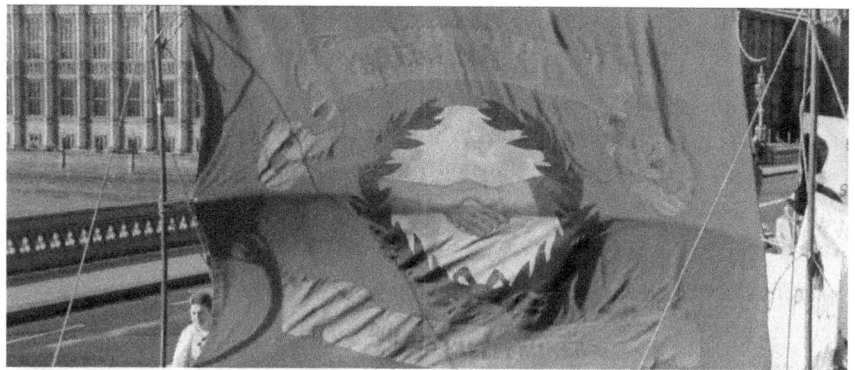

Figure 20 *Pride*'s closing frame – a banner pointing towards the significance of solidarity for the world.

between LGSM and the organizing committee, who unexpectedly inform LGSM that their banners are no longer welcome:

Reggie: Have you heard? No politics.
Gethin: What?
Ray: Mark's over with the steward now.
Steph: No politics?
Ray: And no slogans.
Reggie: We're a 'Mardi Gras' apparently.
Steward: There was a general feeling -
Mark: Amongst who?
Steward: Amongst the committee. That people were tired of politics and that the tone this year should be celebratory. With affirmative slogans and a positive atmosphere.
Mark: Horse-shit.
Steward: If you insist on marching with a banner then you have to march at the back with the fringe groups.
Mike: We're LGSM, mate. We fought alongside the miners.
Steward: Congratulations. But now it's time for a party.

In the film, the sudden arrival of the miners thwarts the committee's ambitions of depoliticizing Pride, and the film's celebratory portrayal of this arrival at once serves as criticism against such a goal. In true Hollywood fashion, the miners are depicted as arriving last minute and unannounced, a surprise even to the members of LGSM and LAPC. This stands in contrast with the reality of the miners having been invited to the march by LGSM members and can, coupled with the film's use of emotive music and an exaggeration of the number of miners present at the scene, be read as a means of heightening the emotional effect produced in the viewer by this display of support. As buses filled with Welsh mining lodges force the Pride steward into allowing LGSM to lead the march, it is again turned into a political event against the will of its organizers.

The sequence reflects criticisms regarding the commodification of Pride and its transformation from protest to party that have been levelled against events such as London Pride. While a number of authors have drawn attention to the corporate creation of queer niche markets, and the ways in which companies benefit from their seeming support of queer rights, activists have for years protested against this with some forming counter-demonstrations.[47] Apart from echoing these critiques, the scene also reflects similar criticisms which have developed since the 1980s, specifically the real Mark Ashton's arguments against the 1985 Pride committee. In an article preceding the 1985 march, Ashton argued that 'a much more consumeristic and male-orientated commercial ideology [had begun to dominate the gay community, with] big clubs like Heaven, free papers like *Out* [having become] aware of the spending power of the white, gay, male subculture. Notions of gay pride and gay liberation have been replaced to a large extent with an emphasis on defending the ghetto.'[48] Ashton comments that 'the separation of "politics" from "fun" seems to be preoccupying this year's Pride committee, [as] they blame "politics" for scaring people off the march in the past.' He therefore cautions that 'the division between "politics" and "enjoyment" is something that the right has long argued' and that, by reproducing this division through ignoring issues like AIDS or refusing to even use the words 'lesbian' or 'gay' on Pride posters, the community risks emptying the phrase 'Lesbian and Gay Pride' of all meaning.[49] Through its criticism of middle-class white gay male consumerism, Ashton's article reflects precisely the debates which had for months been going on in the gay community due to the founding of LGSM and its relation to the miners. In the film, the debate between LGSM and the march organizers echoes both Ashton's critique of the commodification of Pride and similar arguments against contemporary Pride marches, therein embodying Robert Burgoyne's description of how 'the historical film, like the mythic figure of Janus, looks both to the past and the present'.[50]

In the end, at least one LGSM member ended up commending the organization of the march, as Colin Clews has praised the organizers behind it due in part to it having attracted 10,000 people as opposed to two or three thousand in previous years.[51] However, while at once reflecting Ashton's criticism of the committee, the film's recreation of the march also (accidentally) pre-empted the debates surrounding its 2015 commemoration. While LGSM were initially invited to lead the 2015 London Pride, their request to do so accompanied with various unions was met with an unfavourable reception. 'We think that the committee liked the idea of the movie – the glamour, the famous actors,' LGSM's Mike Jackson explained, 'but they hadn't thought about the fact that we were still a political group who would want to make a political point.'[52] As the committee insisted that no more than 200 people be part of LGSM's Pride group and should then be followed by sponsors, this led to LGSM recusing themselves from leading the march and marching in the middle. As Clews notes, 'on the 30th anniversary of this historic event and with even greater LGSM support than in 1985, why will Barclays Bank be fronting the parade?'[53] Consequently, it is possible to compare the way in which the activism of LGSM was commemorated at the 2015 Pride march with how the group is memorialized in the film and to view both as indicative of developments within the LGBTQ movement. The co-option of the LGBTQ movement by companies such as Barclays is now a common part of Pride marches, and while the film critiques a willingness to transform the march into merely a parade, it stops short of offering a broader criticism of the very neoliberal policies which led both to such co-option in the twenty-first century and to the Miners' Strike in the 1980s.

Pride thus occupies a somewhat paradoxical position, as it commemorates the work of activists fighting against neoliberal reform, and yet decontextualizes such solidarity from the political reasoning behind it. This disarticulation is especially relevant considering the pervasive influence which neoliberal policies now exert on the contemporary LGBTQ movement in the UK, be it the commercialization of Pride or the effects of austerity on queer activist organizations.[54] In spite of these and other issues, it is nonetheless important to recognize the film's relevance in transforming the story of LGSM from one in which even its own screenwriter did not at first believe into a film available to transnational audiences.[55] In promoting LGSM's legacy, *Pride* can also promote further research and may serve as inspiration for further activism, as it did with Lesbians and Gays Support the Migrants. Through showing the political potential of solidarity, it is thus an extremely potent example of filmic memory work and may serve to inspire others to develop cross-community cooperation.

Contextualizing *Pride*: Patterns of on-screen activism

The concerns raised here about how the LGBTQ movement is commemorated on-screen are of course not exclusive to *Pride* but relate in equal measure to other cinematic and televisual works. Like the vast majority of on-screen representations of activism in British and American media, LGBTQ representation also tends to obscure feminist political action and instead focuses on the activism of men. The question of whether the LGBTQ rights movement is commemorated as a fundamentally male, white and cisgendered endeavour, as well as how debates within the LGBTQ community are depicted, thus stands at the forefront of this analysis. To this end, I aim here to look at how other representations of queer activism have addressed these issues and will focus in particular on patterns of representation which might either bring these works together or set them apart from each other.

With the exception of Nigel Finch's little-known New Queer Cinema version of *Stonewall* (1995), it was not before the advent of the twenty-first century that dramatizations of queer activism started to appear on British and American screens. Of these films, the importance of Van Sant's *Milk* needs to be stressed, both by virtue of the reception it received (ranging from the Oscars for its screenwriter and lead actor to being one of the highest grossing LGBTQ films ever produced in the United States), as well as due to the unprecedented visibility it granted to the figure of Harvey Milk himself. In the Introduction to this book, I have already written of the effect of the film's release on the transnational recognition granted to Harvey Milk's legacy, as well as the ways in which it altered attitudes towards Milk in the United States. Such recognition is intimately tied to the question of how the LGBTQ movement is narrated and which figures are elevated to the position of the movement's 'heroes'. The two-fold importance of Van Sant's film thus becomes clear, as it marks not only the first time such studio resources had been invested in a project tracing the development of the LGBTQ movement, but also due to the ways in which it prioritizes Milk as an individual activist and as an embodiment of the gay rights movement.

While the general critical reception of *Milk* has been resoundingly celebratory, it is important to note the types of criticism the film did receive.[56] The work of female activists and people of colour remains largely invisible in the film: of all of Milk's collaborators, the only female activist seen in the film is campaign manager Anne Kronenberg, while activists such as the African American Gwenn Craig, who worked as Coordinator of San Francisco against Proposition 6, or the lesbian activist Professor Sally Gearhart, who frequently appeared with Milk on forums to argue against the Briggs Initiative, are occluded.[57] Such an exclusion needs to be seen in conjunction with the film's removal of the numerous LGBTQ, Union and Feminist organizations which fought against Proposition 6, a number of which were activists of colour. *Milk* features no prominent representation of

LGBTQ activists of colour; Milk's advisor Michael Wong (Kelvin Yu) has only two spoken lines, and an African American character can be seen uttering only a single line during the course of the film.[58]

In the same vein, the film's depiction of its only prominent Latin American character, Milk's lover Jack Lira (Diego Luna), is extremely problematic, as exemplified by a scene between Milk and former partner Scott (James Franco) during which Milk himself jokingly uses a racial slur to describe Lira ('Don't let Cesar Chavez hear you calling him taco,' replies Scott).[59] When Scott comments later that Milk 'could do better', Harvey's character is depicted as answering that 'when I come home to Jack, I don't have to talk politics; I don't have to talk intelligently; I don't have to talk at all.' Lira is here reduced to an exoticized body and positioned separately from the gay rights movement which the film sees Milk as emblematizing. Susan Lenon thus convincingly argues that 'the movie's overarching narrative frame of a movement coming into political and social visibility, recounted without the tangible presence of bodies of colour or where such bodies mediate the whiteness of gay male self-determination, produces an erroneous discursive construct that equates gay as white'.[60]

Taken together, the film's marginalizing approach to Lira and its near-total exclusion of women and activists of colour misremembers the development of the gay rights movement and commemorates only the activism of white gay men. Through this and the lack of representation granted to other activists that fought against Proposition 6, it also raises the issue of how on-screen depictions of the history of queer activism at once function as statements about the LGBTQ rights movement and its nature. The overwhelmingly positive reception with which *Milk* was met thus cannot be divorced from the fact that it was the first Hollywood film of its kind and as such served as an unprecedented cinematic commemoration of gay activism. Since its release, projects centred on the history of LGBTQ activism have tended to focus on a larger group of activists, as can be seen in *Pride* in the UK context, the television series *When We Rise* and *Pose* in the United States, Robin Campillo's *120 BPM* (*120 battements par minute*, 2017) in France, or Jeffrey Walker's film *Riot* (2018) in Australia. In focusing on multiple protagonists, these representations of activism open up the possibility of a plurality of perspectives and of presenting the queer movement as more heterogeneous.

In *When We Rise*, Dustin Lance Black's second project about LGBTQ history since his screenwriting Oscar for *Milk*, the notion of the LGBTQ movement being synonymous with a single individual is upset by the show's focus on multiple protagonists and on different aspects of the queer rights struggle. The series was released on ABC in 2017 with its eight episodes seen by an average of 2 million people and the show receiving a GLAAD award for outstanding miniseries.[61] It presents the development of queer rights through focusing on three primary figures; gay activist and NAMES Project founder Cleve Jones (Austin P. McKenzie in its first half, the older Guy Pearce in its second), the lesbian feminist activist Roma Guy (Emily Skeggs, then Mary-Louise Parker), and the African American activist and war veteran Ken Jones (Jonathan Majors and Michael K. Williams). Based in part on Cleve Jones's eponymous memoirs, Lance Black's miniseries attempts the mammoth task of retelling almost five decades of LGBTQ activism. Perhaps as a result, it skips over a number of more famous moments such as the Stonewall Riots and a large part of 1980s AIDS activism and instead traces events such as the so-called Lavender Menace lesbian protest at the 1970 National Organisation of Women (NOW) caucus, the invention of the Rainbow flag, the founding of the first Women's Building in San Francisco in 1979, Cleve Jones's development of the AIDS Quilt in 1987, with all of these events eventually culminating in the victory over marriage equality in 2015.

In presenting the history of LGBTQ activism, the series emphasizes the often separate nature of lesbian feminism and gay male activism, while at the same time highlighting how events such as Proposition 6 and the AIDS crisis served as threats which brought these separate groups to act together. In presenting the fight against Proposition 6 in the series, Lance Black focuses his attention precisely on the grassroots action and coalition building which composed the 'No to 6' campaign. As James Poniewozik's *New York Times* review argues, 'if *When We Rise* has a thread, it's coalition-building, getting disparate voices to find a common chord'.[62] Reviewers also noted the 'didactic' and 'educational' tone of the series, with the majority conceding that the show's stylistic shortcomings were outweighed by the relevance of its message, especially during the Trump administration.[63] Its value as a commemorative media work was thus judged by media critics not only with regard to its importance as an unprecedented televisual depiction of the LGBTQ rights struggle or merely in relation to the information it offers about the past, but by virtue of its insistence on there being 'One struggle. One fight' and therefore serving as a potential call to action for future activists.[64]

Nonetheless, the series' presentation of queer history did inspire criticism, as was noted in the beginning of Part Three through Alexandra Billings's article. After first publishing Billings's critique of the series, *The Huffington Post* soon released a response by transgender actor Ivory Aquino, who plays transgender activist Cecilia Chung from episode four onward in *When We Rise*.[65] In it, the Fillipino-American Aquino commented on the privilege she felt at being given the opportunity to play Chung, herself an activist and AIDS survivor, and commented that Billing's criticism emphasizes the need for more trans stories to be told in the future. Nonetheless, it is notable that while the series does feature transgender representation, its principal transgender character is given notably less screen time than the three primary characters around whom the series revolves. Moreover, both the smaller role granted to Chung and Billings's criticism cannot be divorced from the broader issues plaguing the US film and television industry as a whole and from the ways in which it, as Jamie C. Capuzza and Leland G. Spencer point out, renders 'transgender people as a political community' invisible.[66] At the same time, the under-representation of transgender activists in media depicting queer activism needs to be seen in conjunction with what Susan Stryker describes as 'the double sense of marginalization and displacement experienced within transgender political and cultural activism', with their activism often marginalized both within current LGBTQ activist efforts and in the telling of LGBTQ activist history.[67]

A notable exception to such representational trends can be found in Ryan Murphy's series *Pose*, whose second season features an unprecedented televisual depiction of BAME transgender AIDS activism. *Pose*'s focus on activism is especially relevant considering the show's overarching emphasis on how BAME queer communities have surpassed biological conceptualizations of family, instead forming chosen families in which previously homeless queer youths were given sanctuary by the show's central characters, House 'mothers' Blanca (MJ Rodriguez) and Electra (Dominique Jackson). Such a televisual presentation of community building is exceedingly rare, as queer television has historically tended to focus on white, middle-class individuals and their friend groups and has not thus far presented a similar vision of queer family, especially not among impoverished and homeless queer characters of colour. Through establishing a direct link between activism and such community building in its second season, *Pose* thus counters not only the tendency of depoliticized transgender representation noted by Capuzza and Spencer but also presents a vision of queerness which does not present a strict separation between 'regular' queer life and political action.[68] The depiction of ACT UP protests in a narrative not specifically marketed as being 'about activism' thus presents a relevant step in how AIDS activism is represented and *who* is remembered as participating in it.

Taken together, this short comparison of queer activist cinema and television illustrates the broader issues at stake in representing the past of LGBTQ political action and particularly in mythologizing the roles of certain individuals while simultaneously misrepresenting the queer movement as a predominantly white and male endeavour. Such questions are not only relevant for how we think of the past but are more broadly significant for how we conceptualize the LGBTQ community and envision its future. As Ron Eyerman argues, 'social movements draw inspiration and force by infusing themselves with history, referencing past movements and employing inherited ritual performances. In this way the past becomes present as it is embodied in a new generation of activists.'[69] The fact that the US LGBTQ rights movement is commonly thought of as before and after Stonewall speaks volumes of the importance of commemoration and of how the pasts of activism are narrated.[70] In this context, whether or not a certain group is included in these narratives of the past is of the utmost importance, particularly if that group's present position is also precarious, as is the case with transgender communities. Questions of collective action and a multiplicity of perspectives thus stand at the forefront of how queer activist endeavours are commemorated on-screen and should be seen as crucial to the creation of queer activist prosthetic memory.

Throughout this section, I have looked at whose activism is commemorated on-screen and which aspects of queer activism are at risk of being forgotten. In looking at *Pride*, I traced how the film genders activism and how it marginalizes the work of lesbian separatist women while also depicting the labour of heterosexual women as depoliticized and marked by caregiving practices. I examined how the film fails to represent debates that were happening within the gay community during the Miners' Strike and which pertained to questions of cross-community solidarity and the links between neoliberalism and LGBTQ rights. Through disarticulating the work of LGSM and the striking miners from the specificity of the political situation at the time, the film risks misrepresenting this activism as essentially disconnected from broader criticisms of neoliberal politics. In both cases, what is at stake are broader questions of who is included in, or can claim ownership of the queer activist past, and what sort of activism is being remembered. As I have already noted, the significance of film and television in promoting activist legacies and the medium's potential for promoting histories which may otherwise have been consigned to obscurity cannot be ignored. Thus, the willingness of viewers to critique the exclusion of their communities from these works indicates a broader awareness of the importance of commemoration. Questions of memory ownership, of who is part of the queer past, can thus in part be equated with another, perhaps more obviously vital question – to whom does the LGBTQ movement belong now? And who, truly, is part of the queer community? As this analysis shows, on-screen representation can play a complex part in determining whose activism is considered worthy of commemoration and, by extension, in determining who the most 'relevant' members of the LGBTQ community are.

Conclusion

The borders of memory: Transnational trends in LGBTQ representation

In 2017, I sat in the local cinema, eager to see Park Chan-wook's *The Handmaiden* (*아가씨*, 2016). I was curious what the film would be like; adapted from Sarah Waters's *Fingersmith*, an already-iconic tale of lesbianism in Victorian England that had been brought to the screen once before by the BBC, Chan Wook's adaptation was bringing the story into his own, South Korean context. While I had been prepared for this contextual shift, what struck me was the way in which it used its central romance as a lens through which to examine the Japanese occupation of Korea. In the film, questions of collaboration and the sexual subjugation of occupied Korea were presented as inextricable from questions of sexuality and sexist discrimination. As the movie's main characters, the thief Sook-hee (Kim Tae-ri) and the upper-class Lady Hideko (Min-hee Kim) grew closer together, the men attempting to determine their lives were shown not only as sexually violent, but as collaborators with the occupation itself. In one of the film's more striking scenes, Hideko reveals to Sook-hee that she has been forced to read out Japanese pornographic texts to groups of men by her uncle. Upon learning this, her partner destroys the texts in question, stabbing into erotic prints with a letter opener, and spilling ink all across a vast library of pornography, until Hideko herself joins into the destruction. The moment is deeply moving, with Hideko finally managing to escape the exploitation she has suffered since childhood. Once treated merely as pawns for men's enjoyment, the film ends happily for the couple, with the men who abused them perishing while the two women run away together, leaving Korea.

The Handmaiden's approach to national memory left a deep impression on me. In particular, what fascinated me was the way in which the film connected the memory of the Japanese occupation, a deeply traumatic time in Korea's history, with the story of its central lesbian couple and their journey towards liberation. That one could be depicted in conjunction with the other was all the more interesting when taking into account the continued persistence of homophobia in South Korea. Only a year before the film was released, anti-LGBTQ demonstrators arrived in droves to protest a queer festival held in Seoul, while more recent events have seen a distinctly homophobic public response in the country following the rise in Covid-19 cases, which many have blamed on the country's queer population.[1] When taking all of this into account, *The Handmaiden*'s approach to Korean history represents a rhetorical intervention into how national memory is conceptualized, erasing the proposed distinction between national history on the one hand and the queer past on the other.

Chan-wook's film is far from alone in such an approach. As Jelača's path-breaking work on cinema memory in the countries of former Yugoslavia has shown, queer film in the region has regularly tackled issues of how war is remembered alongside the question of homophobic discrimination, therein no longer excluding LGBTQ people from its depictions of national trauma.[2] Similarly, my own work on cinema from this area, more specifically on Srđan Dragojević's *Parade* (Serbia, 2011), argues that far from conflating 'unlike' issues as some critics have written, such approaches to national memory show the fundamentally intersectional nature of discrimination, with issues like homophobia being impossible to contemplate without taking into account the ways in which memories of war, conflict and ethnic discrimination influence the current state of LGBTQ rights.[3] Instead of abating, the 'trend' of looking at queerness through the lens of national memory has continued in films like the Croatian *Constitution* (*Ustav Republike Hrvatske*, 2016), which again thematizes how memories of war shape the current state of homophobia and transphobia in the country.

Such queer interventions into how national history is narrativized are merely one of the ways in which transnational cinema is thematizing queer memory. In films such as *120 BPM* (France, 2017), which explores of the Paris faction of ACT UP; *Riot* (2018, Australia), which looks at Australian gay rights activists; *Tom of Finland* (2017, Finland), which tracks the life of the eponymous artist, and the docudrama *The Circle* (*Der Kreis*, 2014, Switzerland), which tracks a group of Swiss gay rights activists during the 1950s, the focus is on how activism and art have functioned as methods of resistance and community building. These queer films thus function as relevant commemorative texts, with the international attention granted to some of these films (for example to Robin Campillo's *120 BPM*) serving to amplify the reach of these works well beyond national lines.

In turn, this focus on queer history has not gone unnoticed by cinema reporters, with film critic Ben Walters asking himself why 'LGBTQ film [was] trying to reclaim history?'[4] For Walters, queer historical cinema redresses the lack of 'traditional channels for the transmission of the unique heritage of queer experience … [such as] intergenerational gossip', which he argues has withered due to a focus on assimilation and consumerism.[5] In a similar vein, film writer Guy Lodge has also commented on how contemporary queer cinema is marked by 'a mutual concern with the past – an urge to process centuries of persecution and internalised prejudice before looking ahead to whatever the future of queer identity might be'.[6] For Lodge, it is clear that queer cinema's 'calling on the past' is not merely an effect of nostalgia, but rather looks towards 'a radical future'.[7] In noting the interdependency between queer cinema's focus on period pieces, LGBTQ intergenerationality and futurity, these articles thus acknowledge the importance of these links and the need for them to be examined further.

It is precisely the necessity of understanding these connections, of focusing in detail on the queer search for memory in cinema and television, that has been the impetus for this work. When I began my research, it was not initially my intention to focus on mediatized queer memory, but rather to trace the trends marking contemporary LGBTQ representation. It was only through surveying these tendencies, and through looking at recent LGBTQ works, that a preoccupation with memory in queer on-screen representation became apparent to me. I was thus surprised to see that no sustained interrogation of queer on-screen memory existed, especially considering the ways in which film and television not only represent but *create* memory and comment on *how* we remember. This is a question of particular relevance for LGBTQ people, for whom traditional channels of memory (be it state-sponsored or in the family) have often not been available. Drawing from this, I have examined how media works have themselves commented on the mediation of queer memory (Part One), on the passage of queer memory across familial and intergenerational lines (Part Two), and on how activist legacies are commemorated (Part Three). Through examining these issues, I have endeavoured both to better understand the specificity of how LGBTQ memory is constructed by the media and to grasp what this can tell us about the position of the queer community within contemporary society.

As this book makes clear, the proliferation of queer on-screen memory works illustrates the paradoxical position occupied by the LGBTQ movement in the present moment, with the history of queer activism finally being commemorated in cinema, while at once highlighting both the legacies and continued influence of discrimination. In spite of the increased legal protection granted to LGBTQ people, as well as the drastic increase in queer media representation, a 2019 survey undertaken by the Trevor Project has found that 39 per cent of US LGBTQ youths have seriously considered suicide, with this percentage rising to more than 50 per cent for transgender and non-binary youths.[8] A notable rise in hate crime has also been documented in both the American and British context, with the UK organization Stonewall noting a 160 per cent rise in reported cases since 2015.[9] It is within such a context that we must survey the queer search for memory and that we must regard the insistence of queer cinema and television on imagining pasts in which LGBTQ people have always existed. In this sense, the impetus towards creating commemorative and historical media also functions as a broader rhetorical intervention into heterosexist conceptualizations of history and, by extension, of the present and the future. In presenting such queer visions of history, these representations thus serve as powerful affective resources through which queer memory can be made and remade, reflected and recreated. The issue of how queer pasts are reimagined, whose LGBTQ histories are commemorated and how, who profits from such commemoration, and how this influences and shapes community memory are thus of the utmost importance. This book therefore hopes to serve as a springboard for further research on queer on-screen memory across national lines. Far from being over, the tendency towards queer cinematic and televisual engagements with the past seems only to have begun, with LGBTQ representation looking resolutely backwards. The creation of queer memory is thus itself a continuing process, and it is up to us to see how it is being shaped, by whom and, crucially, which political goals for the future it promotes.

Notes

Introduction

1. Benjamin Lee, 'Roland Emmerich: Gay Rights Drama *Stonewall* Needed "Straight-Acting" Hero', *The Guardian*, 24 September 2015, https://www.theguardian.com/film/2015/sep/24/roland-emmerich-gay-rights-drama-stonewall-needed-straight-acting-hero [accessed 10 July 2018].
2. Ibid.; *BBC News*, 'Petition to Boycott *Stonewall* Movie', 9 August 2015, https://www.bbc.com/news/entertainment-arts-33840449 [accessed 6 July 2020]; Kate Groetzinger, 'Photos: What If Makers of the *Stonewall* Movie Took On Other Moments in American History?', *Quartz*, 11 August 2015, https://qz.com/476156/photos-heres-what-would-happen-if-the-makers-of-the-stonewall-movie-took-on-the-rest-history/ [accessed 6 July 2020].
3. Lee, 'Roland Emmerich'.
4. '*Stonewall*', *Box Office Mojo*, https://www.boxofficemojo.com/release/rl1551730177/ [accessed 6 July 2020]; '*Stonewall* (2015)', *Rotten Tomatoes*, https://www.rottentomatoes.com/m/stonewall_2015 [accessed 6 July 2020].
5. Bilge Ebiri, 'Roland Emmerich's *Stonewall* Fails on Almost Every Level', *Vulture*, 25 September 2015, https://www.vulture.com/2015/09/movie-review-stonewall-fails-across-the-board.html [accessed 27 March 2018]; Godfrey Cheshire, '*Stonewall*', *RogerEbert.Com*, 25 September 2015, https://www.rogerebert.com/reviews/stonewall-2015 [accessed 10 July 2018]; Peter Debruge, 'Toronto Film Review: *Stonewall*', *Variety*, 18 September 2015, https://variety.com/2015/film/reviews/stonewall-film-review-1201597094/ [accessed 27 March 2018].
6. While no term or acronym is perfect, this book utilizes the terms 'LGBTQ' (lesbian, gay, bisexual, transgender and queer) and 'queer' to refer to individuals in the rainbow continuum. I have chosen these terms due to their widespread use with activists and academics alike, as well as due to the fact that the films and television series analysed in this book deal specifically with the lesbian, gay, bisexual, transgender and queer members of the community. However, this terminology in no way means to exclude any other terms or acronyms the reader may find preferable.
7. Iwona Irwin-Zarecka, *Frames of Remembrance: The Dynamics of Collective Memory* (New York: Routledge, 2017), p. 2.
8. Christopher Castiglia and Christopher Reed, *If Memory Serves: Gay Men, AIDS, and the Promise of the Queer Past* (Minneapolis: University of Minnesota Press,

2012); John Lynch, 'Memory and Matthew Shepard: Opposing Expressions of Public Memory in Television Movies', *Journal of Communication Inquiry*, 31:3 (2007), 222–38; Matt Richardson, 'Our Stories Have Never Been Told: Preliminary Thoughts on Black Lesbian Cultural Production as Historiography in The Watermelon Woman', *Black Camera*, 2:2 (2011), 100–13; Nishant Shahani, 'Getting Off (on) the Shortbus (John Cameron Mitchell, 2006): The Politics of Hypothetical Queer History', *New Cinemas: Journal of Contemporary Film*, 10:2–3 (2012), 101–14; Scott J. McKinnon, *Gay Men at the Movies: Cinema, Memory and the History of a Gay Male Community* (Chicago: The University of Chicago Press, 2016).

9 Alison Landsberg, *Prosthetic Memory: The Transformation of American Remembrance in the Age of Mass Culture* (New York: Columbia University Press, 2004); Marita Sturken, *Tangled Memories: The Vietnam War, the AIDS Epidemic, and the Politics of Remembering* (Berkeley: University of California Press, 1997); Paul Grainge, *Memory and Popular Film* (Manchester: Manchester University Press, 2003); Gary Richard Edgerton, 'Television as Historian: A Different Kind of History Altogether', in *Television Histories: Shaping Collective Memory in the Media Age* (Lexington: University Press of Kentucky, 2001), pp. 1–18; Amy Holdsworth, *Television, Memory and Nostalgia* (Basingstoke: Palgrave Macmillan, 2011).

10 Maurice Halbwachs, *On Collective Memory* (London: University of Chicago Press, 1992), p. 40.

11 José Esteban Muñoz, 'Ephemera as Evidence: Introductory Notes to Queer Acts', *Women and Performance*, 8:2 (1996), 5–16; Thomas R. Dunn, *Queerly Remembered: Rhetorics for Representing the GLBTQ Past* (Columbia: University of South Carolina Press, 2016).

12 Libby Brooks, 'Scotland to Embed LGBTI Teaching across Curriculum', *The Guardian*, 9 November 2018, https://www.theguardian.com/education/2018/nov/09/scotland-first-country-approve-lgbti-school-lessons [accessed 6 July 2020].

13 Casey Leins, 'States That Require Schools to Teach LGBT History', *US News*, 14 August 2019, https://www.usnews.com/news/best-states/articles/2019-08-14/states-that-require-schools-to-teach-lgbt-history [accessed 6 July 2020].

14 DW, 'Berlin's Holocaust Memorial Vandalized with Nazi Graffiti', 24 August 2008, https://www.dw.com/en/berlins-holocaust-memorial-vandalized-with-nazi-graffiti/a-3589626 [accessed 6 July 2020]; Tamara Zieve, '"Death to LGBT" Scrawled on Tel Aviv Holocaust Memorial', *The Jerusalem Post*, 25 October 2018, https://www.jpost.com/israel-news/death-to-lgbt-scrawled-on-tel-aviv-holocaust-memorial-570315 [accessed 6 July 2020]; Daniel Avery, 'Memorial to Gay Victims of Holocaust Vandalized in Berlin', *Newsweek*, 19 August 2019, https://www.newsweek.com/gay-holocaust-berlin-memorial-vandalized-1455084 [accessed 6 July 2020].

15 James Tweedie, 'The Suspended Spectacle of History: The Tableau Vivant in Derek Jarman's *Caravaggio*', *Screen*, 44:4 (2003), 379–403.

16　Glenda M. Russell and Janis S. Bohan, 'The Gay Generation Gap: Communicating Across the LGBT Generational Divide', *Angles*, 8:1 (2005), 1–8; Ragan Cooper Fox, 'Gay Grows Up: An Interpretive Study on Aging Metaphors and Queer Identity', *Journal of Homosexuality*, 52:3–4 (2007), 33–61; Stephen Farrier, 'Playing with Time: Gay Intergenerational Performance Work and the Productive Possibilities of Queer Temporalities', *Journal of Homosexuality*, 62:10 (2015), 1398–418; Jayson A. Morrison, '*La MaMa's Squirts*: Igniting Queer Intergenerational Dialogue through Performance', *Text and Performance Quarterly*, 35:2–3 (2015), 226–33.

17　Russell and Bohan, 'The Gay Generation Gap: Communicating across the LGBT Generational Divide', p. 2.

18　Rachel Gelfand, *Nobody's Baby: Queer Intergenerational Thinking across Oral History, Archives, and Visual Culture*, PhD diss., Chapel Hill, University of North Carolina, 2018.

19　Sarah Schulman, *Ties That Bind: Familial Homophobia and Its Consequences* (London: The New Press, 2009), p. 39.

20　Marianne Hirsch, 'Projected Memory: Holocaust Photographs in Personal and Public Fantasy', in *Acts of Memory: Cultural Recall in the Present* (Hanover: University Press of New England, 1999), p. 8.

21　Gelfand, *Nobody's Baby*, p. 15.

22　*AfterBuzz TV*, 'Interview with Cleve Jones: The Legendary LGBTQ Activist Talks Harvey Milk, AIDS, & More', 24 April 2017, https://www.youtube.com/watch?v=8EfkWRDGC4g [accessed 12 July 2018].

23　*CNN*, 'Schwarzenegger Signs Bill Honoring Gay-Rights Activist', 12 October 2009, http://edition.cnn.com/2009/POLITICS/10/12/harvey.milk/ [accessed 1 July 2018].

24　Ibid.

25　Alex Shaw, 'Stratford LGBT Student Society Celebrates Third Anniversary with Tribute to Politician and Gay Rights Campaigner Harvey Milk', *Newham Recorder*, 18 September 2018, https://www.newhamrecorder.co.uk/news/education/harvey-milk-honoured-for-london-academy-of-excellence-lae-stratford-lgbt-society-third-anniversary-1-5699746 [accessed 1 November 2018]; *Somosgay*, 'SOMOSGAY Organizes an Artistic and Collective Expression Called "Graffities for Equality"', 9 August 2013, http://somosgay.org/infonews/infodetalle/somosgay-organizes-an-artistic-and-collective-expression-called-graffities [accessed 1 July 2018].

26　*BBC News*, 'Elton John Condemns Russia *Rocketman* Censorship', 1 June 2019, https://www.bbc.com/news/world-europe-48482872 [accessed 6 July 2020]; '*God's Own Country* Distributor Samuel Goldwyn Censors Film on Prime Video',

Metro Weekly, 22 May 2020, https://www.metroweekly.com/2020/05/gods-own-countrys-distributor-samuel-goldwyn-censors-film-on-prime-video/ [accessed 6 July 2020].

27 Ann Cvetkovich, *An Archive of Feelings, An Archive of Feelings: Trauma, Sexuality, and Lesbian Public Cultures* (London: Duke University Press, 2013), p. 242; Anna Reading, 'Identity, Memory and Cosmopolitanism: The Otherness of the Past and a Right to Memory?', *European Journal of Cultural Studies*, 14:4 (2011), 379–94.

28 Marianne Hirsch and Valerie Smith, 'Feminism and Cultural Memory: An Introduction', *Signs: Journal of Women in Culture and Society*, 28:1 (2002), 1–19.

29 Michel Foucault, 'Film and Popular Memory: An Interview with Michel Foucault', *Radical Philosophy*, 11 (1975), 24–9.

30 Ibid., p. 25.

31 Sturken, *Tangled Memories*, p. 86.

32 Landsberg, *Prosthetic Memory*, p. 9.

33 Ibid., p. 2.

34 Ibid., p. 20.

35 Ibid., p. 19.

36 Ibid., p. 20.

37 Carolyn Dinshaw, *Getting Medieval: Sexualities and Communities, Pre- and Postmodern* (London: Duke University Press, 1999); Lee Edelman, *No Future: Queer Theory and the Death Drive* (London: Duke University Press, 2004); Jack Halberstam, *In a Queer Time and Place: Transgender Bodies, Subcultural Lives* (New York: New York University Press, 2005); Carla Freccero, *Queer/Early/Modern* (London: Duke University Press, 2006); Elizabeth Freeman, *Time Binds: Queer Temporalities, Queer Histories* (London: Duke University Press, 2010); Cvetkovich, *An Archive of Feelings*; Gilad Padva, *Queer Nostalgia in Cinema and Pop Culture, Queer Nostalgia in Cinema and Pop Culture* (New York: Palgrave Macmillan, 2014).

38 Carolyn Dinshaw, Lee Edelman, Roderick A. Ferguson, Carla Freccero, Elizabeth Freeman, Jack Halberstam, Annamarie Jagose, Christopher Nealon and Tan Hoang Nguyen, 'Theorizing Queer Temporalities: A Roundtable Discussion', *GLQ*, 13:2 (2007), 178 and 185.

39 Dinshaw, *Getting Medieval*, p. 12; Dinshaw et al., 'Theorizing Queer Temporalities', p. 178.

40 Freeman, *Time Binds*.

41 Louise Fradenburg and Carla Freccero, *Premodern Sexualities* (New York: Routledge, 1996), p. xxi.

42 Freccero, *Queer/Early/Modern*; Carla Freccero, 'Queer Spectrality: Haunting the Past', in *A Companion to Lesbian, Gay, Bisexual, Transgender, and Queer Studies*, ed. George E. Haggerty McGarry and Molly (Oxford: Duke University Press, 2007), pp. 194–213.

43 McKinnon, '*Gay Men at the Movies*'; Lynch, 'Memory and Matthew Shepard'; Richardson, 'Our Stories Have Never Been Told'; Castiglia and Reed, *If Memory Serves*; Shahani, 'Getting Off (on) the *Shortbus*'.

44 Padva, *Queer Nostalgia in Cinema and Pop Culture*; Elisabeth Windle, '"It Never Really Was the Same": *Brother to Brother*'s Black and White and Queer Nostalgia', *Melus*, 41:4 (2016), 6–31; Gilad Padva, 'A Fantastic Fabrication of Weimar Berlin: Queer Nostalgia, Timeless Memories and Surreal Spatiality in the Film *Bent*', *Queer Studies in Media & Popular Culture*, 2:2 (2017), 167–82; Bridget Kies and Thomas J. West III, 'Queer Nostalgia and Queer Histories in Uncertain Times', *Queer Studies in Media & Popular Culture*, 2:2 (2017), 161–5.

45 Padva, *Queer Nostalgia in Cinema and Pop Culture*, p. 231.

46 Kies and West, *Queer Nostalgia and Queer Histories in Uncertain Times*, p. 161.

47 Padva, *Queer Nostalgia in Cinema and Pop Culture*, p. 5.

48 Joanne Garde-Hansen, *Media and Memory* (Edinburgh: Edinburgh University Press, 2011), p. 8.

49 Daniel Levy and Natan Sznaider, *The Holocaust and Memory in the Global Age* (Philadelphia: Temple University Press, 2006).

50 Ross Poole, 'Misremembering the Holocaust: Universal Symbol, Nationalist Icon or Moral Kitsch?', in *Memory and the Future* (New York: Palgrave Macmillan, 2010), pp. 31–49.

51 Jasbir K. Puar, *Terrorist Assemblages: Homonationalism in Queer Times* (London: Duke University Press, 2007).

52 Yifat Gutman, Adam D. Brown and Amy Sodaro, *Memory and the Future: Transnational Politics, Ethics and Society* (New York: Palgrave Macmillan, 2010).

53 Gutman, Brown and Sodaro, *Memory and the Future*, p. 1.

54 José Esteban Muñoz, *Cruising Utopia: The Then and There of Queer Futurity* (New York: New York University Press, 2009), p. 27.

55 Ibid., p. 35.

56 Rachel Mainwaring, 'I Thought It Was a Myth', Says Filmmaker Who's Bringing the True Story of *Pride* to the Big Screen', *Wales Online*, 5 September 2014, https://www.walesonline.co.uk/whats-on/film-news/i-thought-myth-says-filmmaker-7712411 [accessed 10 June 2018].

57 *Lesbians & Gays Support the Migrants*, http://www.lgsmigrants.com [accessed 2 July 2020].

58 Vito Russo, *The Celluloid Closet: Homosexuality in the Movies* (New York: Harper & Row, 1981); Larry Gross, *Up from Invisibility: Lesbians, Gay Men,*

and the Media in America (New York: Columbia University Press, 2001); Harry M. Benshoff and Sean Griffin, *Queer Images: A History of Gay and Lesbian Film in America* (Lanham: Rowman & Littlefield Publishers, 2005); Steven Capsuto, *Alternate Channels: The Uncensored Story of Gay and Lesbian Images on Radio and Television* (New York: Ballantine Books, 2000); Stephen Tropiano, *The Prime Time Closet: A History of Gays and Lesbians on TV* (New York: Hal Leonard Corporation, 2002).

59 Anna Reading and Tamar Katriel, *Cultural Memories of Nonviolent Struggles: Powerful Times* (Basingstoke: Palgrave Macmillan, 2015); Donatella Della Porta, Massimiliano Andretta, Tiago Fernandes, Eduardo Romanos and Markos Vogiatzoglou, *Legacies and Memories in Movements: Justice and Democracy in Southern Europe* (New York: Oxford University Press, 2018); Red Chidgey, *Feminist Afterlives Assemblage Memory in Activist Times* (Cham: Palgrave Macmillan, 2018).

60 Eric O. Clarke, *Virtuous Vice: Homoeroticism and the Public Sphere* (London: Duke University Press, 2000); Lisa Duggan, *The Twilight of Equality?: Neoliberalism, Cultural Politics, and the Attack on Democracy* (Boston: Beacon Press, 2003); Puar, *Terrorist Assemblages*; Rosemary Hennessy, *Profit and Pleasure: Sexual Identities in Late Capitalism* (New York: Routledge, 2000).

Part One

1 Alexander Doty, *Making Things Perfectly Queer: Interpreting Mass Culture* (Minneapolis: University of Minnesota Press, 1993); Daniel Harris, *The Rise and Fall of Gay Culture* (New York: Hyperion, 1997); Brett Farmer, *Spectacular Passions: Cinema, Fantasy, Gay Male Spectatorships* (Durham: Duke University Press, 2000); Manuel Betancourt, *Being in the Picture: The Movie Fan and Queer Literature*, PhD diss., New Brunswick, Rutgers, 2015; Scott J. McKinnon, *Gay Men at the Movies: Cinema, Memory and the History of a Gay Male Community* (Chicago: The University of Chicago Press, 2016).

2 McKinnon, *Gay Men at the Movies*.

3 Ibid., p. 6.

4 Ibid.

5 Vito Russo, *The Celluloid Closet: Homosexuality in the Movies* (New York: Harper & Row, 1981); Larry Gross, *Up from Invisibility: Lesbians, Gay Men, and the Media in America* (New York: Columbia University Press, 2001); Harry M. Benshoff and Sean Griffin, *Queer Images: A History of Gay and Lesbian Film in America* (Lanham: Rowman & Littlefield Publishers, 2005); Steven Capsuto, *Alternate Channels: The Uncensored Story of Gay and Lesbian Images on Radio and Television*

(New York: Ballantine Books, 2000); Stephen Tropiano, *The Prime Time Closet: A History of Gays and Lesbians on TV* (New York: Hal Leonard Corporation, 2002).

6. George Gerbner and Larry Gross, 'Living with Television: The Violence Profile', *Journal of Communication*, 26:2 (1976), 172–99.
7. GLAAD, 'Where We Are on TV Report 2019', 2020, http://glaad.org/files/WWAT/WWAT_GLAAD_2018-2019.pdf [accessed 20 June 2020].
8. GLAAD, 'Studio Responsibility Index 2018', 2019, https://www.glaad.org/files/2018 GLAAD Studio Responsibility Index.pdf [accessed 20 June 2020].
9. Melanie E. S. Kohnen, *Queer Representation, Visibility, and Race in American Film and Television* (Abingdon: Routledge, 2015).
10. Kohnen, *Queer Representation, Visibility, and Race in American Film and Television*, p. 3.
11. GLAAD, *Studio Responsibility Index 2018*.
12. Doty, *Making Things Perfectly Queer*.
13. Farmer, *Spectacular Passions*, pp. 6 and 2.
14. Betancourt, *Being in the Picture*; McKinnon, *Gay Men at the Movies*; Julie Scanlon and Ruth Lewis, 'Whose Sexuality Is It Anyway? Women's Experiences of Viewing Lesbians on Screen', *Feminist Media Studies*, 17:6 (2017), 1005–21; Rebecca Kern, 'Imagining Community: Visibility, Bonding, and *L Word* Audiences', *Sexualities*, 17:4 (2014), 434–50.
15. Annette Kuhn, Daniel Biltereyst and Philippe Meers, 'Memories of Cinemagoing and Film Experience: An Introduction', *Memory Studies*, 10:1 (2017), 3–16.
16. Jackie Stacey, *Star Gazing: Hollywood Cinema and Female Spectatorship* (Abingdon: Routledge, 1993); Annette Kuhn, *An Everyday Magic: Cinema and Cultural Memory* (London: I.B. Tauris, 2002); Helen Richards, 'Memory Reclamation of Cinema Going in Bridgend, South Wales, 1930–1960', *Historical Journal of Film, Radio and Television*, 23:4 (2003), 341–55; Jo Labanyi, 'The Mediation of Everyday Life: An Oral History of Cinema-Going in 1940s and 1950s Spain', *Studies in Hispanic Cinema*, 2:2 (2007), 105–8; Maria Antonia Paz, 'The Spanish Remember: Movie Attendance during the Franco Dictatorship, 1943–1975', *Historical Journal of Film, Radio and Television*, 23:4 (2003), 357–74; Daniela Treveri-Gennari, Catherine O'Rawe and Danielle Hipkins, 'In Search of Italian Cinema Audiences in the 1940s and 1950s: Gender, Genre and National Identity', *Participations: Journal of Audience & Reception Studies*, 8:2 (2011), 539–53; José Carlos Lozano, Philippe Meers and Daniel Biltereyst, 'La Experiencia Social Histórica de Asistencia al Cine En Monterrey (Nuevo León, México) Durante Las Décadas de 1930 a 1960', *Palabra Clave – Revista de Comunicación*, 19:3 (2016), 691–720; Nancy Huggett, 'A Cultural History of Cinema-Going in the Illawarra (1900–1950)', PhD diss., Wollongong, University of Wollongong, 2002.
17. B. Ruby Rich, 'Reflections on a Queer Screen', *GLQ: A Journal of Lesbian and Gay Studies*, 1:1 (1993), 83–91, 86–7.

18 Dijana Jelača, *Dislocated Screen Memory* (Basingstoke: Palgrave Macmillan, 2016).
19 Ibid., p. 13.
20 Ibid.
21 Ibid., p. 11.
22 Ibid., pp. 2–3.
23 McKinnon, *Gay Men at the Movies*.
24 B. Ruby Rich, *New Queer Cinema: The Director's Cut* (Durham: Duke University Press, 2013), p. 18.
25 Ibid.
26 Simon Watney, 'Derek Jarman 1942–94: A Political Death', *Artforum*, May 1994, https://www.artforum.com/print/199405/derek-jarman-1942-1994-a-political-death-33389 [accessed 15 March 2020]; James Tweedie, 'The Suspended Spectacle of History: The Tableau Vivant in Derek Jarman's *Caravaggio*', *Screen*, 44:4 (2003), 379–403; Alexandra Parsons, 'History, Activism, and the Queer Child in Derek Jarman's Queer *Edward II* (1991)', *Shakespeare Bulletin*, 32:3 (2014), 413–28.
27 E. L. Kennedy, 'Telling Tales: Oral History and the Construction of Pre-Stonewall Lesbian History', *Radical History Review*, 62 (1995), 59–79, 60.
28 Michele Aaron, 'New Queer Cinema', in *Contemporary American Cinema* (London: Open University Press, 2006), pp. 398–409, 399; see also Rich, *New Queer Cinema: The Director's Cut*.

Chapter 1

1 Glenn D'Cruz, 'He's Not There: *Velvet Goldmine* and the Spectres of David Bowie', in *In Enchanting David Bowie: Space, Time, Body, Memory* (London: Bloomsbury, 2015), pp. 259–73; Chad Bennett, 'Flaming the Fans: Shame and the Aesthetics of Queer Fandom in Todd Haynes's *Velvet Goldmine*', *Cinema Journal*, 49:2 (2010), 17–39; Edward R. O'Neill, 'Traumatic Postmodern Histories: *Velvet Goldmine*'s Phantasmatic Testimonies', *Camera Obscura*, 19:3 (2004), 156–85; Mary Ann Doane, 'Pathos and Pathology: The Cinema of Todd Haynes', *Camera Obscura*, 19:3 (2004), 1–21.
2 Kurt Loder, 'David Bowie: Scary Monster on Broadway', *Rolling Stone*, 13 November 1980, https://www.rollingstone.com/music/music-news/david-bowie-scary-monster-on-broadway-100929/ [accessed 27 January 2017].
3 Bennett, 'Flaming the Fans'.
4 Bowie Wonderworld, 'BowieNet Live Chat with David Bowie and Boy George', 27 February 1999, http://www.bowiewonderworld.com/chats/dbchatbg0299.htm [accessed 3 July 2020].
5 Richard Dyer, *Stars* (London: British Film Institute, 1998), p. 34.

6 Ibid., p. 34.
7 Marjorie B. Garber, *Vice Versa: Bisexuality and the Eroticism of Everyday Life* (London: Penguin Books, 1997), p. 140.
8 Joel Deshaye, 'The Metaphor of Celebrity, Three Superheroes, and One *Persona* or Another', *Journal of Popular Culture*, 47:3 (2014), 571–90, 572.
9 Ibid., pp. 571–90.
10 Garber, *Vice Versa*, p. 141.
11 Stephen N. DoCarmo, 'Beyond Good and Evil: Mass Culture Theorized in Todd Haynes' *Velvet Goldmine*', *Journal of American & Comparative Cultures*, 25:3–4 (2002), 395–8, 397.
12 Henry Jenkins, *Textual Poachers: Television Fans and Participatory Culture* (New York: Routledge, 1992); see also Anne Elizabeth Jamison, *Fic: Why Fanfiction Is Taking Over the World* (Dallas: Smart Pop, 2013).
13 Jenkins, *Textual Poachers*, pp. 24–5.
14 Ibid., p. 33.
15 Ibid.
16 Barney Hoskyns, *Glam!: Bowie, Bolan and the Glitter Rock Revolution* (London: Faber, 1998), p. xi.
17 D'Cruz, 'He's Not There', p. 268.
18 Kerry Powell, *Acting Wilde: Victorian Sexuality, Theatre, and Oscar Wilde* (Cambridge: Cambridge University Press, 2009); Aaron Jaffe and Jonathan E. Goldman, *Modernist Star Maps: Celebrity, Modernity, Culture* (New York: Ashgate Publishing, 2010); Jonathan Goldman, *Modernism Is the Literature of Celebrity, Modernism Is the Literature of Celebrity* (Austin: University of Texas Press, 2011); Thomas R. Dunn, *Queerly Remembered: Rhetorics for Representing the GLBTQ Past, Queerly Remembered: Rhetorics for Representing the GLBTQ Past* (Columbia: University of South Carolina Press, 2016).
19 Alan Sinfield, *The Wilde Century: Effeminacy, Oscar Wilde, and the Queer Moment* (London: Cassell, 1994), p. vii.
20 Henry Jenkins, *Convergence Culture: Where Old and New Media Collide* (New York: New York University Press, 2006), p. 258.
21 Stan Hawkins, *Queerness in Pop Music: Aesthetics, Gender Norms, and Temporality* (New York: Routledge, 2015), p. 66.
22 David Buckley, *Strange Fascination: David Bowie the Definitive Story* (London: Virgin Books, 2005), p. 106.
23 Kurt Loder, 'David Bowie: Straight Time', *Rolling Stone*, 12 May 1983, https://www.rollingstone.com/music/features/straight-time-19830512 [accessed 27 January 2017].
24 Loder, *David Bowie: Straight Time*.
25 D'Cruz, 'He's Not There', p. 270.
26 DoCarmo, 'Beyond Good and Evil'; O'Neill, 'Traumatic Postmodern Histories'.

27 Christopher Castiglia and Christopher Reed, *If Memory Serves: Gay Men, AIDS, and the Promise of the Queer Past* (Minneapolis: University of Minnesota Press, 2012), p. 40.
28 Ibid., p. 2.
29 Ibid., p. 40.
30 José Esteban Muñoz, *Cruising Utopia: The Then and There of Queer Futurity* (New York: New York University Press, 2009), p. 27.

Chapter 2

1 Laura L. Sullivan, 'Chasing Fae: *The Watermelon Woman* and Black Lesbian Possibility', *Callaloo Literature and Culture*, 23:1 (2000), 448–60.
2 Judith Millermarch, 'Lobbyists Fight Cuts on Arts Day in Capital', *The New York Times*, 13 March 1997, http://www.nytimes.com/1997/03/13/arts/lobbyists-fight-cuts-on-arts-day-in-capital.html [accessed 23 March 2018].
3 Catherine Zimmer, 'Histories of *The Watermelon Woman*: Reflexivity between Race and Gender', *Camera Obscura*, 23:2 (68) (2008), 41.
4 Matt Richardson, *The Queer Limit of Black Memory: Black Lesbian Literature and Irresolution* (Columbus: Ohio State University Press, 2013).
5 Ibid., p. 10.
6 Kobena Mercer, 'Angelus Diasporae', in *Isaac Julien: Riot* (New York: Museum of Modern Art, 2013), p. 59.
7 Alison Landsberg, *Prosthetic Memory: The Transformation of American Remembrance in the Age of Mass Culture* (New York: Columbia University Press, 2004), p. 20.
8 Ibid., p. 19.
9 Ibid., p. 3.
10 Bill Nichols, *Representing Reality: Issues and Concepts in Documentary* (Bloomington: Indiana University Press, 1991), p. 113.
11 Ibid., p. x.
12 Jane Roscoe and Craig Hight, *Faking It: Mock-Documentary and the Subversion of Factuality* (Manchester: Manchester University Press, 2001), p. 53.
13 Clitha Mason, 'Queering the Mammy: New Queer Cinema's Version of an American Institution in Cheryl Dunye's *The Watermelon Woman*', *Black Camera*, 8:2 (2017), 50–74.
14 Kimberly Wallace-Sanders, *Mammy: A Century of Race, Gender, and Southern Memory* (Ann Arbor: University of Michigan Press, 2008), p. 6.
15 Ibid., p. 3.
16 Patricia Hill Collins, *Black Feminist Thought: Knowledge, Consciousness, and the Politics of Empowerment* (New York: Routledge, 2002), pp. 2–3.

17 Richardson, *The Queer Limit of Black Memory*, p. 6.
18 Cheryl Clarke, 'Lesbianism: An Act of Resistance', in *This Bridge Called My Back: Writings by Radical Women of Color* (New York: Kitchen Table, 1981), pp. 134–5.
19 Ibid., p. 135.
20 Ibid.
21 Elizabeth Freeman, *Time Binds: Queer Temporalities, Queer Histories* (London: Duke University Press, 2010).
22 Robert F. Reid-Pharr, 'Makes Me Feel Mighty Real: *The Watermelon Woman* and the Critique of Black Visuality', in *F Is for Phony: Fake Documentary and Truth's Undoing* (Minneapolis: University of Minnesota Press, 2006), p. 138.
23 bell hooks, *Reel to Real: Race, Class and Sex at the Movies* (New York: Routledge, 1996), pp. 21–3.
24 Sara Ahmed, 'Declarations of Whiteness: The Non-Performativity of Anti-Racism', *Borderlands*, 3:2 (2004), 8.
25 Ibid., p. 11.
26 Dagmawi Woubshet, 'The Imperfect Power of *I Am Not Your Negro*', *The Atlantic*, 8 February 2017, https://www.theatlantic.com/entertainment/archive/2017/02/i-am-not-your-negro-review/515976/ [accessed 10 March 2017].
27 Rebecca Nicholson, '*The L Word: Generation Q* Review – It's Here, It's Queer … and It's Loads of Fun', *The Guardian*, 4 February 2020, https://www.theguardian.com/tv-and-radio/2020/feb/04/the-l-word-generation-q-review-its-here-its-queer-and-its-loads-of-fun [accessed 6 July 2020]; Elisabeth Vincentelli, '*The L Word: Generation Q* Review: New Vision, Old Blind Spots', *The New York Times*, 5 December 2019, https://www.nytimes.com/2019/12/05/arts/television/l-word-generation-q-review.html [accessed 6 July 2020]; Judy Berman, '*Generation Q* Proves It: *The L Word* Is a Time Capsule That Should Have Stayed Buried', *Time*, 5 December 2019, https://time.com/5744710/the-l-word-generation-q-review/ [accessed 6 July 2020].

Part Two

1 Adam Liptak, 'Civil Rights Law Protects Gay and Transgender Workers, Supreme Court Rules', *The New York Times*, 15 June 2020, https://www.nytimes.com/2020/06/15/us/gay-transgender-workers-supreme-court.html [accessed 18 July 2020]; Human Rights Watch, 'United States: State Laws Threaten LGBT Equality', 19 February 2018, https://www.hrw.org/news/2018/02/19/united-states-state-laws-threaten-lgbt-equality [accessed 1 November 2018].
2 Dan Savage, '2010: "It Gets Better" Founder Dan Savage Reflects on The Groundbreaking Youth Project', *Out*, 1 October 2017, https://www.out.com/pride/2017/10/01/2010-it-gets-better-founder-dan-savage-reflects-groundbreaking-youth-project [accessed 1 November 2018].

3   David L. Eng, 'Out Here and Over There: Queerness and Diaspora in Asian American Studies', *Social Text*, 52:53 (1997), 31–52; Gayatri Gopinath, *Impossible Desires: Queer Diasporas and South Asian Public Cultures* (London: Duke University Press, 2005); Sarah Schulman, *Ties That Bind: Familial Homophobia and Its Consequences* (London: The New Press, 2009).
4   Rachel Gelfand, *Nobody's Baby: Queer Intergenerational Thinking across Oral History, Archives, and Visual Culture*, PhD diss., Chapel Hill, University of North Carolina, 2018.
5   Glenda M. Russell and Janis S. Bohan, 'The Gay Generation Gap: Communicating across the LGBT Generational Divide', *Angles*, 8:1 (2005), 1–8; Ragan Cooper Fox, 'Gay Grows Up: An Interpretive Study on Aging Metaphors and Queer Identity', *Journal of Homosexuality*, 52:3–4 (2007), 33–61; Stephen Farrier, 'Playing with Time: Gay Intergenerational Performance Work and the Productive Possibilities of Queer Temporalities', *Journal of Homosexuality*, 62:10 (2015), 1398–418; Jayson A. Morrison, '*La MaMa's Squirts*: Igniting Queer Intergenerational Dialogue through Performance', *Text and Performance Quarterly*, 35:2–3 (2015), 226–33.
6   Dion Kagan, 'How to Have Memories in an Epidemic: Recent Documentaries about HIV/AIDS', *Kill Your Darlings*, 13 (2013), 141–52.
7   Christopher Castiglia and Christopher Reed, *If Memory Serves: Gay Men, AIDS, and the Promise of the Queer Past* (Minneapolis: University of Minnesota Press, 2012); *AfterBuzz TV*, 'Interview with Cleve Jones: The Legendary LGBTQ Activist Talks Harvey Milk, AIDS, & More', 24 April 2017, https://www.youtube.com/watch?v=8EfkWRDGC4g [accessed 12 July 2018].
8   Ken Plummer, 'Generational Sexualities, Subterranean Traditions, and the Hauntings of the Sexual World: Some Preliminary Remarks', *Symbolic Interaction*, 33:2 (2010), 163–90; Jon Binnie and Christian Klesse, 'The Politics of Age, Temporality and Intergenerationality in Transnational Lesbian, Gay, Bisexual, Transgender and Queer Activist Networks', *Sociology*, 47:3 (2013), 580–95.
9   Marianne Hirsch, 'Projected Memory: Holocaust Photographs in Personal and Public Fantasy', in *Acts of Memory: Cultural Recall in the Present* (Hanover: University Press of New England, 1999), pp. 3–23.
10 Marianne Hirsch, 'The Generation of Postmemory', *Poetics Today*, 29:1 (2008), 103–28, 111.
11 Ibid.
12 April Guasp, *Lesbian*, 'Gay & Bisexual People in Later Life', *Stonewall*, January 2015, https://www.stonewall.org.uk/sites/default/files/LGB_people_in_Later_Life__2011_.pdf [accessed 1 October 2018]; Sue Westwood, '"We See It as Being Heterosexualised, Being Put into a Care Home": Gender, Sexuality and Housing/Care Preferences among Older LGB Individuals in the UK', *Health & Social Care in the Community*, 24:6 (2016), 155–63.

13 Plummer, 'Generational Sexualities, Subterranean Traditions, and the Hauntings of the Sexual World', p. 172.
14 Ibid., p. 171.
15 Fox, 'Gay Grows Up'.
16 Michael Johnson, Jr., 'Race, Aging and Gay In/Visibility on US Television', in *Television and the Self: Knowledge, Identity, and Media Representation* (Lanham: Lexington Books, 2013), pp. 227–42, 227.
17 Ibid., pp. 227–8.

Chapter 3

1 Stephen Vider, 'Why Is an Obscure 1968 Documentary in the Opening Credits of Transparent?', *Slate*, 23 October 2014, http://www.slate.com/blogs/outward/2014/10/23/transparent_s_opening_credits_are_a_lesson_in_the_history_of_gender.html [accessed 1 October 2016].
2 Ibid.
3 Jamie C. Capuzza and Leland G. Spencer, 'Regressing, Progressing, or Transgressing on the Small Screen? Transgender Characters on U.S. Scripted Television Series', *Communication Quarterly*, 65:2 (2017), 214–30; Paul Martin Lester, 'From Abomination to Indifference: A Visual Analysis of Transgender Stereotypes in the Media', in *Transgender Communication: Histories, Trends, and Trajectories* (Lanham: Lexington Books, 2015), 143–54; Lucy J. Miller, 'Becoming One of the Girls/Guys: Distancing Transgender Representations in Popular Film Comedies', in *Transgender Communication: Histories, Trends, and Trajectories* (Lanham: Lexington Books, 2015), 127–42; Julia Serano, *Whipping Girl: A Transsexual Woman on Sexism and the Scapegoating of Femininity* (Seattle: Seal Press, 2016).
4 Michael Cuby, 'The New Season of *Transparent* Is Ushering in the Trans Revolution', *VICE*, 26 September 2016, https://www.vice.com/en_au/article/mvkbw4/the-new-season-of-transparent-is-ushering-in-the-trans-revolution [accessed 25 March 2017]; Capuzza and Spencer, 'Regressing, Progressing, or Transgressing on the Small Screen?'; GLAAD, 'Victims or Villains: Examining Ten Years of Transgender Images on Television', https://www.glaad.org/publications/victims-or-villains-examining-ten-years-transgender-images-television [accessed 27 March 2019].
5 Jessica Goodman, 'Emmy Winner Jill Soloway: Topple the Patriarchy', *EW*, 18 September 2016, https://ew.com/article/2016/09/18/jill-soloway-topple-patriarchy-emmys/ [accessed 3 July 2020].
6 Maisie Smith-Walters, 'Hollywood Trans Roles under Fire – Again', *BBC News*, 15 September 2016, http://www.bbc.co.uk/news/magazine-37312338 [accessed 23 November 2016]; Neda Ulaby, 'On Television, More Transgender

Characters Come into Focus', *NPR,* 23 April 2014, http://www.npr.org/blogs/monkeysee/2014/04/23/306166533/on-television-more-transgender-characters-come-into-focus [accessed 25 September 2016].
7   Lesley Goldberg, 'Jeffrey Tambor Officially Dropped from *Transparent* in Wake of Harassment Claims', *The Hollywood Reporter,* 15 February 2018, https://www.hollywoodreporter.com/live-feed/jeffrey-tambor-officially-fired-transparent-wake-harassment-claims-1085236 [accessed 20 February 2018].
8   Joey Soloway, *She Wants It: Desire, Power, and Toppling the Patriarchy* (London: Ebury Press, 2019).
9   Cuby, 'The New Season of *Transparent* Is Ushering in the Trans Revolution'.
10 Chaka L. Bachmann and Becca Gooch, 'LGBT in Britain: Hate Crime and Discrimination', *Stonewall,* September 2017, https://www.stonewall.org.uk/sites/default/files/lgbt_in_britain_hate_crime.pdf [accessed 22 November 2018]; Human Rights Campaign Foundation, *A National Epidemic: Fatal Anti-Transgender Violence in America in 2018* https://www.hrc.org/resources/a-national-epidemic-fatal-anti-transgender-violence-in-america-in-2018 [accessed 22 November 2018].
11 Jack Halberstam, *In a Queer Time and Place: Transgender Bodies, Subcultural Lives* (New York: New York University Press, 2005), p. 77.
12 Ibid.
13 Ibid.
14 Carla Freccero, 'Queer Spectrality: Haunting the Past', in *A Companion to Lesbian, Gay, Bisexual, Transgender, and Queer Studies* (Oxford: Blackwell Publishing, 2007), pp. 194–213, 196.
15 Ibid., p. 196.
16 John Stratton, *Jewish Identity in Western Pop Culture* (New York: Palgrave Macmillan, 2008), p. 61.
17 Erik N. Jensen, 'The Pink Triangle and Political Consciousness: Gays, Lesbians, and the Memory of Nazi Persecution', *Journal of the History of Sexuality,* 11:1/2 (2002), 319–49.
18 Judith Butler, 'Imitation and Gender Insubordination', in *Women, Knowledge, and Reality: Explorations in Feminist Philosophy* (London: Routledge, 1996), p. 378.
19 Marianne Hirsch and Valerie Smith, 'Feminism and Cultural Memory: An Introduction', *Signs: Journal of Women in Culture and Society,* 28:1 (2002), 1–19.
20 Trudy Ring, 'This Year's Michigan Womyn's Music Festival Will Be the Last', *The Advocate,* 21 April 2015, http://www.advocate.com/michfest/2015/04/21/years-michigan-womyns-music-festival-will-be-last [accessed 22 December 2016]; Nick Duffy, 'Women-Only Festival Implements "No Transgender" Policy and Then Bans Discussion of It', *Pink News,* 14 December 2015, http://www.pinknews.co.uk/2015/12/14/women-only-festival-implements-no-transgender-policy-and-then-bans-discussion-of-it/ [accessed 22 December 2016].
21 Freccero, 'Queer Spectrality: Haunting the Past', p. 196.

22 Marianne Hirsch, 'Projected Memory: Holocaust Photographs in Personal and Public Fantasy', in *Acts of Memory: Cultural Recall in the Present* (Hanover: University Press of New England, 1999), pp. 3–23, p. 89.

23 Thomas J. Billard, 'Writing in the Margins: Mainstream News Media Representations of Transgenderism', *International Journal of Communication*, 10 (2016), 4193–218; Sonja J. Ellis, Louis Bailey and Jay McNeil, 'Transphobic Victimisation and Perceptions of Future Risk: A Large-Scale Study of the Experiences of Trans People in the UK', *Psychology and Sexuality*, 7:3 (2016), 211–24; Esme Ashcroft, 'Bristol Feminists Protest against "Transphobic" Event Branded "Discriminatory" and "Scaremongering"', *Bristol Live*, 7 February 2018, https://www.bristolpost.co.uk/news/bristol-news/bristol-feminists-protest-against-transphobic-1180236 [accessed 8 February 2018]; Josh Gabbatiss, 'London Pride: Anti-Trans Activists Disrupt Parade by Lying Down in the Street to Protest "Lesbian Erasure"', *The Independent*, 7 July 2018, https://www.independent.co.uk/news/uk/home-news/anti-trans-protest-london-pride-parade-lgbt-gay-2018-march-lesbian-gay-rights-a8436506.html [accessed 10 July 2018].

24 José Esteban Muñoz, *Cruising Utopia: The Then and There of Queer Futurity* (New York: New York University Press, 2009), p. 28.

Chapter 4

1 Juliet Jacques, 'Gareth Williams and the Prurience of the Press', *The Guardian*, 4 May 2012, https://www.theguardian.com/commentisfree/2012/may/04/gareth-williams-death-press-prurience [accessed 1 November 2018].

2 Gareth Jacques, 'Williams and the Prurience of the Press; Kevin Dowling and Steven Swinford, Murdered Spy a Regular at Gay Bar near MI6 HQ', *The Times*, 29 August 2010, https://www.thetimes.co.uk/article/murdered-spy-a-regular-at-gay-bar-near-mi6-hq-kvhj0s6lcn9 [accessed 1 November 2018]; John Twomey and Padraic Flanagan, 'Our Murdered Spy Son Was Not Gay – This Is a Smear, Says His Family', *Express*, 28 August 2010, https://www.express.co.uk/news/uk/196046/Our-murdered-spy-son-was-not-gay-this-is-a-smear-says-his-family [accessed 3 July 2020]; Dani Garavelli, 'The Spy in the Bag: Did MI6 Agent's Kinky Sex Games Lead to His Death?', *The Scotsman*, 29 April 2012, https://www.scotsman.com/news/the-spy-in-the-bag-did-mi6-agent-s-kinky-sex-games-lead-to-his-death-1-2262515 [accessed 1 November 2018].

3 Boris Starling, 'Drama Feeds Off Real-Life Crime, but Has *London Spy* Gone Too Far?', *The Guardian*, 12 November 2015, http://www.theguardian.com/commentisfree/2015/nov/12/london-spy-real-life-murder-gareth-williams [accessed 27 May 2016].

4 Niall Johnson, '*I'm a Celeb* Absence Sees McDonald Net 9pm Glory for ITV', *Mediatel*, 8 December 2015, https://mediatel.co.uk/news/2015/12/08/im-a-celeb-absence-sees-mcdonald-net-9pm-glory-for-itv [accessed 3 July 2020].

5   Michael Johnson, Jr., 'Race, Aging and Gay In/Visibility on US Television', in *Television and the Self: Knowledge, Identity, and Media Representation* (Lanham: Lexington Books, 2013), 227–42.
6   Tom Ue, 'The Truth Will Set You Free: Implicit Faith in *Sherlock* and *London Spy*', *Journal of Popular Film and Television*, 45:2 (2017), 90–100.
7   Sarah Ann Harris, 'The Sun and Daily Mail Have Got It Completely Wrong on Ofcom "Complaints" over *London Spy*', *The Huffington Post*, 11 November 2015, https://www.huffingtonpost.co.uk/2015/11/11/the-sun-mail-ofcom-investigating-london-spy-complaint_n_8531242.html [accessed 1 November 2018].
8   Harry Fletcher, '*London Spy* Complaints Won't Be Investigated by Ofcom, Which Doesn't Discriminate against Gay Sex Scenes', *Digital Spy*, 11 November 2015, http://www.digitalspy.com/tv/news/a773673/london-spy-complaints-wont-be-investigated-by-ofcom-who-dont-discriminate-against-gay-sex-scenes/ [accessed 1 November 2018].
9   James Delingpole, 'James Delingpole Cringes at *London Spy*'s Gay Sex Scenes', *The Spectator*, 14 November 2015, https://www.spectator.co.uk/2015/11/james-delingpole-cringes-at-london-spys-gay-sex-scenes [accessed 1 November 2018].
10 Ibid.
11 Christopher Stevens, 'Christopher Stevens Reviews *London Spy* Starring Ben Whishaw and Jim Broadbent', *Daily Mail*, 10 November 2015, https://www.dailymail.co.uk/news/article-3311291/No-plot-lots-disco-dancing-s-Beeb-s-new-gay-spy-drama-CHRISTOPHER-STEVENS-reviews-night-s-TV.html [accessed 3 July 2020].
12 Aubrey Allegretti, '*Daily Mail* TV Review of *London Spy* Laments the Number of BBC "Gay Dramas," Sparks Reader Backlash', *The Huffington Post*, 10 November 2015, https://www.huffingtonpost.co.uk/2015/11/10/daily-mail-christopher-stevens-london-spy-review-comments-gay-backlash_n_8519876.html [accessed 1 November 2018].
13 Allan Hepburn, *Intrigue: Espionage and Culture* (London: Yale University Press, 2014), p. 193.
14 Ibid.
15 Ibid., p. 194.
16 Samuel Osborne, 'British Spy Exposed by Wife over Secret Gay Sex near MI6 HQ', *The Independent*, 26 March 2016, https://www.independent.co.uk/news/uk/home-news/british-spy-exposed-by-wife-over-secret-gay-sex-near-mi6-hq-a6954256.html [accessed 22 December 2016].
17 Alex von Tunzelmann, '*The Imitation Game*: Inventing a New Slander to Insult Alan Turing', *The Guardian*, 20 November 2014, https://www.theguardian.com/film/2014/nov/20/the-imitation-game-invents-new-slander-to-insult-alan-turing-reel-history [accessed 22 December 2016].
18 Rosie White, *Violent Femmes: Women as Spies in Popular Culture* (Abingdon: Routledge, 2007), p. 7.

19 Hannah McKay, 'UK Foreign Spy Agency Flies Rainbow Flag, Says Diversity Gives It Edge', *Reuters*, 17 May 2016, http://uk.reuters.com/article/uk-britain-gay-spies-idUKKCN0Y811N [accessed 3 October 2017].
20 Eric O. Clarke, *Virtuous Vice: Homoeroticism and the Public Sphere* (London: Duke University Press, 2000); Lisa Duggan, *The Twilight of Equality?: Neoliberalism, Cultural Politics, and the Attack on Democracy* (Boston: Beacon Press, 2003).
21 Nathan Hudson-Sharp and Hilary Metcalf, 'Inequality among Lesbian, Gay Bisexual and Transgender Groups in the UK: A Review of Evidence', *National Institute of Economic and Social Research*, July 2016, http://www.galyic.org.uk/docs/equalityreview.pdf [accessed 10 October 2017].
22 Michael P. Marshal, Laura J. Dietz, Mark S. Friedman, Ron Stall, Helen A. Smith, James McGinley, Brian C. Thoma, Pamela J. Murray, Anthony R. D'Augelli and David A. Brent, 'Suicidality and Depression Disparities between Sexual Minority and Heterosexual Youth: A Meta-Analytic Review', *Journal of Adolescent Health*, 49:2 (2011), 115–23.
23 Heather Love, 'Compulsory Happiness and Queer Existence', *New Formations*, 63 (2007), 52–65.
24 Heather Love, *Feeling Backward: Loss and the Politics of Queer History* (Cambridge: Harvard University Press, 2007), p. 30.
25 Ibid., p. 29.
26 Simon Watney, 'The Spectacle of AIDS', *October*, 43 (1987), 71–86; Peter Beharrell, 'AIDS and the British Press', in *Getting the Message: News, Truth and Power* (London: Routledge, 1993), pp. 191–229.
27 Simon Watney, *Policing Desire: Pornography, AIDS and the Media* (London: Cassell, 1987).
28 Jenny Kitzinger and David Miller, 'AIDS, the Policy Process, and Moral Panics', in *The Circuit of Mass Communication: Media Strategies, Representation and Audience Reception in the AIDS Crisis*, ed. Jenny Kitzinger and David Miller (London: Sage Publications, 1998), pp. 213–22, 217.
29 Samuel Hallsor, 'A Comparison of the Early Responses to AIDS in the UK and the US', *Journal of the Royal Medical Society*, 24:1 (2017), 57–64.
30 Simon Watney, 'AIDS, "Moral Panic" Theory, and Homophobia', in *Critical Readings: Moral Panic and the Media*, ed. by Chas Critcher (Maidenhead: Open University Press, 2006), pp. 256–65, 262.
31 Clarke, *Virtuous Vice*, p. 44.
32 Hallsor, 'A Comparison of the Early Responses to AIDS in the UK and the US'.
33 Ibid.; Marita Sturken, *Tangled Memories: The Vietnam War, the AIDS Epidemic, and the Politics of Remembering* (Berkeley: University of California Press, 1997); Carole Blair and Neil Michel, 'The AIDS Memorial Quilt and the Contemporary Culture of Public Commemoration', *Rhetoric & Public Affairs*, 10:4 (2007), 595–626.
34 Watney, *Policing Desire: Pornography, AIDS and the Media*.

35 Roger Hallas, *Reframing Bodies: AIDS, Bearing Witness, and the Queer Moving Image* (Durham: Duke University Press, 2009), p. 17.
36 Sarah Schulman, *Ties That Bind: Familial Homophobia and Its Consequences* (London: The New Press, 2009).
37 Christopher Castiglia and Christopher Reed, *If Memory Serves: Gay Men, AIDS, and the Promise of the Queer Past* (Minneapolis: University of Minnesota Press, 2012), p. 10.
38 Ann Cvetkovich, *An Archive of Feelings, An Archive of Feelings: Trauma, Sexuality, and Lesbian Public Cultures* (London: Duke University Press, 2013), p. 8.
39 Jenna Carine Ashton, 'Derek Jarman's *Blue*: Negating the Visual', *Journal of Applied Arts & Health*, 3:3 (2013), 295–307.
40 James Tweedie, 'The Suspended Spectacle of History: The Tableau Vivant in Derek Jarman's *Caravaggio*', *Screen*, 44:4 (2003), 379–403.

Part Three

1 Alexandra Billings, 'When We Rose, I Was There', *Huffington Post*, 3 October 2017, https://www.huffingtonpost.com/entry/when-we-rose-i-was-there_us_58c32cb7e4b0a797c1d39cac [accessed 10 July 2018].
2 Ibid.
3 Anna Reading and Tamar Katriel, *Cultural Memories of Nonviolent Struggles: Powerful Times* (Basingstoke: Palgrave Macmillan, 2015).
4 Rosemary Hennessy, *Profit and Pleasure: Sexual Identities in Late Capitalism* (New York: Routledge, 2000); Jasbir K. Puar, *Terrorist Assemblages: Homonationalism in Queer Times* (London: Duke University Press, 2007); Eric O. Clarke, *Virtuous Vice: Homoeroticism and the Public Sphere* (London: Duke University Press, 2000); Lisa Duggan, *The Twilight of Equality?: Neoliberalism, Cultural Politics, and the Attack on Democracy* (Boston: Beacon Press, 2003).
5 Jarrett Lyons, 'Here's Why LGBT Twitter Is Dragging a Human-Rights Organization All over the Internet Today', *Salon*, 14 November 2017, https://www.salon.com/2017/11/14/heres-why-lgbtq-twitter-is-dragging-a-human-rights-organization-all-over-the-internet-today/ [accessed 29 July 2018].
6 Catherine Silverstone, 'Duckie's Gay Shame: Critiquing Pride and Selling Shame in Club Performance', *Contemporary Theatre Review*, 22:1 (2012), 62–78; India Ross, 'The Business of Gay Pride', *Financial Times*, 11 August 2016, https://www.ft.com/content/228207c6-5f46-11e6-ae3f-77baadeb1c93 [accessed 29 July 2018].
7 Fiona Colgan, Chrissy Hunter and Aidan McKearney, '"Staying Alive": The Impact of "Austerity Cuts" on the LGBT Voluntary and Community Sector (VCS) in England and Wales', London Metropolitan University, 26 June 2014, https://www.tuc.org.uk/sites/default/files/StayingAlive_0.pdf [accessed 29 July 2018].

8. Ross Poole, 'Misremembering the Holocaust: Universal Symbol, Nationalist Icon or Moral Kitsch?', in *Memory and the Future* (New York: Palgrave Macmillan, 2010), pp. 31–49, 159 and 152; see also Yifat Gutman, Adam D. Brown and Amy Sodaro, *Memory and the Future: Transnational Politics, Ethics and Society* (New York: Palgrave Macmillan, 2010).
9. Red Chidgey, *Feminist Afterlives Assemblage Memory in Activist Times* (Basingstoke: Palgrave Macmillan, 2018), p. 3.
10. Ibid., p. 2.
11. Susan Stryker, 'Transgender History, Homonormativity, and Disciplinarity', *Radical History Review*, 100 (2008), 145–57.
12. Michel Foucault, 'Film and Popular Memory: An Interview with Michel Foucault', *Radical Philosophy*, 11 (1975), 24–9, 26.
13. Reading and Katriel, *Cultural Memories of Nonviolent Struggles: Powerful Times*, p. 10.
14. Michael D. Snediker, *Queer Optimism: Lyric Personhood and Other Felicitous Persuasions* (Minneapolis: University of Minnesota Press, 2009); Leo Bersani, 'Is the Rectum a Grave?', *October*, 43 (1987), 197–222; Lee Edelman, *No Future: Queer Theory and the Death Drive* (London: Duke University Press, 2004).
15. Simon Watney, *Imagine Hope: AIDS and Gay Identity* (London: Routledge, 2002), p. 251.
16. *Lesbians & Gays Support the Migrants*, http://www.lgsmigrants.com [accessed 2 July 2020].
17. José Esteban Muñoz, *Cruising Utopia: The Then and There of Queer Futurity*, (New York: New York University Press, 2009); Rachel Mainwaring, '"I Thought It Was a Myth," Says Filmmaker Who's Bringing the True Story of *Pride* to the Big Screen', *Wales Online*, 5 September 2014, https://www.walesonline.co.uk/whats-on/film-news/i-thought-myth-saysfilmmaker-7712411 [accessed 10 June 2018].

Chapter 5

1. A partial recording of Whitworth's speech is available here: Durham Pride UK, 'Main Stage Is OPEN', *Facebook,* https://www.facebook.com/watch/live/?v=958270930999597&ref=watch_permalink [accessed 2 July 2020]. The rest is recounted from memory.
2. Diarmaid Kelliher, 'Solidarity and Sexuality: Lesbians and Gays Support the Miners 1984–5', *History Workshop Journal*, 77:1 (2014), 240–62, 254.
3. Ibid., p. 255.
4. *The Mark Ashton Red Ribbon Fund*, https://mark-ashton.muchloved.com/Home [accessed 1 November 2018].
5. Kelliher, 'Solidarity and Sexuality', p. 254.
6. Ibid., p. 253.

7. Matthew Warchus, 'Matthew Warchus: Why I Made a Romcom about Gay Activists and Striking Miners', *The Guardian*, 21 May 2014, https://www.theguardian.com/film/2014/may/21/matthew-warchus-pride-gay-activists-miners-strike [accessed 1 July 2018].
8. *Pride:* Film Screening and Q&A with Mike Jackson and Dave Lewis from LGSM, organized by Marras – Friends of Durham Miners' Gala.
9. *Box Office Mojo*, 'Pride', https://www.boxofficemojo.com/release/rl2339079681/ [accessed 2 July 2020].
10. Jennifer L. Borda, *Women Labor Activists in the Movies: Nine Depictions of Workplace Organizers* (London: McFarland, 2010), p. 14.
11. Sarah Gavron, 'The Making of the Feature Film Suffragette', *Women's History Review*, 24:6 (2015), 985–95, 986.
12. Martha Lott, 'The Relationship between the "Invisibility" of African American Women in the American Civil Rights Movement of the 1950s and 1960s and Their Portrayal in Modern Film', *Journal of Black Studies*, 48:4 (2017), 331–54.
13. Ben Walters, 'Film of the Week: *Pride*', *Sight & Sound*, 21 November 2016, https://www.bfi.org.uk/news-opinion/sight-sound-magazine/reviews-recommendations/film-week-pride [accessed 1 July 2018].
14. Lesbians and Gays Support the Miners, *All Out! Dancing in Dulais*, 1985.
15. Kelliher, 'Solidarity and Sexuality', p. 247.
16. Tim Tate, *Pride: The Unlikely Story of the True Heroes of the Miners' Strike* (London: John Blake Publishing Ltd., 2017), p. 225.
17. Kelliher, 'Solidarity and Sexuality'; Jill C. Humphrey, 'Cracks in the Feminist Mirror?: Research and Reflections on Lesbians and Gay Men Working Together', *Feminist Review*, 66:1 (2000), 95–130.
18. Dave Lewis, 'Review: *Pride*', *The Project*, 4 November 2014, http://www.socialistproject.org/trade-unions/review-pride/ [accessed 17 May 2018].
19. Terry Castle, *The Apparitional Lesbian: Female Homosexuality and Modern Culture* (New York: Columbia University Press, 1993).
20. Tate, *Pride*.
21. Ibid., p. 67.
22. Ibid.
23. Ibid., p. 68.
24. Elise Nakhnikian, '*Pride*', *Slant*, 22 September 2014, https://www.slantmagazine.com/film/review/pride-2014 [accessed 17 May 2018].
25. Florence Sutcliffe-Braithwaite and Natalie Thomlinson, 'National Women against Pit Closures: Gender, Trade Unionism and Community Activism in the Miners' Strike, 1984–5', *Contemporary British History*, 32:1 (2018), 78–100.
26. Ibid., p. 79.
27. Tate, *Pride*, pp. 267–8.
28. Sutcliffe-Braithwaite and Thomlinson, 'National Women against Pit Closures', p. 85.
29. Larry Goldsmith, Brian Flynn and Bob Sutcliffe, 'We Danced in the Miners' Hall', *Radical America*, 19:2–3 (1985), 39–46.

30 Lesbians the Miners and Gays Support, 'Support the Miners', *Capital Gay*, 3 August 1984.
31 Chris, 'Would the Miners Support Us?', *Capital Gay*, 3 August 1984.
32 Pat Waller, 'The Miners Will Never Identify with Us', *Capital Gay*, 17 August 1984; Geoff Portass and Roy Puddefoot, 'Such Nonsense about the Miners Is Dangerous', *Capital Gay*, 17 August 1984.
33 Bob Ashkettle, 'Stick to What You Are Good At', *Capital Gay*, 17 August 1984.
34 Andrew Rixon, 'We Will Be Frightened That Our Views Are Out of Line', *Capital Gay*, 14 September 1984.
35 'Gay Tories Support the Miners', *Capital Gay*, 14 December 1984.
36 Mike Simpson, 'I Am Appalled at Such Rubbish', *Capital Gay*, 24 August 1984.
37 Stephen Gee, 'We Will Wear Your Badge on Our Lapels', *Capital Gay*, 25 January 1985.
38 C. N. Townsend, 'Which Side Are You On?', *Capital Gay*, 8 March 1985.
39 Lesbians the Miners and Gays Support, 'Miners' Attitudes Are Changing Faster than Eric's', *Capital Gay*, 19 October 1984.
40 Mark Ashton, 'The Police Had Raided Once Too Often', *Capital Gay*, 27 June 1985.
41 Goldsmith, Flynn and Sutcliffe, 'We Danced in the Miners' Hall', p. 45.
42 Ibid., p. 44.
43 Clive Bradley, 'Out of the Ghetto', *Socialist Organiser*, p. cxcix.
44 Lesbians and Gays Support the Miners, 'Miners' Attitudes Are Changing Faster than Eric's'.
45 Kelliher, 'Solidarity and Sexuality'; Tate, *Pride*.
46 Lesbians and Gays Support the Miners, 'Support the Miners', *Capital Gay*.
47 Alexandra Chasin, 'Interpenetrations: A Cultural Study of the Relationship between the Gay/Lesbian Niche Market and the Gay/Lesbian Political Movement', *Cultural Critique*, 44 (2000), 145–68; Wan-Hsiu Sunny Tsai, 'Assimilating the Queers: Representations of Lesbians, Gay Men, Bisexual, and Transgender People in Mainstream Advertising', *Advertising & Society Review*, 11:1 (2010); Silverstone, 'Duckie's Gay Shame'.
48 Mark Ashton, 'Gay Solidarity', *Morning Star*.
49 Ibid.
50 Robert Burgoyne, *The Hollywood Historical Film* (Oxford: Blackwell Publishing, 2008), p. 11.
51 Colin Clews, '1985. Lesbian and Gay Pride 85', *Gay in the 80s*, 7 January 2013, http://www.gayinthe80s.com/2013/01/1985-lesbian-and-gay-pride-85/ [accessed 1 July 2018].
52 Tate, *Pride*, p. 284.
53 Colin Clews, '1985. Miners Lead London Pride Parade', *Gay in the 80s*, 25 June 2015, http://www.gayinthe80s.com/2015/06/1985-miners-lead-london-pride-parade/ [accessed 1 July 2018].

54 Fiona Colgan, Chrissy Hunter and Aidan McKearney, '"Staying Alive": The Impact of "Austerity Cuts" on the LGBT Voluntary and Community Sector (VCS) in England and Wales', London Metropolitan University, 26 June 2014, https://www.tuc.org.uk/sites/default/files/StayingAlive_0.pdf [accessed 29 July 2018].
55 Rachel Mainwaring, '"I Thought It Was a Myth," Says Filmmaker Who's Bringing the True Story of *Pride* to the Big Screen', *Wales Online*, 5 September 2014, https://www.walesonline.co.uk/whats-on/film-news/i-thought-myth-says-filmmaker-7712411 [accessed 10 June 2018].
56 Julia Erhart, 'Towards a New LGBT Biopic: Politics and Reflexivity in Gus Van Sant's *Milk*', in *Invented Lives, Imagined Communities: Biopics and American National Identity* (Albany: SUNY Press, 2016), pp. 261–80.
57 Hilton Als, 'Revolutionary Road', *The New York Review of Books*, 12 March 2009, https://www.nybooks.com/articles/2009/03/12/revolutionary-road/ [accessed 10 July 2018]; Angharad N. Valdivia, *Latino/as in the Media* (Cambridge: Polity, 2010); Susan Lenon, 'White as *Milk*: Proposition 8 and the Cultural Politics of Gay Rights', *Atlantis: Critical Studies in Gender, Culture and Social Justice*, 36:1 (2013), 44–54; Clayton Dillard, 'Un-Quaring San Francisco in *Milk* and *Test*', *European Journal of American Studies*, 11:3 (2017), http://ejas.revues.org/11714.
58 Lenon, 'White as *Milk*'.
59 Valdivia, *Latino/as in the Media*; Lenon, 'White as *Milk*'; Dillard, 'Un-Quaring San Francisco in *Milk* and *Test*'.
60 Lenon, 'White as *Milk*', p. 47.
61 Rick Porter, '*When We Rise* Finale Adjusts Down: Friday Final Ratings', *TV by the Numbers*, 3 March 2017, https://tvbythenumbers.zap2it.com/daily-ratings/friday-final-ratings-march-3-2017/ [accessed 10 June 2018].
62 James Poniewozik, 'Review: *When We Rise* Charts the History of Gay and Transgender Rights', *New York Times*, 26 February 2017, https://www.nytimes.com/2017/02/26/arts/television/review-when-we-rise-review-gay-rights.html [accessed 10 July 2018].
63 Ibid.; Daniel D'Addario, 'ABC's *When We Rise* Isn't Subtle. That's Why It Works', *Time*, 27 February 2017, http://time.com/4683144/when-we-rise-review-abc/ [accessed 10 July 2018]; Sonia Saraiya, 'TV Review: ABC's *When We Rise*', *Variety*, 20 February 2017, https://variety.com/2017/tv/reviews/tv-review-abc-when-we-rise-dustin-lance-black-guy-pearce-gus-van-sant-1201989559/ [accessed 10 July 2018].
64 D'Addario, 'ABC's *When We Rise* Isn't Subtle'.
65 Ivory Aquino, 'Ivory Aquino Responds to Alexandra Billings' Concerns about Trans Visibility in *When We Rise*', *Huffington Post*, 21 March 2017, https://www.huffingtonpost.com/entry/ivory-aquino-dear-alexandra-billings_us_58d12a03e4b0537abd9574b5 [accessed 10 July 2018].
66 Jamie C. Capuzza and Leland G. Spencer, 'Regressing, Progressing, or Transgressing on the Small Screen? Transgender Characters on U.S. Scripted Television Series', *Communication Quarterly*, 65:2 (2017), 214–30, 12.

67 Susan Stryker, 'Transgender History, Homonormativity, and Disciplinarity', *Radical History Review*, 100 (2008), pp. 145–57, p. 145.
68 Capuzza and Spencer, 'Regressing, Progressing, or Transgressing on the Small Screen?'.
69 Ron Eyerman, 'Harvey Milk and the Trauma of Assassination', *Cultural Sociology*, 6:4 (2012), 399–421, 79.
70 E. A. Armstrong and S. M. Crage, 'Movements and Memory: The Making of the Stonewall Myth', *American Sociological Review*, 71:5 (2006), 724–51; Stryker, 'Transgender History, Homonormativity, and Disciplinarity'.

Conclusion

1 Timothy Gitzen, 'Tracing Homophobia in South Korea's Coronavirus Surveillance Program', *The Conversation*, 18 June 2020, http://theconversation.com/tracing-homophobia-in-south-koreas-coronavirus-surveillance-program-139428 [accessed 16 July 2020].
2 Dijana Jelača, *Dislocated Screen Memory, Dislocated Screen Memory* (Basingstoke: Palgrave Macmillan, 2016).
3 Ongoing research; see also Kevin Moss, 'Queering Ethnicity in the First Gay Films From Ex-Yugoslavia', *Feminist Media Studies*, 12:3 (2012), 352–70; Kevin Moss and Mima Simić, 'Post-Communist Lavender Menace: Lesbians in Mainstream East European Film', *Journal of Lesbian Studies*, 15:3 (2011), 271–83.
4 Ben Walters, '*The Circle*: Why Is LGBTQ Film Trying to Reclaim History?', *The Guardian*, 4 December 2014, https://www.theguardian.com/film/2014/dec/04/the-circle-why-is-gay-cinema-fixated-on-the-past [accessed 2 December 2018].
5 Ben Walters, 'Out of the Past: Gay Cinema and Nostalgia', *The Guardian*, 3 July 2014, https://www.theguardian.com/film/2014/jul/03/out-of-past-gay-cinema-nostalgia-lgbt [accessed 2 December 2018].
6 Guy Lodge, 'How Gay Cinema Is Calling on the Past to Point at a Radical Future', *The Guardian*, 15 June 2018, https://www.theguardian.com/film/2018/jun/15/gay-cinema-radical-future [accessed 2 December 2018].
7 Ibid.
8 *The Trevor Project*, 'The Trevor Project National Survey 2019', https://www.thetrevorproject.org/survey-2019/ [accessed 16 July 2020].
9 Grace Hauck, 'Anti-Gay Hate Crimes on the Rise, FBI Says, and They Likely Undercount', *USAtoday*, 28 June 2019, https://www.usatoday.com/story/news/2019/06/28/anti-gay-hate-crimes-rise-fbi-says-and-they-likely-undercount/1582614001/ [accessed 16 July 2020]; Sam Francis, 'Homophobic Hate Crimes Increase in London', *BBC News*, 10 January 2020, https://www.bbc.com/news/uk-england-london-51049336 [accessed 16 July 2020].

Bibliography

Aaron, Michele, 'New Queer Cinema', in *Contemporary American Cinema*, ed. by Linda Ruth Williams and Michael Hammond (London, 2006), 398–409.

AfterBuzz TV, 'Interview with Cleve Jones: The Legendary LGBTQ Activist Talks Harvey Milk, AIDS, & More', 24 April 2017, https://www.youtube.com/watch?v=8EfkWRDGC4g [accessed 12 July 2018].

Ahmed, Sara, 'Declarations of Whiteness: The Non-Performativity of Anti-Racism', *Borderlands*, 3:2 (2004), 1–15.

Allegretti, Aubrey, '*Daily Mail* TV Review of *London Spy* Laments the Number of BBC "Gay Dramas," Sparks Reader Backlash', *The Huffington Post*, 10 November 2015, https://www.huffingtonpost.co.uk/2015/11/10/daily-mail-christopher-stevens-london-spy-review-comments-gay-backlash_n_8519876.html [accessed 1 November 2018].

Als, Hilton, 'Revolutionary Road', *The New York Review of Books*, 12 March 2009, https://www.nybooks.com/articles/2009/03/12/revolutionary-road/ [accessed 10 July 2018].

Aquino, Ivory, 'Ivory Aquino Responds to Alexandra Billings' Concerns about Trans Visibility in *When We Rise*', *Huffington Post*, 21 March 2017, https://www.huffingtonpost.com/entry/ivory-aquino-dear-alexandra-billings_us_58d12a03e4b0537abd9574b5 [accessed 10 July 2018].

Armstrong, E. A., and S. M Crage, 'Movements and Memory: The Making of the Stonewall Myth', *American Sociological Review*, 71:5 (2006), 724–51.

Ashcroft, Esme, 'Bristol Feminists Protest against "Transphobic" Event Branded "Discriminatory" and "Scaremongering"', *Bristol Live*, 7 February 2018, https://www.bristolpost.co.uk/news/bristol-news/bristol-feminists-protest-against-transphobic-1180236 [accessed 8 February 2018].

Ashkettle, Bob, 'Stick to What You Are Good At', *Capital Gay*, 17 August 1984.

Ashton, Jenna Carine, 'Derek Jarman's *Blue*: Negating the Visual', *Journal of Applied Arts & Health*, 3:3 (2013), 295–307.

Ashton, Mark, 'Gay Solidarity', *Morning Star*, 20 September 1984.

Ashton Mark, 'The Police Had Raided Once Too Often … ', *Capital Gay*, 27 June 1985.

Avery, Daniel, 'Memorial to Gay Victims of Holocaust Vandalized in Berlin', *Newsweek*, 19 August 2019, https://www.newsweek.com/gay-holocaust-berlin-memorial-vandalized-1455084 [accessed 6 July 2020].

Bachmann, Chaka L., and Becca Gooch, 'LGBT in Britain: Hate Crime and Discrimination', *Stonewall*, September 2017, https://www.stonewall.org.uk/sites/default/files/lgbt_in_britain_hate_crime.pdf [accessed 22 November 2018].

BBC News, 'Elton John Condemns Russia Censorship', 1 June 2019, https://www.bbc.com/news/world-europe-48482872 [accessed 6 July 2020].

BBC News, 'Petition to Boycott *Stonewall* Movie', 9 August 2015, https://www.bbc.com/news/entertainment-arts-33840449 [accessed 6 July 2020].

BBC News, 'The Police Had Raided Once Too Often', *Capital Gay*.

Beharrell, Peter, 'AIDS and the British Press', in *Getting the Message: News, Truth and Power* (London: Routledge, 1993), 191–229.

Bennett, Chad, 'Flaming the Fans: Shame and the Aesthetics of Queer Fandom in Todd Haynes's *Velvet Goldmine*', *Cinema Journal*, 49:2 (2010), 17–39.

Benshoff, Harry M., and Sean Griffin, *Queer Images: A History of Gay and Lesbian Film in America* (Lanham: Rowman & Littlefield Publishers, 2005).

Bentley, Jean, '*Pose*: 10 Surprising Facts about Ryan Murphy's Trans-Inclusive Series', *The Hollywood Reporter*, 11 July 2018, https://www.hollywoodreporter.com/live-feed/pose-10-little-known-facts-ryan-murphys-trans-inclusive-series-1126281 [accessed 1 December 2018].

Berman, Judy, '*Generation Q* Proves It: *The L Word* Is a Time Capsule That Should Have Stayed Buried', *Time*, 5 December 2019, https://time.com/5744710/the-l-word-generation-q-review/ [accessed 6 July 2020].

Bersani, Leo, 'Is the Rectum a Grave?', *October*, 43 (1987), 197–222.

Betancourt, Manuel, *Being in the Picture: The Movie Fan and Queer Literature*, PhD diss., New Brunswick, Rutgers, 2015.

Billings, Alexandra, 'When We Rose, I Was There', *Huffington Post*, 3 October 2017, https://www.huffingtonpost.com/entry/when-we-rose-i-was-there_us_58c32cb7e4b0a797c1d39cac [accessed 10 July 2018].

Binnie, Jon, and Christian Klesse, 'The Politics of Age, Temporality and Intergenerationality in Transnational Lesbian, Gay, Bisexual, Transgender and Queer Activist Networks', *Sociology*, 47:3 (2013), 580–95.

Blair, Carole, and Neil Michel, 'The AIDS Memorial Quilt and the Contemporary Culture of Public Commemoration', *Rhetoric & Public Affairs*, 10:4 (2007), 595–626.

Borda, Jennifer L., *Women Labor Activists in the Movies: Nine Depictions of Workplace Organizers* (London: McFarland, 2010).

Bowie Wonderworld, 'BowieNet Live Chat with David Bowie and Boy George', 27 February 1999, http://www.bowiewonderworld.com/chats/dbchatbg0299.htm [accessed 3 July 2020].

Brabazon, Tara, *From Revolution to Revelation: Generation X, Popular Memory and Cultural Studies* (Aldershot: Ashgate, 2017).

Bradley, Clive, 'Out of the Ghetto', *Socialist Organiser*.

Brooks, Libby, 'Scotland to Embed LGBTI Teaching across Curriculum', *The Guardian*, 9 November 2018, https://www.theguardian.com/education/2018/nov/09/scotland-first-country-approve-lgbti-school-lessons [accessed 6 July 2020].

Buckley, David, *Strange Fascination: David Bowie the Definitive Story* (London: Virgin Books, 2005).

Burgoyne, Robert, *The Hollywood Historical Film* (Oxford: Blackwell Publishing, 2008).

Butler, Judith, 'Imitation and Gender Insubordination', in *Women, Knowledge, and Reality: Explorations in Feminist Philosophy* (London: Routledge, 1996).

Capsuto, Steven, *Alternate Channels: The Uncensored Story of Gay and Lesbian Images on Radio and Television* (New York: Ballantine Books, 2000).

Capuzza, Jamie C., and Leland G. Spencer, 'Regressing, Progressing, or Transgressing on the Small Screen? Transgender Characters on U.S. Scripted Television Series', *Communication Quarterly*, 65:2 (2017), 214–30.

Castiglia, Christopher, and Christopher Reed, *If Memory Serves: Gay Men, AIDS, and the Promise of the Queer Past* (Minneapolis: University of Minnesota Press, 2012).

Castle, Terry, *The Apparitional Lesbian: Female Homosexuality and Modern Culture* (New York: Columbia University Press, 1993).

Chasin, Alexandra, 'Interpenetrations: A Cultural Study of the Relationship between the Gay/Lesbian Niche Market and the Gay/Lesbian Political Movement', *Cultural Critique*, 44 (2000), 145–68.

Cheshire, Godfrey, 'Stonewall', *RogerEbert.Com*, 25 September 2015, https://www.rogerebert.com/reviews/stonewall-2015 [accessed 10 July 2018].

Chidgey, Red, *Feminist Afterlives: Assemblage Memory in Activist Times* (Basingstoke: Palgrave Macmillan, 2018).

Chris, 'Would the Miners Support Us?', *Capital Gay*, 3 August 1984.

Clarke, Cheryl, 'Lesbianism: An Act of Resistance', in *This Bridge Called My Back: Writings by Radical Women of Color* (New York: Kitchen Table, 1981), 128–37.

Clarke, Eric O., *Virtuous Vice: Homoeroticism and the Public Sphere* (London: Duke University Press, 2000).

Clews, Colin, '1985. Lesbian and Gay Pride 85', *Gay in the 80s*, 7 January 2013, http://www.gayinthe80s.com/2013/01/1985-lesbian-and-gay-pride-85/ [accessed 1 July 2018].

Clews, Colin, '1985. Miners Lead London Pride Parade', *Gay in the 80s*, 2 June 2015, http://www.gayinthe80s.com/2015/06/1985-miners-lead-london-pride-parade/ [accessed 1 July 2018].

CNN, 'Schwarzenegger Signs Bill Honoring Gay-Rights Activist', 12 October 2009, http://edition.cnn.com/2009/POLITICS/10/12/harvey.milk/ [accessed 1 July 2018].

Colgan, Fiona, Chrissy Hunter, and Aidan McKearney, '"Staying Alive": The Impact of "Austerity Cuts" on the LGBT Voluntary and Community Sector (VCS) in England and Wales', London Metropolitan University, 26 June 2014, https://www.tuc.org.uk/sites/default/files/StayingAlive_0.pdf [accessed 29 July 2018].

Collins, Patricia Hill, *Black Feminist Thought: Knowledge, Consciousness, and the Politics of Empowerment* (New York: Routledge, 2002).

Cuby, Michael, 'The New Season of *Transparent* Is Ushering in the Trans Revolution', *VICE*, 26 September 2016, https://www.vice.com/en_au/article/mvkbw4/the-new-season-of-transparent-is-ushering-in-the-trans-revolution [accessed 25 March 2017].

Cvetkovich, Ann, *An Archive of Feelings: Trauma, Sexuality, and Lesbian Public Cultures* (London: Duke University Press, 2013).

D'Addario, Daniel, 'ABC's *When We Rise* Isn't Subtle. That's Why It Works', *Time*, 27 February 2017, http://time.com/4683144/when-we-rise-review-abc/ [accessed 10 July 2018].

D'Cruz, Glenn, 'He's Not There: *Velvet Goldmine* and the Spectres of David Bowie', in *In Enchanting David Bowie: Space, Time, Body, Memory* (London: Bloomsbury, 2015), 259–73.

Debruge, Peter, 'Toronto Film Review: *Stonewall*', *Variety*, 18 September 2015, https://variety.com/2015/film/reviews/stonewall-film-review-1201597094/ [accessed 27 March 2018].

Delingpole, James, 'James Delingpole Cringes at *London Spy*'s Gay Sex Scenes', *The Spectator*, 14 November 2015, https://www.spectator.co.uk/2015/11/james-delingpole-cringes-at-london-spys-gay-sex-scenes [accessed 1 November 2018].

Della Porta, Donatella, Massimiliano Andretta, Tiago Fernandes, Eduardo Romanos, and Markos Vogiatzoglou, *Legacies and Memories in Movements: Justice and Democracy in Southern Europe* (New York: Oxford University Press, 2018).

Deshaye, Joel, 'The Metaphor of Celebrity, Three Superheroes, and One *Persona* or Another', *Journal of Popular Culture*, 47:3 (2014), 571–90.

Dillard, Clayton, 'Un-Quaring San Francisco in *Milk* and *Test*', *European Journal of American Studies*, 11:3 (2017), http://ejas.revues.org/11714.

Dinshaw, Carolyn, *Getting Medieval: Sexualities and Communities, Pre- and Postmodern* (London: Duke University Press, 1999).

Dinshaw, Carolyn, Lee Edelman, Roderick A. Ferguson, Carla Freccero, Elizabeth Freeman, Judith Halberstam, and Annamarie Jagose, Christopher Nealon and Tan Hoang Nguyen, 'Theorizing Queer Temporalities: A Roundtable Discussion', *GLQ*, 13:2 (2007), 177–95.

Doane, Mary Ann, 'Pathos and Pathology: The Cinema of Todd Haynes', *Camera Obscura*, 19:3 (2004), 1–21.

DoCarmo, Stephen N., 'Beyond Good and Evil: Mass Culture Theorized in Todd Haynes' *Velvet Goldmine*', *Journal of American & Comparative Cultures*, 25:3–4 (2002), 395–98.

Doty, Alexander, *Making Things Perfectly Queer: Interpreting Mass Culture* (Minneapolis: University of Minnesota Press, 1993).

Dowling, Kevin, and Steven Swinford, 'Murdered Spy a Regular at Gay Bar near MI6 HQ', *The Times*, 29 August 2010, https://www.thetimes.co.uk/article/murdered-spy-a-regular-at-gay-bar-near-mi6-hq-kvhj0s6lcn9 [accessed 1 November 2018].

Duffy, Nick, 'Women-Only Festival Implements "No Transgender" Policy and Then Bans Discussion of It', *Pink News*, 14 December 2015, http://www.pinknews.co.uk/2015/12/14/women-only-festival-implements-no-transgender-policy-and-then-bans-discussion-of-it/ [accessed 22 December 2016].

Duggan, Lisa, *The Twilight of Equality?: Neoliberalism, Cultural Politics, and the Attack on Democracy* (Boston: Beacon Press, 2003).

Dunn, Thomas R., *Queerly Remembered: Rhetorics for Representing the GLBTQ Past* (Columbia: University of South Carolina Press, 2016).

Durham Pride UK, 'Main Stage Is OPEN', *Facebook*, https://www.facebook.com/watch/live/?v=958270930999597&ref=watch_permalink [accessed 2 July 2020].

Dyer, Richard, *Stars* (London: British Film Institute, 1998)

DW, 'Berlin's Holocaust Memorial Vandalized with Nazi Graffiti', 24 August 2008, https://www.dw.com/en/berlins-holocaust-memorial-vandalized-with-nazi-graffiti/a-3589626 [accessed 6 July 2020].

Ebiri, Bilge, 'Roland Emmerich's *Stonewall* Fails on Almost Every Level', *Vulture*, 25 September 2015, https://www.vulture.com/2015/09/movie-review-stonewall-fails-across-the-board.html [accessed 27 March 2018].

Edelman, Lee, *No Future: Queer Theory and the Death Drive* (London: Duke University Press, 2004).

Edgerton, Gary Richard, 'Television as Historian: A Different Kind of History Altogether', in *Television Histories: Shaping Collective Memory in the Media Age* (Lexington: University Press of Kentucky, 2001), 1–18.

Ellis, Sonja J., Louis Bailey, and Jay McNeil, 'Transphobic Victimisation and Perceptions of Future Risk: A Large-Scale Study of the Experiences of Trans People in the UK', *Psychology and Sexuality*, 7:3 (2016), 211–24.

Eng, David L., 'Out Here and Over There: Queerness and Diaspora in Asian American Studies', *Social Text*, 52:53 (1997), 31–52.

Erhart, Julia, 'Towards a New LGBT Biopic: Politics and Reflexivity in Gus Van Sant's *Milk*', in *Invented Lives, Imagined Communities: Biopics and American National Identity* (Albany: SUNY Press, 2016), 261–80.

Eyerman, Ron, 'Harvey Milk and the Trauma of Assassination', *Cultural Sociology*, 6:4 (2012), 399–421.

Farmer, Brett, *Spectacular Passions: Cinema, Fantasy, Gay Male Spectatorships* (Durham: Duke University Press, 2000).

Farrier, Stephen, 'Playing with Time: Gay Intergenerational Performance Work and the Productive Possibilities of Queer Temporalities', *Journal of Homosexuality*, 62:10 (2015), 1398–418.

Fletcher, Harry, '*London Spy* Complaints Won't Be Investigated by Ofcom, Which Doesn't Discriminate against Gay Sex Scenes', *Digital Spy*, 11 November 2015, http://www.digitalspy.com/tv/news/a773673/london-spy-complaints-wont-be-investigated-by-ofcom-who-dont-discriminate-against-gay-sex-scenes/ [accessed 1 November 2018].

Flynn, Brian, Larry Goldsmith, and Bob Sutcliffe, 'We Danced in the Miners' Hall', *Radical America*, 19:2–3 (1985), 39–46.

Foucault, Michel, 'Film and Popular Memory: An Interview with Michel Foucault', *Radical Philosophy*, 11 (1975), 24–9.

Fox, Ragan Cooper, 'Gay Grows Up: An Interpretive Study on Aging Metaphors and Queer Identity', *Journal of Homosexuality*, 52:3–4 (2007), 33–61.

Fradenburg, Louise, and Carla Freccero, *Premodern Sexualities* (New York: Routledge, 1996).

Francis, Sam, 'Homophobic Hate Crimes Increase in London', *BBC News*, 10 January 2020, https://www.bbc.com/news/uk-england-london-51049336 [accessed 16 July 2020].

Freccero, Carla, 'Queer Spectrality: Haunting the Past', in *A Companion to Lesbian, Gay, Bisexual, Transgender, and Queer Studies* (Oxford: Blackwell Publishing, 2007), 194–213.

Freccero, Carla, *Queer/Early/Modern* (London: Duke University Press, 2006).

Freeman, Elizabeth, *Time Binds: Queer Temporalities, Queer Histories* (London: Duke University Press, 2010).

Gabbatiss, Josh, 'London Pride: Anti-Trans Activists Disrupt Parade by Lying Down in the Street to Protest "Lesbian Erasure"', *The Independent*, 7 July 2018, https://www.independent.co.uk/news/uk/home-news/anti-trans-protest-london-pride-parade-lgbt-gay-2018-march-lesbian-gay-rights-a8436506.html [accessed 10 July 2018].

Garavelli, Dani, 'The Spy in the Bag: Did MI6 Agent's Kinky Sex Games Lead to His Death?', *The Scotsman*, 29 April 2012, https://www.scotsman.com/news/the-spy-in-the-bag-did-mi6-agent-s-kinky-sex-games-lead-to-his-death-1-2262515 [accessed 1 November 2018].

Garber, Marjorie B., *Vice Versa: Bisexuality and the Eroticism of Everyday Life* (London: Penguin Books, 1997).

Garde-Hansen, Joanne, *Media and Memory* (Edinburgh: Edinburgh University Press, 2011).

Gavron, Sarah, 'The Making of the Feature Film Suffragette', *Women's History Review*, 24:6 (2015), 985–95.

'Gay Tories Support the Miners', *Capital Gay*, 14 December 1984.

Gee, Stephen, 'We Will Wear Your Badge on Our Lapels', *Capital Gay*, 25 January 1985.

Gelfand, Rachel, 'Nobody's Baby: Queer Intergenerational Thinking across Oral History, Archives, and Visual Culture' (unpublished PhD thesis, University of North Carolina, 2018).

Gerbner, George, and Larry Gross, 'Living with Television: The Violence Profile', *Journal of Communication*, 26:2 (1976), 172–99.

Gitzen, Timothy, 'Tracing Homophobia in South Korea's Coronavirus Surveillance Program', *The Conversation*, 18 June 2020, http://theconversation.com/tracing-homophobia-in-south-koreas-coronavirus-surveillance-program-139428 [accessed 16 July 2020].

GLAAD, 'Studio Responsibility Index 2018', 2019, https://www.glaad.org/files/2018GLAADStudioResponsibilityIndex.pdf [accessed 20 June 2020].

GLAAD, 'Victims or Villains: Examining Ten Years of Transgender Images on Television', https://www.glaad.org/publications/victims-or-villains-examining-ten-years-transgender-images-television [accessed 27 March 2019].

GLAAD, 'Where We Are on TV Report 2019', 2020, http://glaad.org/files/WWAT/WWAT_GLAAD_2018-2019.pdf [accessed 20 June 2020].

'*God's Own Country* Distributor Samuel Goldwyn Censors Film on Prime Video', *Metro Weekly*, 22 May 2020, https://www.metroweekly.com/2020/05/gods-own-countrys-distributor-samuel-goldwyn-censors-film-on-prime-video/ [accessed 6 July 2020].

Goldberg, Lesley, 'Jeffrey Tambor Officially Dropped from *Transparent* in Wake of Harassment Claims', *The Hollywood Reporter*, 15 February 2018, https://www.hollywoodreporter.com/live-feed/jeffrey-tambor-officially-fired-transparent-wake-harassment-claims-1085236 [accessed 20 February 2018].

Goldman, Jonathan, *Modernism Is the Literature of Celebrity, Modernism Is the Literature of Celebrity* (Austin: University of Texas Press, 2011).

Goodman, Jessica, 'Emmy Winner Jill Soloway: Topple the Patriarchy', *EW*, 18 September 2016, https://ew.com/article/2016/09/18/jill-soloway-topple-patriarchy-emmys/ [accessed 3 July 2020].

Gopinath, Gayatri, *Impossible Desires: Queer Diasporas and South Asian Public Cultures* (London: Duke University Press, 2005).

Grainge, Paul, *Memory and Popular Film* (Manchester: Manchester University Press, 2003).

Groetzinger, Kate, 'Photos: What If Makers of the Stonewall Movie Took On Other Moments in American History?', *Quartz*, 11 August 2015, https://qz.com/476156/photos-heres-what-would-happen-if-the-makers-of-the-stonewall-movie-took-on-the-rest-history/ [accessed 6 July 2020].

Gross, Larry, *Up from Invisibility: Lesbians, Gay Men, and the Media in America* (New York: Columbia University Press, 2001).

Guasp, April, 'Lesbian, Gay & Bisexual People in Later Life', *Stonewall*, January 2015, https://www.stonewall.org.uk/sites/default/files/LGB_people_in_Later_Life__2011_.pdf [accessed 1 October 2018].

Gutman, Yifat, Adam D. Brown, and Amy Sodaro, *Memory and the Future: Transnational Politics, Ethics and Society* (New York: Palgrave Macmillan, 2010).

Halberstam, Jack, *In a Queer Time and Place: Transgender Bodies, Subcultural Lives* (New York: New York University Press, 2005).

Halbwachs, Maurice, *On Collective Memory* (London: University of Chicago Press, 1992).

Hallas, Roger, *Reframing Bodies: AIDS, Bearing Witness, and the Queer Moving Image* (Durham: Duke University Press, 2009).

Hallsor, Samuel, 'A Comparison of the Early Responses to AIDS in the UK and the US', *Journal of the Royal Medical Society*, 24:1 (2017), 57–64.

Harris, Daniel, *The Rise and Fall of Gay Culture* (New York: Hyperion, 1997).

Harris, Sarah Ann, '*The Sun* and *Daily Mail* Have Got It Completely Wrong on Ofcom "Complaints" over *London Spy*', *The Huffington Post*, 11 November 2015, https://www.huffingtonpost.co.uk/2015/11/11/the-sun-mail-ofcom-investigating-london-spy-complaint_n_8531242.html [accessed 1 November 2018].

Hauck, Grace, 'Anti-Gay Hate Crimes on the Rise, FBI Says, and They Likely Undercount', *USA Today*, 28 June 2019, https://www.usatoday.com/story/news/2019/06/28/anti-gay-hate-crimes-rise-fbi-says-and-they-likely-undercount/1582614001/ [accessed 16 July 2020].

Hawkins, Stan, *Queerness in Pop Music: Aesthetics, Gender Norms, and Temporality* (New York: Routledge, 2015).

Hennessy, Rosemary, *Profit and Pleasure: Sexual Identities in Late Capitalism* (New York: Routledge, 2000).

Hepburn, Allan, *Intrigue: Espionage and Culture* (London: Yale University Press, 2014).

Hirsch, Marianne, 'Projected Memory: Holocaust Photographs in Personal and Public Fantasy', in *Acts of Memory: Cultural Recall in the Present* (Hanover: University Press of New England, 1999), 3–23.

Hirsch, Marianne, 'The Generation of Postmemory', *Poetics Today*, 29:1 (2008), 103–28.

Hirsch, Marianne, and Valerie Smith, 'Feminism and Cultural Memory: An Introduction', *Signs: Journal of Women in Culture and Society*, 28:1 (2002), 1–19.

Holdsworth, Amy, *Television, Memory and Nostalgia* (Basingstoke: Palgrave Macmillan, 2011).

hooks, bell, *Reel to Real: Race, Class and Sex at the Movies* (New York: Routledge, 1996).

Horvat, Anamarija, 'Haunting and Queer Histories: Representing Memory in Jill Soloway's *Transparent*', *Feminist Media Studies*, 20:3 (2020), 398–413.

Hoskyns, Barney, *Glam!: Bowie, Bolan and the Glitter Rock Revolution* (London: Faber, 1998).

Hudson-Sharp, Nathan, and Hilary Metcalf, *Inequality among Lesbian, Gay Bisexual and Transgender Groups in the UK: A Review of Evidence*, National Institute of Economic and Social Research, July 2016, http://www.galyic.org.uk/docs/equalityreview.pdf.

Huggett, Nancy, 'A Cultural History of Cinema-Going in the Illawarra (1900–1950)', PhD diss., Wollongong, University of Wollongong, 2002.

Human Rights Campaign Foundation, *A National Epidemic: Fatal Anti-Transgender Violence in America in 2018*, https://www.hrc.org/resources/a-national-epidemic-fatal-anti-transgender-violence-in-america-in-2018 [accessed 22 November 2018].

Human Rights Watch, 'United States: State Laws Threaten LGBT Equality', 19 February 2018, https://www.hrw.org/news/2018/02/19/united-states-state-laws-threaten-lgbt-equality [accessed 1 November 2018].

Humphrey, Jill C., 'Cracks in the Feminist Mirror?: Research and Reflections on Lesbians and Gay Men Working Together', *Feminist Review*, 66:1 (2000), 95–130.

Irwin-Zarecka, Iwona, *Frames of Remembrance: The Dynamics of Collective Memory* (New York: Routledge, 2017).

Jacques, Juliet, 'Gareth Williams and the Prurience of the Press', *The Guardian*, 4 May 2012, https://www.theguardian.com/commentisfree/2012/may/04/gareth-williams-death-press-prurience [accessed 1 November 2018].

Jaffe, Aaron, and Jonathan E. Goldman, *Modernist Star Maps: Celebrity, Modernity, Culture* (New York: Ashgate Publishing, 2010).

Jamison, Anne Elizabeth, *Fic: Why Fanfiction Is Taking Over the World* (Dallas: Smart Pop, 2013).

Jelača, Dijana, *Dislocated Screen Memory* (Basingstoke: Palgrave Macmillan, 2016).

Jenkins, Henry, *Convergence Culture: Where Old and New Media Collide* (New York: New York University Press, 2006).

Jenkins, Henry, *Textual Poachers: Television Fans and Participatory Culture* (New York: Routledge, 1992).

Jensen, Erik N., 'The Pink Triangle and Political Consciousness: Gays, Lesbians, and the Memory of Nazi Persecution', *Journal of the History of Sexuality*, 11:1/2 (2002), 319–49.

Johnson, Michael Jr., 'Race, Aging and Gay In/Visibility on US Television', in *Television and the Self: Knowledge, Identity, and Media Representation* (Lanham: Lexington Books, 2013), 227–42.

Johnson, Niall, '*I'm a Celeb* Absence Sees McDonald Net 9pm Glory for ITV', *Mediatel*, 8 December 2015, https://mediatel.co.uk/news/2015/12/08/im-a-celeb-absence-sees-mcdonald-net-9pm-glory-for-itv [accessed 3 July 2020].

Kagan, Dion, 'How to Have Memories in an Epidemic: Recent Documentaries about HIV/AIDS', *Kill Your Darlings*, 13 (2013), 141–52.

Kelliher, Diarmaid, 'Solidarity and Sexuality: Lesbians and Gays Support the Miners 1984–5', *History Workshop Journal*, 77:1 (2014), 240–62.

Kennedy, E. L., 'Telling Tales: Oral History and the Construction of Pre-Stonewall Lesbian History', *Radical History Review*, 62 (1995), 59–79.

Kern, Rebecca, 'Imagining Community: Visibility, Bonding, and *L Word* Audiences', *Sexualities*, 17:4 (2014), 434–50.

Kies, Bridget, and Thomas J. West III, 'Queer Nostalgia and Queer Histories in Uncertain Times', *Queer Studies in Media & Popular Culture*, 2:2 (2017), 161–5.

Kitzinger, Jenny, and David Miller, 'AIDS, the Policy Process, and Moral Panics', in *The Circuit of Mass Communication: Media Strategies, Representation and Audience Reception in the AIDS Crisis* (London: Sage Publications, 1998), 213–22.

Kohnen, Melanie E. S., *Queer Representation, Visibility, and Race in American Film and Television: Screening the Closet* (Abingdon: Routledge, 2015).

Kuhn, Annette, *An Everyday Magic: Cinema and Cultural Memory* (London: I.B. Tauris, 2002).

Kuhn, Annette, Daniel Biltereyst, and Philippe Meers, 'Memories of Cinemagoing and Film Experience: An Introduction', *Memory Studies*, 10:1 (2017), 3–16.

Labanyi, Jo, 'The Mediation of Everyday Life: An Oral History of Cinema-Going in 1940s and 1950s Spain', *Studies in Hispanic Cinema*, 2:2 (2007), 105–8.

Landsberg, Alison, *Prosthetic Memory: The Transformation of American Remembrance in the Age of Mass Culture* (New York: Columbia University Press, 2004).

Lee, Benjamin, 'Roland Emmerich: Gay Rights Drama Stonewall Needed "Straight-Acting" Hero', *The Guardian*, 24 September 2015, https://www.theguardian.com/film/2015/sep/24/roland-emmerich-gay-rights-drama-stonewall-needed-straight-acting-hero [accessed 10 July 2018].

Leins, Casey, 'States That Require Schools to Teach LGBT History', *US News*, 14 August 2019, https://www.usnews.com/news/best-states/articles/2019-08-14/states-that-require-schools-to-teach-lgbt-history [accessed 6 July 2020].

Lenon, Susan, 'White as *Milk*: Proposition 8 and the Cultural Politics of Gay Rights', *Atlantis: Critical Studies in Gender, Culture and Social Justice*, 36:1 (2013), 44–54.

Lesbians & Gays Support the Migrants, http://www.lgsmigrants.com [accessed 2 July 2020].

Lesbians and Gays Support the Miners, 'Miners' Attitudes Are Changing Faster than Eric's', *Capital Gay*, 19 October 1984.

Lesbians and Gays Support the Miners, 'Support the Miners', *Capital Gay*, 3 August 1984.

Lester, Paul Martin, 'From Abomination to Indifference: A Visual Analysis of Transgender Stereotypes in the Media', in *Transgender Communication: Histories, Trends, and Trajectories*, ed. Leland G. Spencer and Jamie C. Capuzza (Lanham: Lexington Books, 2015), 143–54.

Levy, Daniel, and Natan Sznaider, *The Holocaust and Memory in the Global Age* (Philadelphia: Temple University Press, 2006).

Lewis, Dave, 'Review: *Pride*', *The Project*, 4 November 2014, http://www.socialistproject.org/trade-unions/review-pride/ [accessed 17 May 2018].

Liptak, Adam, 'Civil Rights Law Protects Gay and Transgender Workers, Supreme Court Rules', *The New York Times*, 15 June 2020, https://www.nytimes.com/2020/06/15/us/gay-transgender-workers-supreme-court.html [accessed 18 July 2020].

Loder, Kurt, 'David Bowie: Scary Monster on Broadway', *Rolling Stone*, 13 November 1980, https://www.rollingstone.com/music/music-news/david-bowie-scary-monster-on-broadway-100929/ [accessed 27 January 2017].

Loder, Kurt, 'David Bowie: Straight Time', *Rolling Stone*, 12 May 1983, https://www.rollingstone.com/music/features/straight-time-19830512 [accessed 27 January 2017].

Lodge, Guy, 'How Gay Cinema Is Calling on the Past to Point at a Radical Future', *The Guardian*, 15 June 2018, https://www.theguardian.com/film/2018/jun/15/gay-cinema-radical-future [accessed 2 December 2018].

Lott, Martha, 'The Relationship between the "Invisibility" of African American Women in the American Civil Rights Movement of the 1950s and 1960s and Their Portrayal in Modern Film', *Journal of Black Studies*, 48:4 (2017), 331–54.

Love, Heather, 'Compulsory Happiness and Queer Existence', *New Formations*, 63 (2007), 52–65.

Love, Heather, *Feeling Backward: Loss and the Politics of Queer History* (Cambridge: Harvard University Press, 2007).

Lozano, José Carlos, Philippe Meers, and Daniel Biltereyst, 'La Experiencia Social Histórica de Asistencia al Cine En Monterrey (Nuevo León, México) Durante Las Décadas de 1930 a 1960', *Palabra Clave–Revista de Comunicación*, 19:3 (2016), 691–720.

Lynch, John, 'Memory and Matthew Shepard: Opposing Expressions of Public Memory in Television Movies', *Journal of Communication Inquiry*, 31:3 (2007), 222–38.

Lyons, Jarrett, 'Here's Why LGBT Twitter Is Dragging a Human-Rights Organization All over the Internet Today', *Salon*, 14 November 2017, https://www.salon.com/2017/11/14/heres-why-lgbtq-twitter-is-dragging-a-human-rights-organization-all-over-the-internet-today/ [accessed 29 July 2018].

Mainwaring, Rachel, 'I Thought It Was a Myth,' Says Filmmaker Who's Bringing the True Story of *Pride* to the Big Screen', *Wales Online*, 5 September 2014, https://www.walesonline.co.uk/whats-on/film-news/i-thought-myth-says-filmmaker-7712411 [accessed 10 June 2018].

Marshal, Michael P., Laura J. Dietz, Mark S. Friedman, Ron Stall, Helen A. Smith, James McGinley, Brian C. Thoma, Pamela J. Murray, Anthony R. D'Augelli, and David A. Brent, 'Suicidality and Depression Disparities between Sexual Minority and Heterosexual Youth: A Meta-Analytic Review', *Journal of Adolescent Health*, 49:2 (2011), 115–23.

Mason, Clitha, 'Queering the Mammy: New Queer Cinema's Version of an American Institution in Cheryl Dunye's *The Watermelon Woman*', *Black Camera*, 8:2 (2017), 50–74.

McKay, Hannah, 'UK Foreign Spy Agency Flies Rainbow Flag, Says Diversity Gives It Edge', *Reuters*, 17 May 2016, http://uk.reuters.com/article/uk-britain-gay-spies-idUKKCN0Y811N [accessed 3 October 2017].

McKinnon, Scott J., *Gay Men at the Movies: Cinema, Memory and the History of a Gay Male Community* (Chicago: The University of Chicago Press, 2016).

Mercer, Kobena, 'Angelus Diasporae', in *Isaac Julien: Riot*, ed. by Isaac Julien Rose and Cynthia (New York).

Miller, Lucy J., 'Becoming One of the Girls/Guys: Distancing Transgender Representations in Popular Film Comedies', in *Transgender Communication: Histories, Trends, and Trajectories* (Lanham: Lexington Books, 2015), 127–42.

Millermarch, Judith, 'Lobbyists Fight Cuts on Arts Day in Capital', *The New York Times*, 13 March 1997, http://www.nytimes.com/1997/03/13/arts/lobbyists-fight-cuts-on-arts-day-in-capital.html [accessed 23 March 2018].

Morrison, Jayson A., '*La MaMa's Squirts*: Igniting Queer Intergenerational Dialogue through Performance', *Text and Performance Quarterly*, 35:2–3 (2015), 226–33.

Moss, Kevin, 'Queering Ethnicity in the First Gay Films from Ex-Yugoslavia', *Feminist Media Studies*, 12:3 (2012), 352–70.

Moss, Kevin, and Mima Simić, 'Post-Communist Lavender Menace: Lesbians in Mainstream East European Film', *Journal of Lesbian Studies*, 15:3 (2011), 271–83.

Muñoz, José Esteban, *Cruising Utopia: The Then and There of Queer Futurity* (New York: New York University Press, 2009).

Muñoz, José Esteban, 'Ephemera as Evidence: Introductory Notes to Queer Acts', *Women and Performance*, 8:2 (1996), 5–16.

Nakhnikian, Elise, '*Pride*', *Slant*, 22 September 2014, https://www.slantmagazine.com/film/review/pride-2014 [accessed 17 May 2018].

Nichols, Bill, *Representing Reality: Issues and Concepts in Documentary* (Bloomington: Indiana University Press, 1991).

Nicholson, Rebecca, '*The L Word: Generation Q Review* – It's Here, It's Queer … and It's Loads of Fun', *The Guardian*, 4 February 2020, https://www.theguardian.com/tv-and-radio/2020/feb/04/the-l-word-generation-q-review-its-here-its-queer-and-its-loads-of-fun [accessed 6 July 2020].

O'Neill, Edward R., 'Traumatic Postmodern Histories: *Velvet Goldmine*'s Phantasmatic Testimonies', *Camera Obscura*, 19:3 (2004), 156–85.

Osborne, Samuel, 'British Spy Exposed by Wife over Secret Gay Sex near MI6 HQ', *The Independent*, 26 March 2016, https://www.independent.co.uk/news/uk/home-news/british-spy-exposed-by-wife-over-secret-gay-sex-near-mi6-hq-a6954256.html [accessed 22 December 2016].

Padva, Gilad, 'A Fantastic Fabrication of Weimar Berlin: Queer Nostalgia, Timeless Memories and Surreal Spatiality in the Film *Bent*', *Queer Studies in Media & Popular Culture*, 2:2 (2017), 167–82.

Padva, Gilad, *Queer Nostalgia in Cinema and Pop Culture* (New York: Palgrave Macmillan, 2014).

Parsons, Alexandra, 'History, Activism, and the Queer Child in Derek Jarman's Queer *Edward II* (1991)', *Shakespeare Bulletin*, 32:3 (2014), 413–28.

Paz, Maria Antonia, 'The Spanish Remember: Movie Attendance during the Franco Dictatorship, 1943–1975', *Historical Journal of Film, Radio and Television*, 23:4 (2003), 357–74.

Plummer, Ken, 'Generational Sexualities, Subterranean Traditions, and the Hauntings of the Sexual World: Some Preliminary Remarks', *Symbolic Interaction*, 33:2 (2010), 163–90.

Poniewozik, James, 'Review: *When We Rise* Charts the History of Gay and Transgender Rights', *New York Times*, 26 February 2017, https://www.nytimes.com/2017/02/26/arts/television/review-when-we-rise-review-gay-rights.html [accessed 10 July 2018].

Poole, Ross, 'Misremembering the Holocaust: Universal Symbol, Nationalist Icon or Moral Kitsch?', in *Memory and the Future* (New York: Palgrave Macmillan, 2010), 31–49.

Portass, Geoff, and Roy Puddefoot, 'Such Nonsense about the Miners Is Dangerous', *Capital Gay*, 17 August 1984.

Porter, Rick, '*When We Rise* Finale Adjusts Down: Friday Final Ratings', *TV by the Numbers*, 3 March 2017, https://tvbythenumbers.zap2it.com/daily-ratings/friday-final-ratings-march-3-2017/ [accessed 10 June 2018].

Powell, Kerry, *Acting Wilde: Victorian Sexuality, Theatre, and Oscar Wilde* (Cambridge: Cambridge University Press, 2009).

'*Pride*', *Box Office Mojo*, https://www.boxofficemojo.com/release/rl2339079681/ [accessed 2 July 2020].

Puar, Jasbir K., *Terrorist Assemblages: Homonationalism in Queer Times* (London: Duke University Press, 2007).

Reading, Anna, 'Identity, Memory and Cosmopolitanism: The Otherness of the Past and a Right to Memory?', *European Journal of Cultural Studies*, 14:4 (2011), 379–94.

Reading, Anna, and Tamar Katriel, *Cultural Memories of Nonviolent Struggles: Powerful Times* (Basingstoke: Palgrave Macmillan, 2015).

Reid-Pharr, Robert F., 'Makes Me Feel Mighty Real: *The Watermelon Woman* and the Critique of Black Visuality', in *F Is for Phony: Fake Documentary and Truth's Undoing* (Minneapolis: University of Minnesota Press, 2006), 130–42.

Rich, B. Ruby, *New Queer Cinema: The Director's Cut* (Durham: Duke University Press, 2013).

Rich, B. Ruby, 'Reflections on a Queer Screen', *GLQ: A Journal of Lesbian and Gay Studies*, 1:1 (1993), 83–91.

Richards, Helen, 'Memory Reclamation of Cinema Going in Bridgend, South Wales, 1930–1960', *Historical Journal of Film, Radio and Television*, 23:4 (2003), 341–55.

Richardson, Matt, 'Our Stories Have Never Been Told: Preliminary Thoughts on Black Lesbian Cultural Production as Historiography in *The Watermelon Woman*', *Black Camera*, 2:2 (2011), 100–13.

Richardson, Matt, *The Queer Limit of Black Memory: Black Lesbian Literature and Irresolution* (Columbus: Ohio State University Press, 2013).

Ring, Trudy, 'This Year's Michigan Womyn's Music Festival Will Be the Last', *The Advocate*, 21 April 2015, http://www.advocate.com/michfest/2015/04/21/years-michigan-womyns-music-festival-will-be-last [accessed 22 December 2016].

Rixon, Andrew, 'We Will Be Frightened That Our Views Are Out of Line', *Capital Gay*, 14 September 1984.

Roscoe, Jane, and Craig Hight, *Faking It: Mock-Documentary and the Subversion of Factuality* (Manchester: Manchester University Press, 2001).

Ross, India, 'The Business of Gay Pride', *Financial Times*, 11 August 2016, https://www.ft.com/content/228207c6-5f46-11e6-ae3f-77baadeb1c93 [accessed 29 July 2018].

Russell, Glenda M., and Janis S. Bohan, 'The Gay Generation Gap: Communicating across the LGBT Generational Divide', *Angles*, 8:1 (2005), 1–8.

Russo, Vito, *The Celluloid Closet: Homosexuality in the Movies* (New York: Harper & Row, 1981).

Saraiya, Sonia, 'TV Review: ABC's *When We Rise*', *Variety*, 20 February 2017, https://variety.com/2017/tv/reviews/tv-review-abc-when-we-rise-dustin-lance-black-guy-pearce-gus-van-sant-1201989559/ [accessed 10 July 2018].

Savage, Dan, '2010: "It Gets Better" Founder Dan Savage Reflects on The Groundbreaking Youth Project', *Out*, 1 October 2017, https://www.out.com/

pride/2017/10/01/2010-it-gets-better-founder.-dan-savage-reflects-groundbreaking-youth-project [accessed 1 November 2018].

Scanlon, Julie, and Ruth Lewis, 'Whose Sexuality Is It Anyway? Women's Experiences of Viewing Lesbians on Screen', *Feminist Media Studies*, 17:6 (2017), 1005–21.

Schulman, Sarah, *Ties That Bind: Familial Homophobia and Its Consequences* (London: The New Press, 2009).

Shahani, Nishant, 'Getting Off (on) the *Shortbus* (John Cameron Mitchell, 2006): The Politics of Hypothetical Queer History', *New Cinemas: Journal of Contemporary Film*, 10:2–3 (2012), 101–14.

Shaw, Alex, 'Stratford LGBT Student Society Celebrates Third Anniversary with Tribute to Politician and Gay Rights Campaigner Harvey Milk', *Newham Recorder*, 18 September 2018, https://www.newhamrecorder.co.uk/news/education/harvey-milk-honoured-for-london-academy-of-excellence-lae-stratford-lgbt-society-third-anniversary-1-5699746 [accessed 1 November 2018].

Silverstone, Catherine, 'Duckie's Gay Shame: Critiquing Pride and Selling Shame in Club Performance 1', *Contemporary Theatre Review*, 22:1 (2012), 62–78.

Simpson, Mike, 'I Am Appalled at Such Rubbish', *Capital Gay*, 24 August 1984.

Sinfield, Alan, *The Wilde Century: Effeminacy, Oscar Wilde, and the Queer Moment* (London: Cassell, 1994).

Smith-Walters, Maisie, 'Hollywood Trans Roles under Fire – Again', *BBC News*, 15 September 2016, http://www.bbc.co.uk/news/magazine-37312338 [accessed 23 November 2016].

Snediker, Michael D., *Queer Optimism: Lyric Personhood and Other Felicitous Persuasions* (Minneapolis: University of Minnesota Press, 2009).

Soloway, Joey, *She Wants It: Desire, Power, and Toppling the Patriarchy* (London: Ebury Press, 2019).

Somosgay, 'SOMOSGAY Organizes an Artistic and Collective Expression Called "Graffities for Equality"', *Somosgay*, 9 August 2013, http://somosgay.org/infonews/infodetalle/somosgay-organizes-an-artistic-and-collective-expression-called-graffities [accessed 1 July 2018].

Stacey, Jackie, *Star Gazing: Hollywood Cinema and Female Spectatorship* (Abingdon: Routledge, 1993).

Starling, Boris, 'Drama Feeds Off Real-Life Crime, but Has *London Spy* Gone Too Far?', *The Guardian*, 12 November 2015, http://www.theguardian.com/commentisfree/2015/nov/12/london-spy-real-life-murder-gareth-williams [accessed 27 May 2016].

Stevens, Christopher, 'Christopher Stevens Reviews *London Spy* Starring Ben Whishaw and Jim Broadbent', *Daily Mail*, 10 November 2015, https://www.dailymail.co.uk/news/article-3311291/No-plot-lots-disco-dancing-s-Beeb-s-new-gay-spy-drama-CHRISTOPHER-STEVENS-reviews-night-s-TV.html [accessed 3 July 2020].

'Stonewall', *Box Office Mojo*, https://www.boxofficemojo.com/release/rl1551730177/ [accessed 6 July 2020].

'Stonewall (2015)', *Rotten Tomatoes*, https://www.rottentomatoes.com/m/stonewall_2015 [accessed 6 July 2020].

Stratton, John, *Jewish Identity in Western Pop Culture* (New York: Palgrave Macmillan, 2008).

Stryker, Susan, 'Transgender History, Homonormativity, and Disciplinarity', *Radical History Review*, 100 (2008), 145–57.

Sturken, Marita, *Tangled Memories: The Vietnam War, the AIDS Epidemic, and the Politics of Remembering* (Berkeley: University of California Press, 1997).

Sullivan, Laura L., 'Chasing Fae: *The Watermelon Woman* and Black Lesbian', *Source: Callaloo Literature and Culture*, 23:1 (2000), 448–60.

Sutcliffe-Braithwaite, Florence, and Natalie Thomlinson, 'National Women against Pit Closures: Gender, Trade Unionism and Community Activism in the Miners' Strike, 1984–5', *Contemporary British History*, 32:1 (2018), 78–100.

Tate, Tim, *Pride: The Unlikely Story of the True Heroes of the Miners' Strike* (London: John Blake Publishing Ltd., 2017).

The Mark Ashton Red Ribbon Fund, https://mark-ashton.muchloved.com/Home [accessed 1 November 2018].

The Trevor Project, 'The Trevor Project National Survey 2019', https://www.thetrevorproject.org/survey-2019/ [accessed 16 July 2020].

Townsend, C. N., 'Which Side Are You On?', *Capital Gay*, 8 March 1985.

Treveri-Gennari, Daniela, Catherine O'Rawe, and Danielle Hipkins, 'In Search of Italian Cinema Audiences in the 1940s and 1950s: Gender, Genre and National Identity', *Participations: Journal of Audience & Reception Studies*, 8:2 (2011), 539–53.

Tropiano, Stephen, *The Prime Time Closet: A History of Gays and Lesbians on TV* (New York: Hal Leonard Publishing, 2002).

Tsai, Wan-Hsiu Sunny, 'Assimilating the Queers: Representations of Lesbians, Gay Men, Bisexual, and Transgender People in Mainstream Advertising', *Advertising & Society Review*, 11:1 (2010).

von Tunzelmann, Alex, '*The Imitation Game*: Inventing a New Slander to Insult Alan Turing', *The Guardian*, 20 November 2014, https://www.theguardian.com/film/2014/nov/20/the-imitation-game-invents-new-slander-to-insult-alan-turing-reel-history [accessed 22 December 2016].

Tweedie, James, 'The Suspended Spectacle of History: The Tableau Vivant in Derek Jarman's *Caravaggio*', *Screen*, 44:4 (2003), 379–403.

Twomey, John and Padraic Flanaghan, 'Our Murdered Spy Son Was Not Gay – This Is a Smear, Says His Family', *Express*, 28 August 2010, https://www.express.co.uk/news/uk/196046/Our-murdered-spy-son-was-not-gay-this-is-a-smear-says-his-family [accessed 3 July 2020].

Ue, Tom, 'The Truth Will Set You Free: Implicit Faith in *Sherlock* and *London Spy*', *Journal of Popular Film and Television*, 45:2 (2017), 90–100.

Ulaby, Neda, 'On Television, More Transgender Characters Come into Focus', *NPR*, 23 April 2014, http://www.npr.org/blogs/monkeysee/2014/04/23/306166533/on-television-more-transgender-characters-come-into-focus [accessed 25 September 2016].

Valdivia, Angharad N., *Latino/as in the Media* (Cambridge: Polity, 2010).

Vider, Stephen, 'Why Is an Obscure 1968 Documentary in the Opening Credits of *Transparent*?', *Slate*, 23 October 2014, http://www.slate.com/blogs/outward/2014/10/23/transparent_s_opening_credits_are_a_lesson_in_the_history_of_gender.html [accessed 1 October 2016].

Vincentelli, Elisabeth, '*The L Word: Generation Q* Review: New Vision, Old Blind Spots', *The New York Times*, 5 December 2019, https://www.nytimes.com/2019/12/05/arts/television/l-word-generation-q-review.html [accessed 6 July 2020].

Wallace-Sanders, Kimberly, *Mammy: A Century of Race, Gender, and Southern Memory* (Ann Arbor: University of Michigan Press, 2008).

Waller, Pat, 'The Miners Will Never Identify with Us', *Capital Gay*, 17 August 1984.

Walters, Ben, 'Film of the Week: *Pride*', *Sight & Sound*, 21 November 2016, https://www.bfi.org.uk/news-opinion/sight-sound-magazine/reviews-recommendations/film-week-pride [accessed 1 July 2018].

Walters, Ben, 'Out of the Past: Gay Cinema and Nostalgia', *The Guardian*, 3 July 2014, https://www.theguardian.com/film/2014/jul/03/out-of-past-gay-cinema-nostalgia-lgbt [accessed 2 December 2018].

Walters, Ben, '*The Circle*: Why Is LGBTQ Film Trying to Reclaim History?', *The Guardian*, 4 December 2014, https://www.theguardian.com/film/2014/dec/04/the-circle-why-is-gay-cinema-fixated-on-the-past [accessed 2 December 2018].

Warchus, Matthew, 'Matthew Warchus: Why I Made a Romcom about Gay Activists and Striking Miners', *The Guardian*, 21 May 2014, https://www.theguardian.com/film/2014/may/21/matthew-warchus-pride-gay-activists-miners-strike [accessed 1 July 2018].

Watney, Simon, 'AIDS, "Moral Panic" Theory, and Homophobia', in *Critical Readings: Moral Panic and the Media* (Maidenhead: Open University Press, 2006), 256–65.

Watney, Simon, 'Derek Jarman 1942–94: A Political Death', *Artforum*, May 1994, https://www.artforum.com/print/199405/derek-jarman-1942-1994-a-political-death-33389.

Watney, Simon, *Imagine Hope: AIDS and Gay Identity* (London: Routledge, 2002).

Watney, Simon, *Policing Desire: Pornography, AIDS and the Media* (London: Cassell, 1987).

Watney, Simon, 'The Spectacle of AIDS', *October*, 43 (1987), 71–86.

Westwood, Sue, '"We See It as Being Heterosexualised, Being Put into a Care Home": Gender, Sexuality and Housing/Care Preferences among Older LGB Individuals in the UK', *Health & Social Care in the Community*, 24:6 (2016), 155–63.

White, Rosie, *Violent Femmes: Women as Spies in Popular Culture* (Abingdon: Routledge, 2007).

Wilde, Oscar, *The Picture of Dorian Gray* (Oxford: Oxford University Press, 2008).

Windle, Elisabeth, '"It Never Really Was the Same": *Brother to Brother's* Black and White and Queer Nostalgia', *Melus*, 41:4 (2016), 6–31.

Woubshet, Dagmawi, 'The Imperfect Power of *I Am Not Your Negro*', *The Atlantic*, 8 February 2017, https://www.theatlantic.com/entertainment/archive/2017/02/i-am-not-your-negro-review/515976/ [accessed 10 March 2017].

Zieve, Tamara, '"Death to LGBT" Scrawled on Tel Aviv Holocaust Memorial', *The Jerusalem Post*, 25 October 2018, https://www.jpost.com/israel-news/death-to-lgbt-scrawled-on-tel-aviv-holocaust-memorial-570315 [accessed 6 July 2020].

Zimmer, Catherine, 'Histories of *The Watermelon Woman*: Reflexivity between Race and Gender', *Camera Obscura*, 23:268 (2008), 41–66.

Film and television references

120 BPM, dir. Robin Campillo (*120 battements par minute*, Les Films de Pierre, 2017).
A Man of No Importance, dir. Suri Krishnamma (BBC Films, 1994).
All Out! Dancing in Dulais, dir. Lesbians and Gays Support the Miners (Converse Pictures Ltd., 1985).
Another Country, dir. Marek Kanievska (National Film Finance Corporation, 1984).
Beginners, dir. Mike Mills (Olympus Pictures, 2010).
Ben-Hur, dir. William Wyler (Metro-Goldwyn-Mayer, 1959).
Bessie, dir. Dee Rees (HBO Films, 2015).
Billy Elliot, dir. Stephen Daldry (BBC Films, 2000).
Blue, dir. Derek Jarman (Basilisk Communications Ltd., 1993).
Brideshead Revisited, created by John Mortimer (Granada Television, 1981).
Brother to Brother, dir. Rodney Evans (Miasma Films, 2004).
Caravaggio, dir. Derek Jarman (British Film Institute, 1986).
Circumstance, dir. Maryam Keshavarz (شرایط, Marakesh Films, 2011).
Citizen Kane, dir. Orson Welles (Mercury Productions, 1941).
Cleopatra Jones, dir. Jack Starrett (Warner Bros., 1973).
Cucumber, created by Russell T. Davies (Channel 4, 2015).
Daughters of the Dust, dir. Julie Dash (Kino International, 1991).
Edward II, dir. Derek Jarman (BBC Films, 1991).
Ellen, created by Neal Marlens, Carol Black and David S. Rosenthal (ABC, 1994–8).
Fuller House, created by Jeff Franklin (Netflix, 2016–2020).
Ghostbusters, dir. Paul Feig (Sony Pictures Releasing, 2016).
God's Own Country, dir. Francis Lee (British Film Institute, 2017).
Gods and Monsters, dir. Bill Condon (Lions Gate Films, 1998).
Gone with the Wind, dir. Victor Fleming (Metro-Goldwyn-Mayer, 1939).
Grandma, dir. Paul Weitz (Depth of Field, 2015).
Hidden Figures, dir. Theodore Melfi (Fox 2000 Pictures, 2016).
Hollywood, created by Ian Brennan and Ryan Murphy (Netflix, 2020).
I Am Not Your Negro, dir. Raoul Peck (Independent Lens, 2016).
London Spy, created by Tom Rob Smith (BBC, 2015).
Looking for Langston, dir. Isaac Julien (British Film Institute, 1989).
Love and Death on Long Island, dir. Richard Kwietniowski (Telefilm Canada, 1996).
Love Is Strange, dir. Ira Sachs (Film50, 2014).
Man in the Orange Shirt, dir. (BBC, 2017).
Milk, dir. Gus Van Sant (Focus Features, 2008).

Nitrate Kisses, dir. Barbara Hammer (Frameline, 1992).
Orange Is the New Black, created by Jenji Kohan (Netflix, 2013–19).
Pariah, dir. Dee Rees (Northstar Pictures, 2011).
Paris Is Burning, dir. Jennie Livingston (Art Matters Inc, 1990).
Persona, dir. Ingmar Bergman (AB Svensk Filmindustri, 1966).
Personal Best, dir. Robert Towne (The Geffen Company, 1982).
Pose, created by Steven Canals, Brad Falchuk, and Ryan Murphy (FX, 2018–).
Precious, dir. Lee Daniels (Lionsgate, 2009).
Prejudice and Pride: The People's History of LGBTQ Britain, created by Stephen K. Amos and Susan Calman (BBC, 2017).
Pride, dir. Matthew Warchus (Pathé, 2014).
Queer as Folk, created by Ron Cowen and Daniel Lipman (Showtime, 2000–5).
Queer as Folk, created by Russell T. Davies (Channel 4, 1999–2000).
Queer Eye, created by David Collins and Michael Williams (Bravo, 2003–7).
Queer Eye, created by David Collins (Netflix, 2018–).
Queers, created by Mark Gatiss (BBC, 2017).
Rear Window, dir. Alfred Hitchcock (Paramount Pictures, 1954).
Riot, dir. Jeffrey Walker (Werner Film Productions, 2018).
Rocketman, dir. Dexter Fletcher (Paramount Pictures, 2019).
Rope, dir. Alfred Hitchcock (Warner Bros. Pictures, 1948).
Sebastiane, dir. Derek Jarman (Cinegate, 1976).
Selma, dir. Ava Duvernay (Pathé, 2014).
Sense8, created by Lana Wachowski, Lilly Wachowski and Michael Straczynski (Netflix, 2015–18).
Set It Off, dir. F. Gary Gray (New Line Cinema, 1996).
Stonewall, dir. Nigel Finch (BBC, 1995).
Stonewall, dir. Roland Emmerich (ACE Entertainment, 2015).
Suffragette, dir. Sarah Gavron (Pathé, 2015).
Superstar: The Karen Carpenter Story, dir. Todd Haynes (Iced Tea Productions, 1987).
Swoon, dir. Tom Kalin (Fine Line Features, 1992).
Tales of the City, created by Lauren Morelli (Netflix, 2019).
Tales of the City, dir. Alastair Reid (PBS, 1993).
The Attendant, dir. Isaac Julien (British Film Institute, 1993).
The Birth of a Nation, dir. Nate Parker (BRON Studios, 2016).
The Butler, dir. Lee Daniels (Follow through Productions, 2013).
The Celluloid Closet, dir. Rob Epstein and Jeffrey Friedman (HBO Pictures, 1995).
The Circle, dir. Stefan Haupt (*Der Kreis*, Contrast Film, 2014).
The Colour Purple, dir. Steven Spielberg (Warner Bros, 1985).
The Constitution, dir. Rajko Grlić (*Ustav Republike Hrvatske*, Interfilm, 2016).
The Dead Boys' Club, dir. Mark Christopher (Frameline Distribution, 1992).
The Handmaiden, dir. Park Chan-wook (아가씨, Moho Film, 2016).

The Hours and Times, dir. Christopher Münch (Good Machine, 1991).
The Imitation Game, dir. Morten Tyldum (The Weinstein Company, 2014).
The Incredibly True Adventure of Two Girls in Love, dir. Maria Maggenti (Fine Line Features, 1995).
The L Word, created by Ilene Chaiken, Michele Abbot and Kathy Greenberg (Showtime, 2004–9).
The L Word: Generation Q, created by Ilene Chaiken, Michele Abbot and Kathy Greenberg (Showtime, 2019–).
The Parade, dir. Srđan Dragojević (*Parada*, Delirium, 2011).
The Queen, dir. Frank Simon (Vineyard, 1968).
The Watermelon Woman, dir. Cheryl Dunye (Peccadillo Pictures, 1996).
Tom of Finland, dir. Dome Karukoski (Anagram, 2017).
Transparent, created by Joey Soloway (Amazon Prime, 2014–19).
Twelve Years a Slave, dir. Steve McQueen (Regency Enterprises, 2013).
Velvet Goldmine, dir. Todd Haynes (Goldwyn Films, 1998).
Vicious, created by Gary Janetti and Mark Ravenhill (ITV, 2013–16).
Watermelon Man, dir. Melvin Van Peebles (Columbia Pictures, 1970).
When We Rise, created by Dustin Lance Black (ABC, 2017).
Will & Grace, created by David Kohan and Max Mutchnick (NBC, 1998–2005, 2017–20).

Index

A Man of No Importance 64
ACT UP (AIDS Coalition to Unleash Power) 94, 97, 133, 137
affect
   and fan memory 21, 23, 26, 32–40
   and media memory 7–15, 59, 83, 92, 97, 104, 139
   and postmemory 63, 66, 68, 72–3, 78–81
   and racism 45, 49, 55
ageing 63–5, 101–2
Ahmed, Sara 55
AIDS crisis
   London Spy 66, 92–101
   and memory 5–6, 22, 62
   Pose 133
   Velvet Goldmine 37–8
   When We Rise 103
All Out! Dancing in Dulais 110, 114
Another Country 87
Aquino, Ivory 132–3
'archive of feeling' 83, 97, 100
Ashton, Mark
   activist 123–4, 128
   legacy 110
   Pride 113, 115, 121, 125

Baldwin, James 56–7
Beginners 64
Ben-Hur 11
Bessie 42
Billings, Alexandra 103, 105, 132–3
Billy Elliot 109
blackmail 86–7, 90–91
Bowie, David
   artist 36–7
   Velvet Goldmine 14, 23, 25, 27–8, 32–3, 36–7
Boy George 28
Brideshead Revisited (1981) 3
Bronski Beat 116
Brother to Brother 42, 64

Capital Gay 110, 122, 125
Castiglia, Christopher 37–8, 97
Castle, Terry 117
celebrity 23, 30, 31–7, 40
censorship 7
Chambers, Stephanie
   activist 114, 117–18
   Pride 112, 113, 117, 122, 127
Chung, Cecilia 132–3
Circumstance 11
Citizen Kane 27, 29, 30–1, 35
Clarke, Cheryl 51–2
Cleopatra Jones 49
Clews, Colin 128–9
coming out
   Transparent 67, 69–70
   Velvet Goldmine 25–6, 30–1, 36–7
   Will & Grace 61
commodification of LGBTQ rights movement 104, 127–9
Conservative Group for Homosexual Equality (CGHE) 123
Conservative Party 110, 122
Cucumber 65, 101
Cvetkovich, Ann 7, 97

Daily Mail 85–6, 93
dandy 34–6
Daughters of the Dust 41, 42
depression 91
Dinshaw, Carolyn 9
documentary 45–6
Durham Miners' Association 109, 111
Dyer, Richard 29

Edelman, Lee 106
Ellen 65
erasure
   AIDS victims 83, 97–102
   Black LGBTQ Memory 1–2, 41–3, 47–57, 105, 130–1, 133–5
   interracial relationships 49–56

lesbian activist memory 1, 74, 105, 107, 112–20, 130–1, 134
queer memory 7, 15, 58, 66, 83, 97–102
transgender memory 1, 66, 68, 70, 72–3, 78–81, 103, 105, 132–5

family
  and memory 4–5, 14, 62–6, 138
  Transparent 67–74, 78–81, 102
  Velvet Goldmine 30–3, 52
fan 13–14, 17–19, 23, 25–6, 28–34, 36–40, 58–9
fanfiction 33, 34, 36, 59
'feeling backward' 91–2
feminism on-screen
  Pride 112–20
  queer activist cinema 130–2
  Transparent 68–9, 74, 76–81
50 Shades of Gay Season (Channel 4) 6
Foucault, Michel 8, 35, 105
Fradenburg, Louise 9
Freccero, Carla 9, 71, 80
Freeman, Elizabeth 9, 54
Fuller House 58

Garber, Marjorie 29, 32
Gavron, Sarah 112
Gay Britannia Season (BBC) 6
Ghostbusters 58
God's Own Country 7
Gods and Monsters 64
Gone with the Wind 44, 46
Grandma 64
Greenham Common Women's Peace Camp 117–18
Guardian 8, 82, 87, 134

Halberstam, Jack 70
Halbwachs, Maurice 2–3
Haran, Brett 124
haunting 71, 80
Haynes, Todd
  Carol 3
  Superstar: The Karen Carpenter Story 33
  Velvet Goldmine 13–14, 25–40, 57–9
Hays Code 13, 18
hegemony of Anglo-American cinema 11–12
Hidden Figures 57
Hill Collins, Patricia 47–8

Hirsch, Marianne 4–5, 63, 76, 80
Hirschfeld, Magnus 3, 70–2, 78–9
Hockney, David 99
Hollywood 58–9, 98
homonationalism 12, 104
homonormativity 19, 38, 94–5, 104
Hudson, Rock
  death 93, 98
  Hollywood 58–9
Huffington Post 86, 103, 132–3
Human Rights Campaign (HRC) 104

I Am Not Your Negro 56–7
Iggy Pop 28, 33
Independent 86
intergenerationality
  London Spy 83, 91, 98–102
  and memory 4–5, 7, 10, 14–16, 61–6
  Transparent 68–73, 78–81
interracial relationships 14, 23, 42–3, 49–56
Irwin-Zarecka, Iwona 2
'It Gets Better' 61–2

Jackson, Mike
  activist 110–11, 129
  Pride 113, 127
James, Sian 117–19
Jarman, Derek
  Blue 15, 66, 83, 92, 96–101
  Caravaggio 22
  as director, 3, 20, 22
  Edward II 22, 27
Jelača, Dijana 20–1, 137
Jenkins, Henry 34, 36
Jones, Cleve
  activist 5–6
  When We Rise 132
Julien, Isaac
  The Attendant 49, 53–4
  Looking for Langston 22, 27, 42

Labour Party 110, 126
Lance Black, Dustin
  Milk 5–6, 11, 107, 130–1
  When We Rise 65, 103, 105, 107, 131–3
Landsberg, Alison 8–9, 45, 63
Lapovsky Kennedy, Elizabeth 22
Lesbians against Pit Closures (LAPC) 114–17, 122, 127

Index

Lesbians and Gays Support the Migrants (LGSMigrants) 12, 13, 106, 129
Lesbians and Gays Support the Miners (LGSM) 12, 13, 15, 109–29, 134
Levy, Daniel 11
Lewis, Dave 111, 117
LGBT history education
   UK 3
   USA 3
Lodge, Guy 138
London Spy 14–15, 65–6, 82–102
Love and Death on Long Island 17, 64
Love Is Strange 64
Lysette, Trace 68–9

mammy 44, 46–8, 51, 55
Man in the Orange Shirt 6
McKinnon, Scott 17–18, 20, 21
memory
   and activism 1–2, 4–6, 12–13, 15–16, 72, 93–4, 97, 109–35
   and futurity 8, 12–13, 16, 38–9, 81, 104, 106, 132, 134, 138–9
   global 11–12
   postmemory 4–5, 14, 15, 62–3, 65, 66, 67, 72, 73, 80, 81, 83, 90, 102
   prosthetic 8–9, 45, 49, 51, 134
   right to 7
   screen 20–1, 23, 30, 40
Mercer, Kobena 42–3
Milk, Harvey
   legacy 5–6
   Milk 130–1
Muñoz, Jose Esteban 12, 39, 81, 106

NAMES Project AIDS Memorial Quilt 5, 96
National Women against Pit Closures (NWAPC) Movement 119
neoliberalism 15, 37, 104, 112, 125–9, 134
New Queer Cinema 13–14, 21, 22, 26, 42, 98, 130
Nichols, Bill 46
Nitrate Kisses 22
nostalgia 9–10, 58, 138

120 Beats per Minute 131, 137
Orange Is the New Black 68
Oxenberg, Jan 18

Padva, Gilad 10
Paglia, Camille 48
Pariah 41
Paris Is Burning 98
Persona 31
Personal Best 49
Plummer, Ken 63–4
Pose 3, 57, 68, 98, 101, 131, 133
Precious 42
Prejudice and Pride: The People's History of LGBTQ Britain 6
Pride 3, 12, 15, 109–29, 131, 134
Pride march 104, 109, 113, 122, 126–9
promiscuity 38, 94–5
Proposition 6, 130–2

Queer as Folk (UK) 65
Queer as Folk (US) 65
Queer Eye 58
queer anti-social turn 106
Queers 6

Reading, Anna 7, 106
Rear Window 88
reboot 58–9
Reed, Christopher 37–8, 97
Reed, Lou 28
Rich, B. Ruby 20, 21
Richardson, Matt 42, 48
Riot 131, 137
Rocketman 7
Rope 22

Scargill, Arthur 113, 115
Schulman, Sarah 4, 97
Schwarzenegger, Arnold 6
Sebastiane 22
Section 28 110
Selma 57
Sense8 68
seropositivity 5, 66, 92–101, 103, 118
Set It Off 42
sexology 70–1
Sinfield, Alan 35–6
solidarity 13, 106, 121–2, 125, 126, 129, 134
Soloway, Joey
   showrunner 68–9
   Transparent 3, 14, 65–81, 98, 101, 102
Spectator 85–6

spectrality 71, 80
spy 82–3, 86–7
Stonewall Riots 1, 12, 61, 134
Stonewall (1995) 130
Stonewall (2015) 1–2, 103, 105
Stryker, Susan 133
Suffragette 112
Sun 85, 93
surveillance 87–8, 90
Swoon 22, 27
Sznaider, Natan 11

Tales of the City 58
Tambor, Jeffrey 68–9
temporality 9–10, 12, 70–2, 104
Thatcher, Margaret 113, 123, 124
The Birth of a Nation 57
The Butler 57
The Celluloid Closet 18
The Circle 137
The Colour Purple 42
The Constitution 137
The Dead Boys' Club 22
The Handmaiden 136–7
The Hours and Times 22, 27
The Imitation Game 87
The Incredibly True Adventure of Two Girls in Love 42
The L Word 58

The L Word: Generation Q 58
The Parade 11, 137
The Queen 67, 98
The Watermelon Woman 14, 23, 41–59
Tom of Finland
    art 53
    film 137
trans-exclusionary feminism 77–81
Tunzelmann, Alex 87
Twelve Years a Slave 57

utopia 10, 14, 39–40, 106

Vicious 65, 101

Walters, Ben 113, 138
Watermelon Man 43
Weissman, David 62
Wilde, Oscar
    reputation 35–6
    The Picture of Dorian Gray 27, 30
    Velvet Goldmine 34–6, 39
Will & Grace 58, 61–2, 65
Williams, Gareth 82–6, 93, 101
women-only
    activist groups 114–20
    spaces 77–81
workplace harassment 68–9
world cinema 11–12, 131, 136–7

www.ingramcontent.com/pod-product-compliance
Lightning Source LLC
Chambersburg PA
CBHW070639300426
44111CB00013B/2175